Cooking With Wilma
Family and Friends

෧

Wilma Coates

authorHOUSE®

AuthorHouse™
1663 Liberty Drive
Bloomington, IN 47403
www.authorhouse.com
Phone: 1-800-839-8640

First published by AuthorHouse 8/19/2010

ISBN: 978-1-4520-0126-5 (sc)
ISBN: 978-1-4520-0127-2 (e)

Printed in the United States of America
Bloomington, Indiana

This book is printed on acid-free paper.

Donita Adams

Neoma Bray

Diana Brown

Penny Campbell

Pearl Cavender

Colleen Coates

Shane Coates

Viola Coates

Wilma Coates

Beverly Crandall

Dora Crandall

Stephanie Crays

Tina Ellenwood

Kristine Frolov

Elizabeth Frolov

Sylvia Garner

Leslie Garringer

Debbie Green

Julie Hahn

Cheryl Hamilton

Tina Hansford

Barbara Jeans

Lee Johnson

Loreen Korell

Dean Lebreton

Carole Lloyd

Annette Lutes

Udo Lutes

Norma McBeth

Rodney Murray

Tasha Murray

John & Tracy Nunez

Olga Peters

Virgina Quenzer

Nastasha Rowley

Ryan

Al Schneider

Susan Standley

Paula Starcher

Barbara Travis

Jana Watson

Randy Wilson

Rodney   Lawrence   Shane

Kristine   Jana   Wilma

Felix

I dictate this book to my mother who taught me to love the art of cooking, to my sisters that have supported and shown me the love that only sisters can. I would also like to dedicate this book to those challenged students who continue to inspire me to believe in what others may think is impossible. Reach for the stars but be accepting of the moon, never ever let anyone tell you that you can not achieve your dreams and DREAM BIG!!!

Top row: Eric, Stephanie Crays – Para Pro, Cody, Jenna, Robert, Carole Lloyd – Para Pro, Willa Farrell – Bus Driver, Wilma Coates – Para Pro
Middle row: Ricco, Shelly, Adale
Bottom row: Ryan, David, Miguel, Deanna, John

Tina Hansford
Para Pro

Annette Lutes
Teacher

Randy Wilson
Para Pro

Cooking With Wilma
Family and Friends

Common food equivalent	approximate measure
1 lb butter	2 cups cheese
1 cup shredded	1 cup shredded
1 lb cottage cheese	2 cups
6 oz choc chips	1 cup
8 oz unsweetened choc	8 squares
4 oz coconut	1/3 cups
1 lb coffee	80 tbsp
½ pt whip cream	1 cup (2 cup whipped
8 oz sour cream	1 cup
1 lb flour	3 ½ cups
1 med lemon juice	2 – 3 tbsp
1 lb almonds	1 ¾ cups
1 lb pecans	2 ¼ cups
1 lb peanuts	2 ¼ cups
1 lb walnuts	1 2/3 cups packed
1 lb confect sugar	4 cups
1 lb granular sugar	2 cups
1 ½ tsp cornstarch	1 tbsp flour
1 cup milk	½ c canned milk + ½ c water
unsweetened choc	3 tbsp cocoa + 1 tsp oil

3 tsp	1 tbsp
16 tbsp	1 cup
2 cups	1 pint
4 cups	1 quart
2 pints	1 quart
4 tbsp	¼ cup

Apple Salad

About 4 apples chopped, (red and green for color) Mix together – 1 cup mayonnaise – 2 tbl sugar – ¼ can orange juice concentrate – 1 to 2 tsp celery seed. Mix with whisk or beater and mix in apples. Refrigerate and serve. Can also add sliced bananas, oranges ect.
Randy Wilson
Emmett, ID

Apricot Salad

1 c apricot pie filling – 2 c small marshmallows – 1 c mandarin oranges – 4 sliced bananas. Drain fruits very dry. Mix all together and chill. Can add whipped cream if you want.
Marie Workenton
Brookings, OR

Baked Potato Salad

5 lb potatoes – ½ c chopped celery – ¼ c oil – ¼ c chopped green pepper – ½ c chopped green onions – 1 tbl flour – 1 tbl sugar – 1 tsp salt – ½ c water – ½ tsp dry mustard – ¼ tsp paprika – ¼ c vinegar. Boil potatoes in salted water till barely tender. Drain and peel. Cut into 1 inch cubes. Sauté onions, celery, green pepper in oil till tender. Blend in flour and seasonings. Gradually add water and vinegar stirring till thickened. Toss gently with potatoes. Place in 1 ½ qt casserole. Bake at 350* for 15 to 20 minutes. makes 8 servings.
Lass
Hoar, Germany

Bean Salad

2 cans mushroom pieces – 1 bunch celery chopped – 1 green pepper chopped – 1 med onion chopped – 2 cans lima beans drained – 2 cans Mexican beans drained – 1 can butter beans drained – 1 can pinto beans drained – 1 can wax beans drained – 1 can green beans drained. Mix all beans together with pepper, onions, mushrooms and celery. Mix juice to marinate in 2 c wine vinegar – 2 c sugar – 1 c veg oil – 1 tsp salt – 1 tsp pepper. Mix & pour over beans. Refrigerator for 24 hours.
Barbara Travis
Halsey, OR

Bread Salad

1 lg loaf sandwich type white bread – 1 lg onion chopped – 4 hard boiled eggs chopped – 2 sm cans shrimp – 1 can (7 ½ oz) crab – 1 c chopped celery – 3 c salad dressing. Remove crust from bread and cube; add onion and egg, place in fridge overnight. Add shrimp, crab, celery and bread. Mix. place in fridge again for a few hours. Mix with salad dressing on top.
Paula Starcher
Emmett, ID

Blueberry Salad

2 (3 oz) grape Jell-O – 2 c boiling water – 1 (16 oz) can blueberry pie filling – 1 c sour cream (1 cut cream to ¾ c) – ½ c sugar – 1 (8 oz) pkg cream cheese – 1 tsp vanilla. In 9x13 pan mix gelatin and water till dissolved. Add undrained pineapple and pie filling. Stir and let set in refrigerator. Mix sour cream with softened cream cheese, vanilla and sugar. Spread on top. chill in refrig. (We like it better without sour cream)
Lavonne
Emmett, ID

Broccoli Salad

1 bunch broccoli cut bite size – 1 c sliced celery – 1 green onion chopped – 1 c raisins soaked in 1 c water – 1 ½ c seedless grapes cut in half – ¼ c bacon bits. Mix together and set aside. Dressing. 6 tbl salad dressing – 1 tbl white vinegar – 3 pkg equal – ¼ c plain yogurt. Mix together and pour over broccoli and toss till mixed. Chill 1 to 2 hours.
Beverly
Beach, ND

Broccoli Salad

2 bunches of broccoli, finely chopped – 1 red onion finely chopped – 10 strips of crisp cooked bacon – 2 tsp sugar (opt) – 1 c mayo – ¼ c milk – ¼ c raisins. Combine mayo, milk and sugar into a small bowl and let stand while preparing salad. Combine broc, onion, bacon and raisins. Add mayo mixture and toss well. This is best made the day before you plan to serve it.
Olga Peters
Salem, OR

Broccoli Salad

1 bunch broccoli – ¼ c onions – 1 c raisins – 10 slices bacon fried - 1 c sunflower seeds. mix with dressing – ½ c mayo – 1 tbl vinegar – 3 to 4 tbl sugar. Mix and pour over salad. Best if it sets overnight in refrigerator.
Lavonne
Emmett, ID

Cabbage Pineapple Salad

3 c shredded cabbage – 1 small can crushed pineapple drained - 1 c miniature marshmallow – ½ to ¾ c mayo. Toss lightly but thoroughly until mayo coats all.
Barbara
Cornelius, OR

Christmas Ribbon Salad

2 pkg each of raspberry, lemon and lime Jell-O – 1/3 c mayo – 1 (#2) can crushed pineapple drain save juice – 8 oz cream cheese – 3 bananas – 1 oz mar chino cherries. dissolve raspberry Jell-O in a cup of hot and 2 c cold water. Put in oblong pan set till firm. Set lemon with 1 c hot and 2 c cold. Let set like jelly. Whip and mix mayo and cheese well before adding to lemon Jell-O. Than whip till fluffy. Slice bananas on top of raspberry Jell-O and than pour lemon Jell-O and let set. Than set lime with 2 ½ c water (1 hot and 1 ½ c cold) and 1 c pineapple juice if not enough juice to make cup add water. When Jell-O is lightly set add pineapple and cherries let cool for a few minutes and pour over rest of Jell-O and set till firm. Top with whip cream.
Olive
Sentinel Butte, ND

Cole Slaw

Shred-- cabbage, carrots, dice green pepper, and onion. dressing ½ c oil – 1 tbl water – ¾ c vinegar – 1 tsp salt – 1 c sugar – 1 tsp celery seed – pour over veg. I use a small head cabbage – 1 carrot – ½ green peppers – 1 sm onion.
Bud
Beach, ND

Cranberry Jell-O

1 pkg red Jell-O – 1 c canned cranberries – juice of a lemon – ½ c diced celery – ½ c diced pineapple – fix Jell-O using 1 c boiling water and lemon juice. Add rest of ingredients. Don't drain pineapple.
Herchall
Troutdale, OR

Cranberry Pear Salad

1 box (6 oz) raspberry Jell-O – ½ c cold water – 1 ¾ c boiling water – 1 tsp lemon juice – 1 can whole cranberry sauce - 1 can (29 oz) pear halves – nuts. Stir boiling water into Jell-O until dissolved. Add cold water, cranberries sauce and lemon juice. Stirring until cranberry sauce has melted. Chill till slightly thickened but not set. Drain pears and cut into chunks. Fold pears and nuts into Jell-O and chill until firm.
Lorine
Hebron, ND

Cranberry Salad

1 pkg cherry Jell-O – 1 c hot water – 1 c sugar – 1 c pineapple juice - 1 c raw cranberries – 1 c crushed pineapple – 1 c celery – ½ c nuts. Dissolve Jell-O in hot water. Add juice and cool. Add sugar to ground cranberries and let stand while Jell-O is cooling. Mix all ingredients together and cool.
Marie Workenton
Brookings, OR

Cranberry Salad

2 c sugar – 1 pkg cranberries (grind) – 1 can crushed pineapple drained – 1 pkg miniature marshmallows – 1 pt whipping cream whipped. soak cranberries, pineapple and marshmallows in 1 tbl of sugar overnight. Whip cream add rest of the sugar and fold into the cranberries. Place in freezer. Take out 20 minutes before eating.
Emma
Hillsboro, OR

Cranberry Salad

1 lb uncooked cranberry – 2 oranges – 3 c water – 1 c sugar or a little more – 2 pkg strawberry Jell-O – 1 (#2) can crushed pineapple – 1 c pineapple juice – ½ c each nuts and celery chopped. Peel oranges, remove seeds and skin membrane. Put orange and cranberries through food chopped, add sugar. Let stand awhile, prepare Jell-O. Add crushed pineapple, juice and combine to the first mixture. Add celery and nuts when cool.
Dolores
Mitchell, SD

Crown Jewell Salad

3 (3 oz) pkg Jell-O (different flavors) – 4 c boiling water – ½ c pineapple juice – 1 pkg lemon Jell-O – 2 envelopes dream whip – 1 ½ c cold water – ¼ c sugar – 1/3 c melted oleo – 1 ½ c graham crackers (opt). Prepare the 3 pkg Jell-O separately using 1 c boiling water and ½ c cold for each box. Pour each one into an 8 inch sq pan. Chill overnight. In morning combine lemon Jell-O, sugar and 1 c boiling water and stir until Jell-O and sugar are dissolved. stir in pineapple juice, chill till slightly thickened. Mix cracker crumbs and oleo and press into pan. Cut the 3 Jell-O's into ½ inch cubes. Prepare topping as directed on pkg and blend into the lemon Jell-O, fold in Jell-O cubes. Pour in cracker crust and chill at least 5 hours.
Lola
Desmet, SD

Cucumber Salad

1 lg cucumber – ¼ tsp pepper – ½ tsp salt – 3 tbl oil – 3 tbl white vinegar – 5 tbl sugar. Mix together. Chill.
Kathy
Lake Preston, SD

Cucumber Salad

Cucumber cubed – tomatoes cubed – ham cubed – onion cubed (opt) – mayo, salt and pepper to taste. Chill at least one hour or overnight.
Norma McBeth
Dallas, OR

Dressing

For dip or salad dressing – 1 c mayo – 1 c sour cream – 1 c mayo – double pkg hidden valley dressing mix, some garlic (opt).
Pearl Cavender
Keizer, OR

Easy Day Salad

1 c fruit cocktail – 1 c mandarin oranges – 1 c pineapple tidbits – pkg vanilla instant pudding. Drain fruit. Mix fruit with pudding powder. Stir and chill. Bananas or apples maybe used for variety.
Gail
Lake Preston, SD

Finger Jell-o

1st layer – 1 envelope Knox gelatin – 1 (3 oz) Jell-O pkg – 1 c boiling water – ¼ c sugar – ¼ c cold water mix boiling water with gelatin and Jell-O. add sugar and mix well. Add cold water. Pour into 8x8' square pan. Cool and chill 30 min. in refrigerator 2nd layer – 1 envelope Knox gelatin – ½ c sugar – ¼ c cold water – ¾ c boiling water – 6 tbl canned milk (evaporated) dissolve gelatin with cold water. Add boiling water, sugar & canned milk mix well. Cool and pour onto 1st layer. 30 min. in refrigerator 3rd layer—same as 1st layer. I double the recipe and use 1 (6 oz) box of Jell-O and a 10x13 pan.
Penny Campball
Emmett, ID

French Dressing

1 c sugar – ½ c vinegar – 1 c oil – 1 c ketch up – 2 tsp salt – 1 tbl paprika. Mix all ingredients with mixer. Store in refrigerator. Very good.
Beverly Crandall
Keizer, OR

Fresh Fruit Salad

Layer in a dish. Bananas than strawberries. Mix instant coconut Jell-O pudding, pour ½ over fruit. Than another layer of fruit and than pudding. Top with whip cream. Can also use this as a dessert using coconut cookies on the side.
Lavonne
Emmett, ID

Fresh Veg Salad

Broccoli – cauliflower – carrots – radishes – celery – onion -mushrooms (fresh or canned) cut up vegs into serving pieces. Mix with Italian cream dressing. Mix the day before you want to serve it. Refrigerate. Keeps well for several days. Makes as small or as lg a salad as you like.
Irene
Hebron, ND

Fruit Salad

1 pkg lemon Jell-O – 1 c heated pineapple juice (finish filling with water) – 1 ½ c sm marshmallows – 1 (8 oz) pkg cream cheese – 1 c salad dressing – 2 c crushed pineapple – dream whip (can use cool whip or a ½ pt whipping cream your choice) dissolve Jell-O in hot juice. Pour over marshmallows & cream cheese. Blend with beater. Add salad dressing & whipped cream, fold in pineapple. Pour into 9x9 pans. Chill. Take 2 pkg of Jell-O (rasp) & 2 c boiling water & 1 pkg frozen rasp pour over other mixture & chill till firm.
Bernice
Klamath Falls, OR

Fruit Salad

1 c pineapple juice – ½ c sugars – 2 tbl cornstarch. cook till thick. Cool and pour over pineapple chunks and any fresh fruit you want to add.
Eva line
Lake Preston, SD

Fruit Salad

1 can pineapple tidbits save juice – 1 pkg sm marshmallows – 4 bananas – dressing. 2 eggs – 2 tbl cornstarch – ½ c sugars – 1 c pineapple juice finish filling with water. Mix well cornstarch, eggs and sugar. Add juice and heat till thick. Put on fruit. If to thick add a little cream.
Marlys
Lake Preston, SD

German Potato Salad

8 potatoes cooked, diced or sliced – 2/3 c oil – 2/3 c sugar – ¾ c vinegar – 1/8 tsp pepper – salt to taste – 1 lg onion chopped. Combine oil, sugar, and vinegar, and pepper, salt and chopped onion. Stir very well to dissolve sugar. Pour over cooked and cooled potatoes.
Hilda
Hebron, ND

German Potato Salad

1 lb diced bacon – 3 tbl flour – 3 tsp salt – 1 c chopped onion – ½ tsp pepper – 2/3 c sugar – 2/3 c vinegar – 1 1/3 c water – parsley – 1 c diced celery – 8 sliced potatoes cooked in skins. Fry bacon drain. Use 4 tbl fat in skilled add celery and onions. Cook gently. Add sugar, vinegar, salt and flour. Bring to a boil, pour over potatoes and bacon. Cover and bake in 3 qt casserole 30 minutes at 350*.
Carol
St. Paul, MN

German Potato Salad

Toss 4 c hot cooked diced potatoes with ½ c chopped celery – ¼ c chopped onions – ¼ chopped pimento – ½ c diced dill pickles. Heat commercial oil and vinegar dressing. Toss into salad. I did my own dressing. 2 tbl vinegar – ½ tsp salt and pepper – 1 tsp mustard – 6 tbl oil. Mix all except oil. Than gradually add oil with wire whisk to thicken and mix with salad.
Olga Peters
Salem, OR

German Potato Salad

Slice 8 potatoes (cooked) – 1 med onion till golden brown. add potatoes & enough water to cover potatoes about 2 c – 1 c sugar, salt and pepper to taste – 1 c vinegar, a pinch parsley & bacon. Simmer 4 to 5 hours. This is my great grandma recipe.
Alice
Elgin, ND

Glorified Rice Salad

Cook rice and cool, add ½ tsp salt. Dissolve 1 pkg lemon and orange Jell-O in ½ pint boiling water. Add ½ tsp pineapple juice. When liquid is cold, whip to the consistency of heavy whipping cream. fold into the Jell-O mixture – 2 c cold boiled rice – 1 c crushed pineapple – 1 c sugar and 1 c whipping cream. Set in refrig when harden serve with whipping cream. Any fruit can be used instead of pineapple.
Gladys
Northfields, MN

Hot Potato Salad

8 c cold diced potatoes salad and peeled – ½ lb diced Velveeta cheese – a little cut up onion – 1 c mayo – mix and bake at 325* for 1 ½ hours, stir while in baking process. Can use crock pot on low heat for all day.
Gladys
Northfields, MN

Hot Potato Salad

Boil potatoes with jackets and cool, peel & slice – stew a med onion and add about 1 c water – ½ c vinegar – ¼ c sugar – salt pepper. Than add potatoes to that juice and simmer slowly. You can add more vinegar and sugar if you like.
Ida
Rapid City, SD

Jell-O and Cabbage Salad

1 pkg lime Jell-O – 1 c hot water – 1 c pineapple juice, let set until jelled around edges. Add 1 c drained pineapple – ½ c nuts – ½ c whipped cream – ½ c mayo – 1 c chopped cabbage. Mix all together and sprinkle with nuts on top.
Irene
Forest Grove, OR

Jell-O Rhubarb Salad

1 pkg berry Jell-O – 1 ½ c hot sweetened rhubarb – ½ c crushed pineapples – 2 egg whites beaten stiff. Mix Jell-O, rhubarb and pineapple together, cool than add egg whites fold these in.
Barbara
Cornelius, OR

Knox Blox

4 envelopes Knox unflavored gelatin – 3 (3 oz) pkg Jell-O any kind – 4 c boiling water – combine gelatin and Jell-O add water stir till dissolved. Pour into lg pan 9x13 and chill till firm. Cut into sq for fruity blox use only 2 pkg of the gelatin flavored and stir in 1 can of fruit cocktail undrain (17 oz).
Charla
Forest Grove, OR

Krunchy Cherry Salad

2 small pkg cherry Jell-O – 2 ½ c boiling water – 1 can cherry pie filling – 1 c diced celery – nuts – 2 c diced apples – lettuce. Dissolve Jell-O in water and add cherry filling, fold in celery and nuts and apple. Pour into 9x13 pans. Let set, cut and serve on lettuce.
Myrl
Lake Preston, SD

Macaroni Salad

2 c lg macaroni cook till done. Drain and add grated carrots, radishes, onions and cooked frozen peas. Add salad dressing to taste.
Eunice
Lake Preston, SD

Marinated Cole Slaw

3 lb cabbage – 2 med onions – 1 green pepper. shred together. mix in 1 ½ c sugars and let stand while making dressing. dressing. 1 c salad oil – 1 tsp celery salt – 1 c vinegar – 1 tbl sugar – 1 tsp salt. bring to a boil, remove from heat and pour hot dressing over cabbage. Mix, cool and refrigerator at least one day before serving.
Shelly
Scappoose, OR

Molded Beet Salad

1 can shoestring beets drained, reserving liquid – 1 pkg (3 oz) lemon gelatin – ¼ c sugar – ¼ c vinegar – 1 tbl horseradish. Measure beet liquid and add water to make 1 ½ c. Bring to a boil, remove from heat add lemon gelatin. Stir till dissolved. Add sugar, vinegar and horseradish. Stir into beets. Pour into a dish. Chill in refrig until firm.
Dorletta
Corvallis, OR

Oak Pit Cole Slaw Dressing

½ c whipped cream – ½ c mayo – 2 tbl vinegar – ¼ c sugar – 1 tsp celery seed – whip second four ingredients and blend with the whipped cream. Add a dash of salt and pepper. Let set ½ hour. For garlic dressing. Use same recipe and add pressed garlic to your taste. For Roquefort dressing. Add blue cheese.
Norma McBeth
Dallas, OR

Olive Wreath

2 ½ c crushed pineapple (#2) – 1 pkg lime Jell-O – ½ c grated American cheese – ½ c chopped pimento (opt) – ½ c finely chopped celery – 2/3 c chopped walnuts – ¼ tsp salt – 1 c heavy cream whipped – small stuffed olives sliced. Drain pineapple, heat juice to a boil add boiling water to make 1 ½ c liquid dissolve Jell-O. When Jell-O begins to thicken add pineapple, cheese, pimento, celery, nuts and salt. Fold in whipped cream. Place row of cut olives in bottom of ring mold. Pour carefully into mold. Chill till firm.
Mabel
Scappoose, OR

Orange Dream Cycle Jell-O

1 box orange Jell-O – 1 box vanilla pudding – 1 box tapioca pudding – 2 ½ c water. Heat and stir until thickened. Set aside to cool. When cool, add 1 small can mandarin oranges, cut into pieces and drained. 1 small can crushed pineapple drained. 1 or 2 cups cool whip folded in. Let set in frig until time to serve.
Pearl Cavender
Keizer, OR

Orange Salad

2 pkg orange Jell-O – 1 c juice – 1 (2 ½ oz) can dice drained pineapple – 2 c boiling water – 1 (2 ½ oz) can apricots drained – ½ pkg small marshmallows. Combine ingredients and put in a 9x13 pan. Add topping below before serving. Topping. 1 egg beaten – ½ c sugar – 2 tbl flour – 2 c fruit juice. Cook till thick as pudding, cool and add 1 c whipped topping. Spread on Jell-O and on top with shredded cheese. I use both the pineapple and apricot juice.
Kay
Lake Preston, SD

Orange Sherbet Jell-O Salad

1 lg box orange Jell-O – 1 pt (2 c) orange sherbet ice cream – ½ pt whipping cream – 1 can mandarin oranges. Boil 2 cups water. Pour water into glass square pan and stir in Jell-O. Dissolve thoroughly. Stir in ice cream until melts. Refrigerate until practically set and remove from refrigerator. Stir in whipping cream (whip first) until mixed thoroughly. Add mandarin oranges. Refrigerate.
Olga Peters
Salem, OR

Paradise Salad

1 pkg lemon Jell-O – ½ pt whip cream – 1 (#2) can crushed pineapple drained – ¼ c cottage cheese – maraschino cherries. Dissolve Jell-O in one cup hot water. Drain pineapple. Force cheese thru sieve. Whip cream. Fold in whip cream, pineapple cottage cheese, nuts and cherries when Jell-O is cool.
Dottie
ST Helens, OR

Pear Cheese Salad

1 can (29 oz) pear halves save juice – 1 c pear juice – 1 (6 oz) pkg lime Jell-O – 2 ½ c boiling water – ½ c chopped nuts – 1 (8 oz) pkg cream cheese. Drain pears and save juice, arrange pears in Jell-O ring. Dissolve Jell-O in water add 1 c juice blend and refrig. till like thick syrup. Takes about 1 to 1 ½ hour. Measure ½ Jell-O mixture set aside. Pour the rest over pears. Seal and refrig till set but not firm. Will take about 1 hour. Blend thoroughly the cream cheese and the reserved ½ of the Jell-O. Carefully spoon and spread over the pear mixture. The cheese will be easier to work with if cut into chunks and taken out of refrig an hour before using. Sprinkle nuts over the cheese. Cover and refrig. Until firm.
Lass
Hoar, Germany

Pistachio Salad

#2 can crushed pineapple undrained – 1 box instant pistachio Jell-O – 2 c miniature marshmallows – 1 lg cool whip. Mix Jell-O dry into pineapple, fold in marshmallow and cool whip. Chill at least 2 to 3 hours. even better overnight.
Elaine
Lake Preston, SD

Rainbow in a Cloud

1 (3 oz) box Jell-O any flavor – 1 1/3 c cool whip – 1 c boiling water – ½ c cold water. Make Jell-O with water and pour into 8 inch pan. Chill for 3 hours. Cut into cubes. To remove quickly dip pan in warm water spoon cool whip in dessert dishes leaving a depression in center. Spoon Jell-O cubes in dish and top with cool whip.
Linda
Desmet, SD

Sauerkraut Salad

1/3 c veg oil – 1/3 c vinegar – 1 lg can sauerkraut drained a little 1 c chopped onion – 1 c shredded carrots – 1 c diced celery – 1 c diced green pepper – 1 c sugar – celery seed. Bring celery seed, oil and vinegar to a boil. Cool. Pour over remaining ingredients. Refrigerate 24 hours or overnight. toss occasionally to mix.
Melba
ST Helens, OR

Shortbread Cookie Salad

2 c buttermilk – 2 pkg banana or vanilla instant pudding – 1 lg tub cool whip – 2 cans mandarin oranges drained real well – 1 pkg fudge stripped shortbread cookies broken in small pieces. Take buttermilk and add pudding. Fold in cool whip and add orange than add cookies. Keeps real well.
Lola
Lake Preston, SD

Simple Quick Fruit Salad

1 can cherry pie filling – 1 pkg small marshmallows. 1 can pineapple chunks drained – mix all together and chill.
Eleen
Bryant, SD

Spinach Salad

in a shaker combine – ¾ c olive oil – 2 tbl vinegar – 1 tbl each of sugar, lemon, pepper and seasoning salt. Chill. Serve over fresh salad of spinach and sliced mushrooms.
Skip
Hillsboro, OR

Strawberry Jell-O Salad

1 sm box strawberry Jell-O – 16 lg marshmallows – 2 pkg dream whip – ¼ c boiling water – 1 lg can crushed pineapple – 1 (8 oz) cream cheese (room temp) dissolve Jell-O in boiling water. Add marshmallows & complete can of pineapple. Heat until marshmallows dissolve cool completely. Blend cream cheese in whipped dream whip, as stated on pkg. Blend whipped cream in with Jell-O mixture. Pour into dish. Chill.
Pearl Cavender
Keizer, OR

Strawberry Salad

2 sm pkg strawberry Jell-O dissolved in 1 c boiling water – 1 (10 oz) frozen strawberries – 2 c sweetened cooked rhubarb – 1 (6 oz) can crushed pineapple undrained. mix together and pour into 9x13 cake pan. Prepare 1 pkg dream whip and 1 pkg 3 oz cream cheese soften at room temp. Spread on top after mixture has set.
Leanne
Lake Preston, SD

Taco Salad

1 c chopped onion – 4 c cut up tomatoes – 1 c salad dressing taco sauce – 1 can kidney beans drained – 1 head shredded lettuce – 5 oz pkg Doritos – 4 c shredded or grated cheese – 2 lbs hamb cooked. Mix dressing with taco sauce. Mix with cheese, add onion, tomatoes and lettuce. Crumble the Doritos; add meat and beans put on top.
Martha
Lake Preston, SD

Taco Salad

2 c chili – 2 lbs hamb – make very hot – 1 head lettuce – 2 tomatoes – 1 onion – 1 bottle 1000 island dressing – 1 bag plain tortilla chips, fry meat, drain and add chili and heat real hot. Mix lettuce, onion and tomatoes. When ready to eat, add dressing to the above.
Mary
Richardton, ND

Taco Salad

1 head lettuce torn in pieces – 1 can kidney beans drained – 1 lb hamb cooked and drained – 4 tomatoes diced – 1 can black olives – 1 pkg corn or taco chips – 1 (8 oz) bottle French dressing serving, toss all ingredients together season with salt and pepper and taco sauce. May prepare ahead and refrigerate. ingred. in separate bowls.
Shelly
Scappoose, OR

Taco Salad

2 c hamb – 1 c (7 oz) chili salsa – 1 head lettuce – 3 lg tomatoes - 1 lg avocado – 4 green onion – 2 c grated cheese – 1 can (15 oz) kidney beans – cucumber – olives – 1 (10 oz) pkg tortilla chips. Mix hamb with taco seasoning. Cook hamb and salsa. Add rest of the ingredients toss. Add chips, top with dressing of your choice.
Paula Starcher
Emmett, ID

Taco Salad

1 lb hamb – 1 can (15 oz) kidney beans – 1 head lettuce – 2 tomatoes – 2 c grated cheese – 1 pkg (10 oz) tortilla chips – bottle (sm) French dressing – Tabasco to taste (mix with dressing) cook hamb, add kidney beans, drain and cool. Chop lettuce, dice tomatoes, and add cheese and dressing. Add hamb mixture and crushed tortilla chips.
Wilma Coates
Emmett, ID

Tropical Fruit Salad

1 can fruit cocktail – 1 can pineapple tidbits – 1 can mandarin oranges – 1 pkg vanilla pudding – 1 pkg orange or vanilla tapioca pudding. Drain juice off the fruits, add enough juice to make 3 c liquid and cook with the 2 puddings. Cool then add the fruits – 1 pkg of dream whip, whipped and 2 c of mini -marshmallows. You can also use fresh fruit.
Ona
Parkston, SD

Turkey or Chicken Salad

1 c mayo – 2 tbl lemon juice – ½ tsp salt – ¼ tsp pepper – 3 c turkey diced and cooked – 1 ½ c sliced celery – ½ c chopped onions – ¼ c chopped parsley – 3 hard boiled eggs – ½ c cubed cheese – ½ can French shoe string potatoes. Mix all together.
Ruth
Owatonna, MN

Turkey Salad Polynesian

2 ½ c uncooked mataccioli pasta tube shaped macaroni – 2 c cubed cooked turkey – ¾ c sliced celery – ¾ c chopped walnuts – ¼ c thinly sliced green onions – 11 oz can mandarin orange segments, drained – 8 oz can pineapple tidbits in its own juice, drained reserving 2 tbl juice for dressing. Dressing. ½ c reduced calorie mayo – 1/3 c low fat dairy sour cream – 2 tbl reserved pineapple juice – ½ tsp salt. Cook mataccile to desired doneness as directed on pkg. Drain rinse with cold water. in large bowl, combine all salad ingredients. In small bowl, combine all dressing ingredients, blend well. Pour dressing over pasta mixture, toss gently. (Can use curly macaroni)
Claudia
Emmett, ID

Watergate Salad

4 (8 oz) cool whip – 3 pkg instant pistachio Jell-O – 2 (15 ½ oz) cans barely drained crushed pineapple – 1 c nuts – 2 lg can drained fruit cocktail – 1 ½ bags fruit flavored marshmallows. Mix ingredients together, leaving marshmallows till last. Chill 2 hours. This serves a lot.
Wilma Coates
Emmett, ID

Waldorf Salad

2 c apples – 1 c chopped celery – ½ c chopped nuts – ½ c raisins – 1 c mayo or whipped cream. Pare apples if desired. Combine ingredients and chill thoroughly serve on crisp lettuce leaf. If preparing apples in advance squeeze lemon juice over to keep from turning brown.
Barbara
Cornelius, OR

Baked Beans

4 c white beans soaked overnight in 12 c water – 1 med onion stuck with 2 whole cloves – 1 bay leaf – 1 clove of garlic – 1 tsp salt – 2 tbl oil. Simmer the above until nearly tender about 1 hour. Remove from heat and discard onion, garlic and bay leaf. Pour beans into a strainer saving water to make 3 cups. Put beans pot place 1 onion with beans on top. Mix the following. ½ c ketch up – ½ tsp Worcestershire sauce, add to mixture. Add ½ lb salt pork and the bean water. Push pork down into the beans, letting only the top edge to show. Cover tightly with foil and bake all day or overnight at 250* for at least 6 to 8 hours.
Barbara
Cornelius, OR

Baked Beans

pork and beans – dash Heinz 57 sauce – dash a1 sauce – 1 tsp dry mustard – bacon strips – 1 c brown sugar – salt and pepper to taste. Bake 350* for 40 minutes.
Jimmy
Beaverton, OR

Baked Cabbage

1 med head cabbage – 1 tbl flour – salt and pepper to taste – 1 tbl sugar – 1 c sweet cream – sliced bacon. Shred cabbage and put in baking dish. Mix sugar and flour and combine with cream, salt and pepper. Pour over cabbage. Cover cabbage with slices of bacon and bake in covered dish at 350* for 1 hour. Remove cover when cabbage is nearly done to crisp bacon.
Anggie
Richardton, ND

Batter for Onion Rings

½ c flour – 1 tsp sugar – ½ tsp salt – 1 egg – ¼ c water – Mix together with fork till smooth.
Wilma Coates
Emmett, ID

BBQ Beans

1 c green beans drained – 1 can kidney beans drained – 1 can lima beans drained – 1 can pork and beans. Mix 1 tbl mustard dry or prepared – 1 tbl Worcestershire sauce – ½ c ketch up – 3 tbl vinegar – ½ tsp salt – 1 c brown sugar. Pour sauce over beans. Add cooked chopped bacon. Cover and bake 30 minutes at 350*.
Jana Watson
Boise, ID

Beans

2 lbs white beans – ¾ c brown sugar – ¾ c sugar – 1 tbl salt – ¼ lb bacon – ¾ c ketch up. Cook beans till all most tender. Add the remaining ingredients and bake at 350* for 1 hour.
Thelma
Richardton, ND

Bean Hot Dish

1 lg can baked beans – 1 can kidney beans – 1 can butter beans – ½ lb bacon fried and drained. cook the following for 20 minutes – ½ c vinegar – 2 c chopped onion – 1 c brown sugar – ½ tsp dry mustard – scant tsp garlic salt than mix with beans and bake at 350* for 1 hour.
Dorthea
Coolidge, AZ

Beef and Beans

2 cans pork and beans – 1 tbl mustard – 1 tbl Worcestershire sauce – 1 med onion chopped – ½ lb hamb – ½ c ketch up – ½ c brown sugar. Mix beans with mustard, ketch up, sugar, sauce and onions. Brown meat. Add to beans. Place in a 3 qt dish. Bake at 400* for 45 minutes.
Jan-nita
ST Helens, OR

Bell Pepper Stuffing

1 lb hamburger – 1 med green pepper diced – 1 med onion diced – 1 tbs spoon minced garlic – salt & pepper to taste – 1 14.5 oz stewed tomatoes + 1 can water – 2 tbs spoons Worchester sauce – 1 ½ c instant rice – 2 c grated co jack cheese: cook first 5 ingredients until done. Add Worchester sauce, tomatoes and water, bring to a boil, add rice. Cover and turn off heat. let set 5 minutes, fluff with spoon (add more water to rice if necessary). Top with cheese when served.
Barbara Jeans
Emmett, ID

Bread Dressing

sauté onion and celery until brown. Cooked gizzards (you can use hamb instead) heat milk, cream of mushroom soup- cream of celery soup. You can use the broth from boiling necks, and backs of chicken. Combine veg and liquid. Add celery salt, onion, salt, poultry seasoning, sage and bread cubes. mix well. Bake at 375* for 35 min or until done.
Nastasha Rowley
Emmett, ID

Broccoli and Ham Rolls

10 oz pkg frozen chopped broccoli – 10 ¾ oz can cream of mushroom soup (can use chicken or onion soup cream style) chunked ham or chicken – 4 eggs – oleo – ½ c water. In 2 qt sauce pan prepare broccoli as directed. Drain. Add undiluted soup and meat with a little juice. Cook stirring off and on until meat is heated thru and broken into small pieces. Keep warm. In small bowl with fork beat eggs and water until well blended. In skillet over med heat melt 1 tsp oleo tilting pan to grease sides. Pour 2 to 3 tbl egg mixture into pan tilting to make thin pancakes. When top is set and underside is brown. Make 7 cakes. Fill each one with broccoli mixture, roll and arrange in 1 layer on warm dish, top with sour cream or a cream sauce.
Charla
Forest Grove, OR

Cabbage Curry

5 c finely shredded cabbage – 4 tsp oleo – pinch of pepper – 2 tbl minced onion – ¾ c milk – 4 tsp flour – ¾ tsp curry powder – 1 tsp salt. Cook cabbage till barely tender in ½ inch boiling water about 6 minutes. Meanwhile melt oleo in double boiler, stir in flour, pepper, curry, onion and salt, stir until smooth and thickened, stirring constantly. Heap sauce over cabbage, toss and serve.
Nellie
Hillsboro, OR

Cabbage Soup

Cook 1 whole chicken in water, enough to cover. When chicken is done, remove from pan and allow to cool enough to take meat off bones. Reserve the broth in the pan. Put deboned chicken back in pan and add 1 tbl poultry seasoning and 1 tbl sage. Add salt and pepper to taste. Add garlic seasoning and minced onion seasoning (opt). Add chopped cabbage, diced potatoes, and 1 can whole or chopped tomatoes. Allow to simmer until cabbage and potatoes are fork tender. Add ½ to ¾ cup milk before serving. Olga Peters
Salem, OR

Cheesy BBQ Potatoes

2 c cheddar cheese shredded – 1 can cream of mushroom soup 2 tbl bbq sauce – 4 c sliced raw potatoes – ½ tsp paprika – 1/3 c milk – 1/8 tsp pepper – ¼ tsp oregano – ¼ tsp salt – in lg bowl mix together 1 ½ c cheese, soup, milk, bbq sauce, oregano, salt and pepper. Stir in spuds until well coated turn into shallow baking dish, cover with foil. Bake at 350* for 45 minutes. Sprinkle with cheese remaining and paprika. Let stand 5 minutes.
Jackie
Sentinel Butte, ND

Cream of Potato Soup

1 stalk celery – 2 tbl butter – 3 med potatoes – 2 tbl flour – ¼ onion – 2 c milk – ¼ tsp salt – 1/8 tsp pepper – 2 ½ c boiling water – peel and dice pot (about 2 c) wash & dice one stalk of celery & mince ¼ of an onion – put pot, celery, onion, salt, pepper in boiling water. Simmer covered for 10 to 15 minutes or until fork tinder. Stir every couple of min. so soup won't stick. While the pot are cooking, heat butter in a sauce pan on med heat. Add flour & salt to the butter stir until well blended. Pour all milk into mixture while stirring with wire wisk. Heat mixtures to boiling stirring constantly cook 1 to 2 min after it begins to boil. Combine white sauce, pot and pot water. Heat to serving temp.
Tasha Murray
Middleton, ID

Cheese & Brown Frilattata

6 eggs – 1 c milk – 1 minced green onion – 2 tbl melted oleo – ½ tsp salt – 1 tsp pepper – 14 oz pkg shredded cheese – ½ of a 3 oz can crumbled bacon bits or bacon fried crisp and broke into pieces. Grease 9x9 baking pan. Beat egg, milk, onion, oleo, salt and pepper till well blended. Pour mixture into pan. Sprinkle cheese and bacon evenly over the top. Bake 20 minutes till set and golden. Bake at 400*.
Mary
Portland, OR

Chili Pie Casserole

3 c corn chips – ½ c chopped onions – 1 c grated cheese – 1 can (19 oz) chili. place chips in a 9x13 pan. Arrange onions, and ½ of the cheese on chips. Pour the chili over top. Top with remaining cheese and chips. Bake at 350* for 15 to 20 minutes.
Linda
Bessiemer, AK

Deep Fry Batter

1 c buttermilk pancake mix – 1 tbl oil – 1 egg – ½ tsp paprika – ¾ c milk – ¼ tsp pepper – 1 tsp salt. Beat egg and milk together. Add oil and mix till dry ingredients are moistened. Stir in salt, pepper and paprika.
Jan-nita
ST Helens, OR

Free Soup

12 oz tomato juice – dehydrated onions – parsley flakes – celery chopped – green pepper chopped – 1 sm head cabbage chopped – 1 chicken bouillon cube – 2 beef bouillon cubes – salt and pepper – 1 to 2 pkg French style green beans. Add approximately 1 c water to the above ingredients in a sauce pan. Boil one hour. Can also add watercress, Chinese peas, cauliflower and broccoli.
Olga Peters
Salem, OR

Five Bean and Bacon Bake

1 pkg bacon – 3 lg onions thinly sliced – ¾ c brown sugar – ½ c vinegar – ½ tsp garlic powder – 1 can (16 oz) each of butter beans, green beans, green lima beans, kidney beans and baked beans. Fry bacon until done, not crisp drain & set aside. Reserve 2 tbl of dripping. Reduce heat & add onions, brown sugar, vinegar, garlic powder to skillet, stir well, cover & cook 2 min. then drain & combine the beans except baked. Add baked beans undrained to the rest of the beans. Combine mix & ½ of the bacon slices crumbled in a 3 qt casserole, top with remaining bacon sliced. Cook uncovered 1 hour at 350*
Alice
Coolidge, AZ

Four Beans

1 can kidney beans drained – 1 can lima beans drained – 1 can butter beans drained – 1 can pork and beans with molasses (do not drain) mix beans in casserole. Make a sauce with ½ lb chopped bacon, ham or span with 2 lg onions. Add garlic salt, ½ tsp dry mustard, ½ c ketch up and ¾ c brown sugar. Simmer 10 to 20 minutes. Add to beans. Bake 1 hour at 350*
Wilma Coates
Emmett, ID

Fried Onion Rings

¾ c flour – 2/3 c milk – 1 egg – ¼ tsp salt – 2 tbl oil – 2 onions peeled and sliced ¼ inch thick. Sift flour and salt in a bowl. Add milk, oil and egg beaten until smooth. Separate onions into rings. Dip each in batter. Fry 2 to 3 minutes in oil heated to 370* Turing occsa. Drain and sprinkle with salt.
Grace
Gray, KY

Fried Rice

2 c cooked rice – sauté 1 small onion diced – 1 stalk celery diced ¼ c strips of green pepper – 1 strip bacon cut real fine – 1 egg. Mix together, add rice last and fry in a small amount of butter.
Mary
Portland, OR

Green Bean and Potatoes

combine 1 ½ c cooked green beans – 1 c diced boiled potatoes and 1 c sliced celery in a casserole. Fry 4 sliced bacon, drain and crumble. sauté 2 tbl finely chopped onions in 1 tbl of bacon dripping. Stir in 1 tbl flour, add 1 c milk slowly stir constantly. Cook until thickens and smooth. Add 1 c shredded cheese stir until melted. Pour over veg in casserole, mix well. Sprinkle ½ c potato chips and bacon crumb. Bake at 350* for 30 minutes. Melba
ST Helens, OR

Grilled Cheese Sandwich

2 pieces of bread (any type) butter on one side. Place butter side down on hot frying pan. Place cheese on bread. Place other piece of bread butter side up on top. Brown turn over and brown other side. enjoy.
Shane Coates
Boise, ID

Harvard Beets

3 tbl sugar – 1 tbl cornstarch – ¼ tsp salt – dash of pepper – 2 c (16 oz) sliced beets drained – ½ c liquid (reserved from beets) – 3 c vinegar. in sauce pan, combine sugar, cornstarch and seasonings. Stir in beet liquid and vinegar. Cook over med low until thickened. mix in beets and heat through.
Wilma Coates
Emmett, ID

Harvard Beets

3 c cooked diced beets – 1 c beet liquid and water if needed to finish the cup. 3 tbl flour – 2 tbl sugar – 1 tsp each salt and pepper – 1/3 c vinegar. Heat until thickened.
Shirley
Willmar, MN

Home Made Noodles

Sift 2 c flour into a bowl. Make a well and drop 4 eggs and 2 tsp salt into it. Mix by hand and knead into a hard dough. Divide into 4 balls and roll out very thin. Lay on a clean cloth to partly dry. Fold in half and half again. Roll up and cut off very thin noodles. Spread out loosely. Bring water or broth to a boil. Cook to a rolling boil and serve.
Olga Peters
Salem, OR

Homemade Stove Top Dressing

1 ¾ c water – 2 tbl chopped onion – 1 ½ tsp chicken or beef bouillon – ¼ tsp garlic powder – ¼ c butter – 2 tbl celery or a ¼ tsp celery salt – ½ tsp dried parsley flakes – ½ tsp salt – dash of pepper. Combine all ingredients and boil 8 minutes. Stirring now and then. Pour over 6 c dried bread crumbs, mix well. Cover and let stand 5 minutes. Fluff with fork and serve.
Eva
Golva, ND

Hot Bean Dish

1 can (16 oz) kidney beans drained – 1 can (16 oz) pork and beans drained – 1 can lima or butter beans drained – but keep juice to add later in case liquid is needed. 1 lb bacon (prefried) – 1 lb hamb and 1 lg onion prefried together. 1 c catsup and brown sugar. Make in slow cooker.
Wilma Coates
Emmett, ID

Irish Colcannon

2 lbs potatoes – 3 tsp salt – 4 c shredded cabbage – 1 ½ c sliced green onion – 1/3 c milk – ½ c butter – ¼ tsp pepper. Boil potatoes cover with 1 tsp salt 15 minutes or till fork tender. Drain. Heat slowly just enough to fry out. Boil cabbage and ¼ tsp salt 10 minutes. Drain. Heat onions, milk and ½ tsp salt. Bring to boil and simmer 10 minutes. Drain onions reserving milk. Beat potatoes and 2 tbl butter, 1 tsp salt and pepper. Beat in onions and part of the reserved milk. Stir in cabbage and pour rest of melted butter over and serve hot.
Mary
Portland, OR

Klep Suppe (Milk Soy w/Dumplings)

2 eggs beaten – ½ c milk – ½ tsp salt – 1 tsp sugar – ¼ tsp baking powder – flour to make fairly stiff dough. Combine ingredients and mix until smooth. Scald 2 qts milk and ½ tsp salt. Drop by tsp. Spoon into milk and cook until done about 15 minutes.
Sonja
ST Helens, OR

Macaroni and Tomato Soup

Beef stock bring to a boil. Cook macaroni in the stock. Add celery, onion, and tomato puree and tomato soup.
Nellie
Hillsboro, OR

Marinated Carrots

2 cans (15 oz) carrot round, boil and cool – 1 c sugar and ½ c vinegar. mix carrots, - 1 c sliced green peppers – 1 lg onion sliced – 1 c celery chopped. mix in 1 can tomato soup. set 1 day before using. keep 2 to 3 weeks in fridge. Great for get tog ethers.
Loretta
Dickenson, ND

Pearl Onions in Cream Sauce

3 tbl oleo – 3 tbl flour – 1 ½ c milk heat almost to boiling small pearl onions, salt and pepper to taste – dash nutmeg – cook onions in boiling water for 10 minutes whole and than drain. Cream sauce, melt oleo over med heat. When melted, add flour, stirring constantly with wire wisk, till oleo is dissolved. Turn heat down low and add milk slowly. Add seasoning. Fold in onions and mix well. I add peas cooked and drained a little parsley.
Wilma Coates
Emmett, ID

Pesole'

Small Pork roast – boil and pull apart (do not drain) – add tp the mixture – 1-2 cans tomato sauce (8 oz) – 1 package chili seasoning – 1 tsp vinegar – 1-2 large cans hominy – Italian seasoning and Oregano to taste. Bring to a complete boil for several minutes. Serve in bowls topped with gratted cabbage and a squeeze of lime.
Randy Wilson
Emmett, ID

Potato Casserole

2 lbs frozen hash brown potatoes – 1 tsp salt – 1 can cream of chicken soup undiluted – 2 c grated cheddar cheese – 2 c sour cream, onion if desired – 2 c crushed corn flakes. Thaw potatoes and combine all ingredients except corn flakes into baking dish. Put corn flakes over top. Bake at 350* for 45 minute or 1 hour.
Virginia Quenzer
Emmett, ID

Potatoes Romanof

6 large potatoes – 1 pint sour cream – 1 bunch green onions (chopped fine) – 1 ½ c grated sharp cheese – 1 ½ tsp salt – ½ tsp pepper -- cook potatoes unpeeled until tender. Cool, peel, shred on grater or slice very thin into large bowl. Stir in sour cream, onion, 1 c cheese, salt & pepper. Turn into casserole & top with remaining cheese. Sprinkle paprika on top. Cover and refrigerate several hours or overnight. Bake uncovered for 30-40 minutes at 350*.
Kristine Frolov
Notus, ID

Potatoes & Franks

3 c hot mashed potatoes – 1 (8 oz) cheese whiz spread – ¼ c green onions sliced – 1 tbl prepared mustard – 1 lb wieners cut in half length wise. Combine potatoes, cheese, onion and mustard, mix well. In lightly greased 10x6 baking dish layer ½ of the potato mixture and wieners, repeat layers. Bake at 350* for 25 minutes. Garnish with green onions.
Jan-nita
ST Helens, OR

Pumpkin Soup

3 to 4 pieces of chicken boiled with diced onion (dice chicken when done) – add 2 cans diced tomatoes – 1 can tomato sauce – 1 bag frozen broc (chopped fine) – 2 cups cooked pumpkin – 4 to 5 diced potatoes with skin – cook till potatoes are tender, add ¼ to ½ cup sour cream.
Annette lutes
Emmett, ID

Quiche Lorriane

1 unbaked pie shell – 1 tbl soft butter – 12 slices bacon – 4 eggs – pinch of nutmeg – pinch of sugar – pinch of pepper (cayenne) – 1/8 tsp pepper – 2 c ½ & ½ cream – ¾ tsp salt – ¼ lb grated Swiss cheese. Rub butter over surface of unbaked pie shell. Fry bacon till crisp and crumble into small pieces. Combine eggs, cream, salt, nutmeg, sugar, peppers with hand beater, just to mix. Sprinkle pie shell with bacon and cheese. Pour in the cream mixture. Bake 15 minutes. at 425*. layer heat to 300* for 40 minutes.
Mabel
Scappoose, OR

Refried Bean Dip

Mix 1 c mayo – 1 c sour cream – and 1 pkg taco seasoning mix. Spread 1 or 2 cans refried beans in a casserole dish. Spread above mixture over the beans. Top with grated cheese. Garnish with diced tomatoes, olives, and green onions. Serve with chips and salsa.
Pearl Cavender
Keizer, OR

Rice & Broccoli Casserole

1 c cooked rice – 1/3 c butter softened – 1 c shredded cheese – 1 egg beaten – 1 can cream of chicken soup – ½ c milk – 1 onion grated – 1 pkg frozen chopped broccoli cooked and drained. Combine all ingredients. Mix well. Spoon mixture into a greased 1 ½ qt casserole. Bake 1 hour at 350*.
Delores
Richardton, ND

Rice & Broccoli Hot Dish

2 c cooked rice – 2 pkg (20 oz) frozen broccoli cooked – 1 can of cream of celery soup – 1 can cream of mushroom soup. Brown and sauté – 1 c chopped onion and 1 c chopped celery in ½ c oleo. Add 1 jar cheese whiz and bake 30 minutes at 350*.
Loretta
Dickenson, ND

Road Side Potatoes

1 pkg (16 oz) or ½ of a 32 oz pkg frozen hash browns – ¼ c (½ stick) butter – 1 sm onion minced – ½ c shredded cheddar cheese – ½ c grated parmesan cheese – salt and pepper – 1/3 c ½ & ½ - 3 tbl firm butter – parsley flakes in a large bowl. Combine the potatoes, melted butter, onions and cheese. Turn into a well buttered 9 in baking dish. Sprinkle with salt and pepper. Add ½ & ½ . dot with butter. Bake at 350* for 1 hour or until the potatoes are slightly crusty on the edges and lightly browned. Sprinkle with parsley. Could add crispy bacon on top.
Olga peters
Salem, OR

Rotemos (Rutabagas)

Cook rutabagas until tender, then drain. Add half as much boiled potatoes and mash together until light and fluffy. Add a little sweet cream and butter. Season to taste. Keep hot till ready to serve. can omit potatoes.
Sonja
ST Helens, OR

Scalloped Corn

1 egg – 1 c sour cream – 1 can cream style corn – 1 can whole kernel corn – 1 stick oleo – salt – pepper – 1 tbl dry onion – 1 pkg corn muffin mix. mix all together and put in 9x9 pan or in casserole dish. Bake at 350* for 50 to 60 minutes.
Vivian
Lake Preston, SD

Skillet Cabbage

2 tbl butter – ½ c onion – 1 c green pepper – 1 ½ tsp salt – 1/8 tsp pepper – 2 c tomatoes – 1 c celery sliced thin – 1 qt shredded cabbage – 1 tsp sugar. Melt butter and add rest of ingredients and cook till veg are tender.
Angie
Richardton, ND

Stuffed Potato W/Cheese

Baking potatoes – butter – salt – pepper – egg yolks – light cream or milk scalded – Romano cheese grated – paprika. Wash and scrub potatoes. pierce with a fork and bake at 400* for 1 hour or till tender. Cut potatoes length wise and scoop out, reserving the shell. Combine potato, butter, salt, pepper, egg yolk, cream and Romano cheese beat till smooth. Put mixture back into shells. Sprinkle with cheddar cheese and paprika. Return to the oven and heat till top is browned about 15 minutes.
Jean
Oklahoma City, OK

Swedish Cabbage Rolls

12 lg cabbage leaves – ¼ c milk – ¼ c chopped onions – 1 lb hamb 1 (8 oz) can tomatoes – 1 tsp salt & pepper – 1 c cooked rice – 1 tbl brown sugar – 1 tsp Worcestershire sauce. Immerse cabbage in lg kettle of boiling water until you can separate leaves and they are limp. Drain. Combine egg, milk, and onion, salt and pepper cooked beef, rice, and canned tomatoes. Place about ¼ meat mixture in center of each leaf, fold in sides and roll ends over meat. place in slow cooker seam sides down. Combine tomato sauce, brown sugar, lemon juice and Worcestershire sauce. Pour over cabbage rolls. Cover and cook on low 7 to 9 hours.
Pearl Cavender
Keizer, OR

Sweet and Sour Beans

8 bacon slices, fry till crisp, drain and chunk – 4 lg onions cut into rings – ½ to 1 c brown sugar – 1 tsp dry mustard – ½ tsp garlic powder – 1 tsp salt – ½ c vinegar. Place onions in skillet bacon were cooked in. Add sugar, mustard, garlic, salt, pepper and vinegar. Cook 20 minutes. Into 3 qt casserole put 2 cans (15 oz) each white lima beans, drained. 1 lg can baked beans undrained – 1 c kidney beans drained add sauce to the bacon which has been added and cook for about 1 hour at 350*.
Olive
Sentinel Butte, ND

Sweet and Sour Baked Beans

8 slices bacon, cooked and crumbles – 2 ½ lg onions – 1 lg green pepper cut into rings – ¾ c brown sugar – 1 tsp garlic powder – ½ c vinegar – 1 tbl salt – 1 tbl dry mustard – 1/3 c bbq sauce – 2 cans (15 oz) lg white lima beans drained – 1 can green lima beans - 1 can red kidney beans drained – 1 can (1 lb 11 oz) baked beans. preboil onions and green pepper rings 10 minutes, drain, add brown sugar, garlic powder, salt, and dry mustard, vinegar and bbq sauce, salt, and pepper to taste. Mix all ingredients except paprika and parsley in lg bowl. Let stand for about 10 to 15 minutes. Put in buttered cake pan. 9x13 top with paprika and parsley. Bake at 325* for 1 ½ to 2 hours or until done.
Francis
Richardton, ND.

Uncommon Ramen

ingredients: 1-2 pounds of meat (any kind, preferably boneless, anything from ground beef to chicken) - 2 packages of ramen (compatible with whatever meat you have selected) - 2 cans of a premium soup (Campbell's select, Progresso, or whatever you have) - 1 pound bag of frozen vegetables (Normandy blend) directions: cook meat as desired. I prefer to grill it on my George foreman grill. When it cooled about 5 minutes and then cube it. (cut it into sizes that would be comfortable to soup) start cooking the ramen following the package directions. I usually steam the veg of the ramen but you can add them in after the ramen is finished. When the ramen is finished, add all the other ingredients. Make sure to add in the seasoning and any other seasonings you may enjoy. I typically will add in some salt and some Mrs. Dash. Cook on medium heat stirring occasionally until everything is done. (make sure the frozen vegetables aren't frozen anymore.)
Udo Lutes
Emmett, ID

Wild Rice Dressing

1 box of Uncle Ben's rice – 2 pkg turkey gravy mix onion and celery. Add amount of water on gravy pkg and than add the mix. Sauté the celery and onion. Mix all together and stuff turkey.
Sandra
Hillsboro, OR

Zucchini Skillet

4 c sliced zucchini – 3 slices bacon chopped – 1 c grated cheese garlic powder and pepper to taste – ½ c chopped onion. Brown bacon and onion. Add zucchini and seasonings on high heat to keep most of moisture cooked out. Fry stirring occasionally. When squash is soft and clear add cheese on top. Serve when cheese is melted.
Marie
Beach, ND

Zucchini Soufflé

4 c cubed zucchini cook until just tender in 2 c boiling water – 2 eggs beaten in a lg bowl – stir in 1 c mayo – salt – pepper – ¼ c chopped green pepper – 1 chopped onion – 1 c grated cheese. Add zucchini to eggs and veg put in a baking dish. Do not grease sides of pan. Sprinkle on bread crumbs and dot with butter. Bake at 350* for 30 minutes. Broccoli can be used instead of zucchini.
Thelma
Beach, ND

Almond Bark Candy

1 lb almond bark – 2 c peanut butter – 2 c rice krispie – 1 c Spanish peanuts – 2 c marshmallows. Melt bark, add peanuts butter and mix. Add rice krispies peanuts, and marshmallows. Spoon onto wax paper. Chill.
Beverly
Richardton, ND

Almond Butter Candies

1 c butter – 1 1/3 c sugar – 1 tbl corn syrup – 3 tbl water – 1 c coarsely chopped almonds toasted – 4 (4 ½ oz) milk choc bars, melted – 1 c finely chopped almonds toasted. in lg sauce pan melt butter. Add sugar, syrup and water. Cook stirring occasionally to the hard crack stage (300*) (watch carefully after 250*) quickly stir in coarsely chopped almonds. Spread in ungreased 13x9x2 pan. Cool thoroughly. Turn out on wax paper. Invert. Spread with ½ of the melted choc. Sprinkle with ½ of the nuts. Cover with waxed paper. Invert. Spread with remaining choc and nuts. Chill to firm, crack in pieces. As a family, we prefer choc and nuts on only 1 side less mess.
Barbara
Emmett, ID

Anise Candy

2 c sugar – 1 c water – ¾ c white syrup. Boil to crack stage 280* remove from heat. Add 1 tbl oil of anise – 10 drops food (red) coloring. Quickly stir to mix. Pour into greased flat pan or greased muffin tins. When making cinnamon candy use 1 sm bile cin oil about 1 tsp.
Isemarie
Moet, ND

Angel Food Candy

1 lb sweet choc bars – ¼ tsp salt – 2 c filberts – ½ lb mini marshmallows. Melt choc over water. Stir constantly. Remove form heat, add salt and stir until smooth. Add nuts. Continue stirring and add marshmallows stir until the marshmallows are entirely coated. Pour into buttered pan. Cut into pieces when cooled.
Polly
Canby, OR

Butterscotch Crisp

1 c butter – 1 c sugar. Cook to hard crack stage 300*. Spread on foil lined cookie sheet. Sprinkle with 6 oz pkg of butterscotch chips. Let melt for 4 minutes. Spread with back of spoon. Sprinkle with finely chopped brazil or hazel nuts. Chill.
Gene
Warren, OR

Candy

½ lb nuts spread in 9x13 pan – 2 c sugar – 2 c butter. Boil until color of brown and beating fast all the time so butter and sugar do not separate. Takes at least 15 minutes to med boil stage or 232* on thermometer. Spread over nuts and cut into squares. Cool and put in pieces.
Helen
Richardton, ND

Candy Recipe

1 (12 oz) pkg choc chips – ½ pkg caramels – ¾ c peanut butter – ¼ c sweetened condensed milk – ½ c heavy whipped cream (whipped stiff) – 2 c chopped walnuts – 1 ½ c coconut. Melt choc chips in double boiler. Add all other ingredients. Mix and melt till creamed together. Drop by spoonfuls onto waxed paper. Cool in refrigerator. Enjoy.
Julie
Emmett, ID

Carmel Candy

1 pkg caramels – 4 tbl milk – 1 c nuts, rice krispies coconut. Melt caramels and milk. Add 2 c rice krispies and nuts. Roll in balls and then in coconut.
Marie Workenton
Brookings, OR

Carmel Corn

Combine in sauce pan and boil for 5 minutes – 2 c brown sugar – 2 cubes butter – ½ c molasses – 1 scant tsp salt – add 1 tsp soda and stir. Pour over 7 ½ qt popped corn. mix. Put on cookie sheets and bake in oven at 200* for 1 hour. Crumble when cool and enjoy.
Cheryl Hamilton
Emmett, ID

Cheerio Christmas Tree

12 tbl butter – 12 c mini marshmallows – (2 bags) melt over double boiler, remove from heat and add 2 tsp vanilla and green food coloring. Add this mixture to 16 c (lg box) of cheerios. Stir to coat and let cool until warm. Cover hands with butter and form trees. Cut green gum drops into slices and press circles onto tree for decorations. (I use all colors gum drops)
Julie
Emmett, ID

Chinese Fried Walnuts

6 c water – 4 c walnuts – ½ c sugar – salad oil – salt – in 4 qt sauce pan over high heat, heat water to boiling, add walnuts and heat to boiling. Cook 1 min. Rinse under running hot water, drain, wash saucepan and dry well. In large bowl with rubber spatula gently stir warm walnuts with sugar, until sugar is dissolved. (if necessary let mixture stand 5 min to dissolve sugar) mean while in same saucepan over med heat, heat about 1 inch salad oil to 350* on deep fat themeter, with slotted spoon add about ½ of the nuts to oil. Fry 5 min or till golden brown, stirring often. With slotted spoon place nuts in coarse sieve over bowl to drain. Sprinkle very lightly with salt. Toss lightly to keep nuts from sticking together. Transfer to paper towel to cool. Fry rest of walnuts.
Mary
Portland, OR

Chocolate Brittle

mico-wave – 1 c sugar – ½ c corn syrup – 1 c pistachio nuts (no red ones –use green) – 2 tbs oleo – 1 tsp vanilla – ½ tsp soda – 1 (6 oz) choc chips – combine sugar and syrup in a 2 qt dish, microwave for 4 minutes. Stir and microwave again for 4 minutes. Stir in nuts, mix in butter and vanilla. Microwave for 1 minute longer remove. Stir in soda. Sprinkle chips over hot candy and let stand for 3 minutes. Spread chips over candy with knife. Refrigerate until firm. Brake into pieces.
Louise
ST Helens, OR

Chocolate Coconut Balls

2 eggs beaten – 1 c powdered sugar – 1 tsp vanilla. Melt 1 pkg (8 oz) choc chips. When cool add to the above mixture. Add 1 c chopped nuts – 1 c mini marshmallow. Make into balls and roll in coconut or drop by spoon or make into a log, and roll in coconut and cut into slices.
Mabel
Scappose, OR

Choc Peanut Butter Balls

½ c butter – 2 c nestles quick – ½ c boiling water – 1 lb powdered sugar – 1 c peanut butter- finely chopped peanuts or coconut. Combine in order. Cool a few minutes. Form into 1 inch balls and roll in finely chopped nuts.
Thea
Emmett, ID

Coconut Balls

1 stick melted oleo – coconut – 2 ¾ c crushed vanilla wafers – orange juice – powdered sugar. Combine wafers, oleo and nuts. Shape into balls. Roll balls in powdered sugar. Dip into orange juice. Roll in coconut and chill.
Glenda
ST Helens, OR

Coconut Cherry Freeze

Prepare cherry fluffy frosting mix as directed on pkg except use ½ c cold water. Beat frosting until fluffy about 3 minutes on high speed, gradually beat in 1 ½ c chilled whipping cream until stiff. Fold in 1 c shredded coconut and the cherry bits. Pour into 12 paper baking cups or a baking pan 8x8x2 inches. Sprinkle with additional coconut and garnish with maraschino cherries. Freeze. Can substitute lemon fluff frosting mix for cherry and 1 can crushed pineapple (drained) for coconut.
Julie
Emmett, ID

Coconut Patties

1 pkg choc chips – 1 ¾ shredded coconut. Heat chips over boiling water until melted. Remove from heat and add coconut, stirring until blended. Drop from tsp on waxed paper. Cool until firm.
Polly
Canby, OR

Date Nut Balls

½ c butter – 1 ½ c cut pitted dates – 1/3 c chopped mar chino cherries – ¾ c sugar – 3 c rice krispies – 1 c chopped pecans. Measure. Oleo (butter) dates, cherries and sugar into sauce pan. Cook over med heat stirring constantly until mixture becomes a soft peak. Remove from heat, add krispie and nuts. mix thoroughly. Portion by level measuring tbl onto wax paper or buttered baking sheet. Shape into balls. Cool.
Dorothy
Vancover, WA

Divinity

2 c sugar – ¾ c white syrup – ½ c water. Boil until mixture thread from spoon. Have ready ¼ tsp salt – 2 beaten egg whites, while beating with elec. mixer. Beat with mixer, tabors and mixture is quite thick. Add 1 tsp vanilla and 1 c nuts. Beat with mixer or by hand until you can drop by tbl and it stands in shape and does not run.
Marge
Bismarck, ND

Divinity

2 c sugar – ½ c light syrup – ½ c water – 1/8 tsp salt – 1 tsp vanilla – 1 tsp powdered sugar. In sauce pan mix first 4 ingredients. Slowly bring to a boil stirring until sugar dissolves. Cook to 250* hard boil stage. Mean while, beat egg whites until stiff. Gradually pour hot syrup into white until stiff. Beat until candy begins to hold shape. Beat in vanilla and powdered sugar. Drop from tsp onto wax paper or pour into buttered pan. Let stand several hours until firm. Store in airtight container. Makes about 50.
Barbara
Corvelius, OR

Divinity Fudge

3 c sugar – 1 c white syrup – ½ c water – ¼ tsp salt – 1 tsp vanilla – 2 egg whites. Combine syrup, water, salt and sugar in a 3 qt pan, boil to 248*. Beat egg whites stiff in a large bowl and gradually beat in the syrup. Beat until it begins to stiffen. Add vanilla than (for verity you can add 1 c nuts, chopped peppermint candy, gum drops or choc chips) beat by hand slightly and pour into slightly buttered dish. Cut into sq when cooled, also can drop by spoons. (Don't scrape sides of pan while boiling syrup) wipe with damp cloth, never use spoon and always change to clean one.
Ellen
Lake Preston, SD

Divinity Pastels

3 c sugar – ¾ c water – 2 egg whites – ¾ c white syrup – 1 pkg Jell-O (any color 3 oz) 1 c chopped nuts or candied fruit, coconut or gum drops (no black). Mix sugar, syrup and water, bring to a boil over low heat, stirring to dissolve sugar. Continue boiling stirring occasionally until a little syrup forms hard ball stage 252* on thermeter. Meanwhile beat egg whites until stiff not dry. Add dry Jell-O 1 tbl at a time and beat until stiff and peaks. Pour syrup in a thin stream into whites, beating constantly, continue beating until mixture holds its shape and looses its gloss about 10 minutes. Add nuts or what you want quickly pour into a well greased pan or drop on wax paper by tsp and let set. Store in covered containers.
Effie
North Plains, OR

Fanny Farmer Caramels

1 can canned milk – 2 c brown sugar – ½ c butter – 1 c white syrup. Melt butter in sauce pan. Add milk, sugar and syrup. Boil and stir for 7 minutes. Add 2 c nuts and 1 tsp vanilla. Pour into cookie sheet. Cool, cut and wrap each separately in plastic wrap.
Marge
Bismarck, ND

Fantasy Fudge

¾ c butter – 3 c sugar – 1 (5 oz) canned milk – 1 (12 oz) semi sweet choc pieces – 1 (7 oz) marshmallow cream – 1 c chopped nuts – 1 tsp vanilla. Combine sugar, butter and milk in heavy 2 ½ to 3 qt sauce pans. Bring to full boil, and stir constantly. Cook. Continue boiling 5 minutes over med heat, stirring constantly to prevent scorching. Remove form heat and stir in choc pieces until melted. Add remaining ingredients and mix until blended. Pour into greased 13x9 inch pan. Cool at room temperature. Candy therm. 234*.
Jana Watson
Boise, ID

Five Minute Fudge

2/3 c canned milk – ½ tsp salt – 1 2/3 c sugar – 1 ½ c miniature marshmallows – 1 ½ c choc chips – 1 tsp vanilla – ½ c chopped nuts. Place milk, sugar and salt over low heat. Bring to a full boil. Cook 5 minutes stirring almost constantly. Remove from heat. Stir in other ingredients till the marshmallows are melted. Pour in well buttered 9 inch square pan. Cool.
Jan-nita
ST Helens, OR

Fudge

11 c sugar – 1 lb margarine – 2 c karo syrup – ½ c cocoa – 2 c milk 2 c nut meats – 1 tbl vanilla. Boil to soft ball, sugar, cocoa, and milk. Add margarine and boil to med ball. Add vanilla. Beat over cold water thickened. For peanut butter fudge, use ½ lb margarine. 1 c chunky peanut butter Omit cocoa (opt).
Pearl Cavender
Keizer, OR

Fudge

Combine in sauce pan. ½ c butter – ¼ c cocoa melt together, remove from heat and mix in 2 c sugar. Add 1 c cream or canned milk stir well. Cook over med heat to soft ball stage. Stir and scrape sides of pan only occasionally. Remove form heat. Add 1 tsp vanilla. Place in pan of cold water and beat until begins to thickens. Add 1 c nuts. (Coconut, rice krispies, corn flakes maybe used instead of nuts.) Pour into 8 inch pan or a platter that has been buttered. Cool and cut into squares.
Marge
Bismark, ND

Fudge Cycles

1 pkg instant choc pudding – 2 ½ c milk – mix as directed on pudding pkg. Pour into ice tube molds. Freeze. Makes 12. Or use 1 qt choc milk – 2 egg yolks (no whites0 1 c sugar. Mix egg yolk. Add other ingredients and stir well. Pour into ice tube molds. Freeze.
Shelly
Scappoose, OR

Frozen French Mints

1 c butter – 2 tsp vanilla – 2 c sugar – 4 eggs – 4 oz unsweetened choc chips – 1 tsp peppermint extract – ¼ c crushed graham crackers. Cream butter and sugar. Melt chips over boiling water, add to creamed mixture. Add eggs one at a time beating well. Add vanilla and peppermint. Continue to beat for 3 to 4 minute. Use cup cake liners or candy cups. Spoon into liners. Sprinkle tops with a pinch of cracker crumbs. Freeze 5 hours before using. (Will keep for at least 2 weeks.)
Polly
Canby, OR

Honey Cracker Jacks

½ c honey – ¼ c butter – 6 c popped corn – 1 c shelled peanuts – heat honey and butter in sauce pan until blended. Cool. pour over popcorn which has been mixed with peanuts, stirring as you pour. When well coated, spread on pan in a single layer. Bake at 350* for 5 to 10 minutes or until crisp, stirring several times.
Pearl Cavender
Keizer, OR

Jell-O Divinity

3 c sugar – ¾ c white corn syrup – ¾ c water – 2 egg whites – ½ pkg Jell-O (sm) – 1 c nuts. Bring syrup, sugar, and water to a boil. Cook to hard ball stage. 252* Beat egg whites until fluffy and Jell-O gradually until mixture holds peak. Pour syrup over egg mixture slowly. Beat until holds shape and looses gloss. Stir in nuts. Drop by tsp onto wax paper.
Neoma Bray
Emmett, ID

Microwave Peanut Brittle

1 c raw peanuts – 1 c sugar – ½ c white corn syrup – 1/8 tsp salt – 1 tsp soda – 1 tsp vanilla – 1 tsp butter. In lg bowl stir peanuts, sugar, syrup, and salt. Cook 8 minutes on high. Stir after 4 minutes. Add butter. Cook 1 minute more. Add baking soda and vanilla and quickly stir until light & foamy. immediately pour on buttered baking sheet. Spread thin. Cool. Crack.
Donita Adams
Emmett, ID

Marshmallow Treats

Melt. ¼ c butter – 1 pkg (10 oz) about 40 regular or 4 c miniature marshmallows – 5 c rice krispies. Mix well pat in 9x13 pan. Chill before cutting.
Wilma Coates
Emmett, ID

Mint Candy

12 oz pkg cream cheese – ¼ tsp flavoring (mint, rum, almond or vanilla) 1 2/3 c powdered sugar for different coloring. Mash cream cheese. Add flavoring and color. Mix in sugar finely kneading with hands until about marble size. Dip in sugar and press firmly into mint molds. Unmold at once on to wax paper
Julie
Kanadoka, MN

Mom's Candy

Put 1 can canned milk in a kettle of water and boil for about an hour. Be sure it doesn't run dry so that it explodes. Put wax paper over top of can when opening. Dip marshmallows in it and roll right away in nuts and put on wax paper.
Barbara
Cornelius, OR

Never Fail Fudge

1/3 c butter – 1 c canned milk – 4 ½ c sugar – 2 tsp vanilla – 1 c marshmallow cream – 13 oz sweet choc, grated – 12 oz semi sweet choc chips – 2 c walnuts, chopped (opt). Combine butter, sugar and milk. Boil 5 ½ minutes. Remove from heat and add remaining ingredients, except nuts. Beat until well mixed. Add nuts. Spoon into a buttered pan. Cool until firm. Then cut.
Barbara Travis
Halsey, OR

No Cook Peanut Butter Kisses

1 c karo syrup – 1 c peanut butter – 1 ½ c powdered milk (dry) – 1 c powdered sugar. Mix karo syrup and peanut butter in a small bowl. Stir in gradually dry milk and powdered sugar. Shape into a roll and roll on chopped nuts or any little candy bits. Chill and cut into sm pieces, or form into balls.
Jana Watson
Boise, ID

Nut Carmel Clusters

1 lb choc – 1 ½ lb walnuts halves – ½ lb Carmel. Melt Carmel. Arrange walnuts on wax paper. Scoop small amount of Carmel on each walnut. Melt choc and dip each one. Let cool on wax paper.
Carol
Emmett, ID

Old Time Fudge

2 c sugar – ¾ c milk – 2 oz unsweetened choc – 1 tsp light corn syrup – 2 tbl butter – 1 tsp vanilla – ½ c chopped nuts. Butter the sides of a heavy 2 qt pan. In it mix sugar, milk choc and corn syrup. Cook and stir over med heat till sugar dissolves and it comes to boil. Continue to cook to 234* (soft ball stage) Remove from heat, add butter and vanilla but do not stir. Cool to luke warm about one hour. Add nuts and beat vigorously till gets thick and just starts to lose its gloss. Immediately spread in a buttered 9x5x3 pan. Score into squares while warm and cut when firm.
Barbara
Emmett, ID

Peanut Brittle

1 ½ c sugar – ¾ c white karo syrup – ½ c water – 1 c raw peanuts lump of butter – 1 tsp soda – 1 tsp vanilla. Cook until it spins a thread. Add raw peanuts. Cook until golden brown. Add butter, soda and vanilla. Pour into greased cookie sheet. Let it harden. Then break to pieces.
Loreen Korell
Emmett, ID

Peanut Brittle

1 c sugar – ½ c light corn syrup – pinch salt – 2 lb butter – 1 tsp vanilla – 1 tsp soda – 1 c unroasted peanuts. Mix sugar, syrup and salt. Put on to cook. Add peanuts and butter. Cook until brittle when dropped into cold water (300*) remove from flame at once. Add soda and vanilla all at once. Pour on to a large greased surface. Pull until thin and turn over. Cool and break into pieces.
Kathy
Emmett, ID

Penuche

2 c brown sugar -1 c white sugar – 1 c cream (can use ½ & ½) 2 tbl white sugar – ¼ tsp salt. Put all in a saucepan do not stir. Cook to 236*. Remove from stove, add 2 tbl butter. Let stand until it reaches 105* then beat. Add vanilla and nuts. Pour into buttered pan. Cut when set.
Helen
Richardton, ND

Reese Candy

Melt. 1 cube margarine – 1 ½ c graham cracker crumbs – 1 c crunchy peanut butter – 2 c powdered Sugar. Mix together well and pat in pan. Frost with melted choc chips. Cut into sq's. When cool.
Sylvia Garner
Emmett, ID

Rocky Road Candy

Melt in lg sauce pan over low heat stirring until smooth. 1 pkg (6 oz) semi sweet choc pieces – 1 sq (1 oz) unsweetened choc – 1 tbl butter. Remove from heat. Beat until foamy 2 eggs. Mix in 1 ½ c confectioner's sugar – ½ tsp salt – 1 tsp vanilla. Blend in choc mixture. Stir in – 2 c salted peanuts – 2 c mini marshmallows. Drop by tsp onto wax paper. Chill until firm. Store in refrig.
Cindy
Emmett, ID

Salted Nut Roll

Combine in double boiler – 30 to 32 caramels – ¼ c evaporated milk. Heat caramels and milk till melted. Remove from heat, add ¼ c butter. Mix well. Add 1 c powdered sugar. Cool slightly. Drop by tsp full's onto a bowl of salted peanuts with skins. Form into sum log and roll with peanuts until coated. Place on wax paper and chill.
Tillie
Hebron, ND

Soda Cracker Candy

Preheat oven to 350* - Cover large cookie sheet with tin foil cover with soda crackers. In a pan combine 1 cup butter – 1 cup brown sugar, boil hard for 2 minutes. Then pour over crackers. Place pan in oven for 5 minutes. Remove from oven and spread 12 oz pkg choc chips over top. Put back in oven for 2 minutes. Then take out of oven spread evenly. Then cut into squares.
Randy Wilson
Emmett, ID

10 Min Peanut Brittle

1 c sugar – ½ c light corn syrup – 1 ½ to 1 ¾ c salted cocktail peanuts (I use Spanish) 1 tbl butter – 1 tsp vanilla – 1 tsp soda. Combine sugar & corn syrup. Microwave on high 5 min. Add peanuts. Microwave on high 1 ½ min. Stir. Microwave 1 ¾ min (peanuts and syrup will be lightly browned) add butter, vanilla & soda. Spread as thinly as possible on buttered cookie sheet.
Barbara Travis
Halsey, OR

Vinegar Taffy

2 c sugar – ¼ tsp cream of tarter – 1 tbl butter – ½ c vinegar – pinch of salt. Cook to hard crack. Pour onto buttered plate. Pull when you can handle until hard. Break into pieces.
Lisa
Emmett, ID

Al's Famous Jerky

2 to 3 lb meat (½ to 3/8 inch cuts) – 2 qt water – 3 ½ c brown sugar – 4 tbl liquid smoke – ¾ c tenderquick – 2 tbl molasses – 1 tbl soy sauce – 2 tbl Worcestershire sauce – ½ tbl red pepper flakes – 2 tbl pepper – 1 tbl garlic powder – 1 tsp Tabasco sauce. Mix the ingredients in a bowl real good then add meat. Soak 24 hour. Skewer strips of meat and place in oven. Cook for 3 hours at a temp of 150* to 200* - leave oven door cracked. After 3 hour check meat, if it's ok take it out if not done add an hour longer. Put tin foil on bottom of oven to catch drops.
Al Schneider
Emmett, ID

Baked Alaska Meat Loaf

2 lb hamb – 2 eggs slightly beaten – 2 tsp salt – ¼ c milk – 1/8 tsp pepper – ¼ c minced onions – 1 ½ c bread crumbs. Bake 1 hour in oven at 350* till done. Drain off liquid completely drain and pat with paper towels, slice meat into casserole bigger than meat loaf. Take 3 ½ c mashed potatoes – 2 egg yolks – Paprika and grated cheese. Whip eggs into potatoes and frost the meat loaf. Sprinkle with paprika and cheese. Bake till surface is golden brown.
Virgina
Tok, AK

Baked Beans Hot Dish

½ lb hamb – ½ lb bacon – 1 onion – salt & pepper – 1 tsp mustard – 2 tbl vinegar – ½ c ketch up – ¼ c brown sugar – 1 can of butter beans – 1 can kidney beans – 1 can pork and beans. Brown hamb and bacon, add salt & pepper, add onions. Add mustard, vinegar, ketch up, sugar and beans. Place in hot dish. Bake 2 hours at 325*. I drain beans a little.
Gayle
Norhtfield, MN

Baked Hamb Squares

2 lb hamb – 1/3 c onions – salt & pepper - 2 c dried fine bread crumbs – 2/3 c milk. Mix hamb, crumbs, milk, salt & pepper together. Pat into cake pan and top with topping below. Topping – ¼ c chopped fine onions – ¾ tsp chili powder- ¼ c vinegar – ½ c ketch up – 1 tbl brown sugar. Mix all and spread on meat mixture. Bake at 350* for 35 minutes.
Vickie
Del Rio, TX

Barbecued Meatballs

1 c soft bread crumbs – ½ c milk – 1 lb hamb – 1 tsp salt – ¼ tsp pepper. Moisten crumbs with milk. Combine with meat, salt and pepper. Shape into balls and place in single layer pan. Combine the following sauce. ½ c ketch up – ½ c chopped onion – ¼ c vinegar – 3 tbl brown sugar – ½ c water. Pour sauce over raw meat balls. Bake at 350* for 50 minutes. Good with baked potatoes.
Mable
Lake Preston, SD

BBQ Spareribs

Boil ribs in water with 1 lemon, onion and smoke (in bottle) to give it a smoke flavor and taste. Boil till done, put BBQ sauce over them (throw away the water) bake for a few minutes (about 20 minutes)
Pat
Lake Preston, SD

BBQ Beef Balls

1 c soft bread crumbs – ½ c milk – 1 lb hamb – 1 tsp salt – 1 tsp pepper. Mix all together and shape into balls and place in pan. Mix together. 1 tbl Worcestershire sauce - ¼ c vinegar – 3 tbl brown sugar – ¼ c ketch up – ½ c water – ½ c onion. Pour over meat balls and bake 30 minutes at 350*.
Maxine
Lake Preston, SD

Bean Hot Dish

Brown 1 lb hamb and onion. Add 1 can each green and wax beans drained. Add can tomatoes soup and about 1 tsp chili powder and salt and pepper to taste. Put in casserole, and top with mashed potatoes dot with butter. Bake at 350* for about 10 minutes.
Rena
Beach, ND

Beef Burger Willington

1 pie crust unbaked – 1 ½ lb hamb – 1 egg – ¼ c milk – salt & pepper 1 tbl ketch up. Preheat oven to 350*. Roll crust into circle as for pie. Cut into 4 portions. Mix rest of ingred. Divide into 4 portions, all so shape in loaves. Remove a bit for the top of each loaf, & make an oblong shape will in each. Fill with any desired filling. Replace the top of each loaf, & press edge to seal & make a smooth loaf. Place pie crust over the top, tucking it in & underneath crust will not cover all. Place pastry side up in baking pan & bake 35 min. turn on broiler for 2 min if pastry needs more browning. A suggested filling, chopped onion, mushroom, celery, cheese, tom pieces, cooked bacon pieces, chopped green peppers. Use any desired comb.
Iris
Beaverton, OR

Beef Flank Steak

Marinate steak and sliced onions in ½ c oil and ¾ c soy sauce for 2 hour, turning every ½ hour. Drip off --- in hot frying pan fry 3 to 4 minutes on side. Lay the onions to one side. Than fry for 3 to 4 minutes longer. Cut away from the grain. You may need to add a little more juice.
Leola
Rapid City, SD

Beef Stroganoff

1 lb hamb – shortening – salt & pepper – 1 c mushroom soup – ½ pt sour cream – wide noodles, rice or potatoes. Brown beef in sm amount of shortening. Add seasonings, soup, and sour cream. Simmer a few minutes and serve over hot potatoes or noodles.
Polly
Canby, OR

Beef Stroganoff

1 ½ lb hamb cut into 1 inch pieces – 1 tsp pepper – ½ c shortening 1 can cream of mushroom soup – med pkg noodles – ½ tsp each onion and garlic salt – 1 can beef broth or bouillon cubes – 1 c sour cream – grated cheese. Dust meat well with pepper and flour mixture, brown in ½ c shortening. Boil med pkg of noodles. Mix meat, seasons, broth together add sour cream. Put noodles on bottom of casserole, meat mixture on top. Place cheese on top. Bake 350* for 1 hour.
Bernee
Mitchell, SD

Beef Thurninger

5 lb hamb – 5 rounded tsp tenderizer salt – 2 ½ tsp garlic salt -2 ½ tsp ground pepper – 2 ½ tsp mustard seed – 1 tsp liquid smoke or hickory salt. Mix together with hands and put in refrigerator with lid. Next day, mix well with hands and put in refrigerator with lid. Next day, mix well with hands again and put back in frig. Next day mix again and form 5 long thin rolls. Place in broiler pan and put in oven on warm 140 to 150* for 24 hours turning 2 or 3 times.
Olga Peters
Salem, OR

Borscht (German Soup)

1 head cabbage – 1 bunch parsley – 1 c tom – 1 chic or 1 ½ lbs beef - 4 med onions – 1 tbl salt – 1 carrot – ½ c sour cream – 1 sm bunch dill leaves – 4 tsp pepper. Cook meat until tender. Add all other ingredients, except cream and boil for 15 min. than add cream. Bring to a boil and serve. Add green pepper (opt)
Olga Peters
Salem, OR

Brisket Chili

5# brisket trimmed – 4 onions diced – 2 green peppers diced – 2 c oil – ½ c minced garlic – 2 ½ c flour – ¼ c sriacha – ¼ c dry oregano – 2 tbsp cumin – 1 #10 can diced tomatoes with juice – 2 # 10 can chili beans – 1 #10 can white beans: fine dice brisket. In large skillet cook beef in oil with onion and peppers until browned. Add flour to thicken. Combine remaining ingredients and stew over low heat, stirring often, 2 hours. Cool and portion for service.
John & Tracy Nunez
Huskie Pizza
Emmett, ID

Cabbage Hot Dish

1 lg head cabbage – 1 med onion – 1 lb hamb – 1 can tomato soup. Sauté the meat and onion in a little butter. Heat it through but not brown. Season to taste with salt and pepper. Grease casserole and put a layer of cabbage on bottom then cover this with the hamb and onion. Add the rest of the cabbage. Pour over the top the soup. Cover and bake in 350* oven till cabbage is tender. About 1 hour.
Nellie
Mankats, MN

Cabbage Rolls

2 lb hamb – 1 c cooked rice – 2 eggs – 1 ½ tsp salt – 2 tbl minced onions – ¼ tsp garlic powder – ¼ tsp pepper – 2 tsp parsley flakes - ½ c milk (can milk is better). Mix together, 1 head of cabbage, cut core out. Place whole head in boiling water with salt and cook, pulling off leaves as they come loose. Put ½ c of meat in each leaf and roll up and tuck in edge so meat doesn't show. Put in lg pan. Mix 2 cans tomato soup and 1 can water over cabbage. Dot with cube of butter or oleo. Cover with foil and bake at 350* for 1 ½ hour.
Kevin
Lake Preston, SD

Chuck Wagon Mac

1 lb hamb – 1 tsp salt – dash pepper – ¼ c chopped green pepper – 2 tbl oil – 2 c whole kernel corn drained – 1 can (6 oz) tomato paste – ½ c sliced celery – ½ c chopped onion – 1 pkg macaroni and cheese – 2 c tomatoes – ½ tsp salt. Season meat with salt and pepper. Shape into 12 balls. Brown in oil, add celery, onion and green pepper, cook till tender. Prepare macaroni and cheese as directed on pkg. Add to meat balls with remaining ingredients, simmer for 15 minutes.
Helen
Fayetivil, AK.

Corn Beef Hot Dish

1 bag of med noodles cooked – 1 can corn beef – 1 can chicken and rice soup – 1 can cream of chicken soup – 1 c American cheese. Make a white sauce. 2 c milk – 4 tbl flour – 4 tbl oleo and cook till thick, add cheese, soup and corn beef. When cheese is melted add to noodles and put potato chips on top and bake 1 hour at 350*.
Lola
Lake Preston, SD

Danish Casserole

1 ½ lb lean ground beef – 1 egg – 1 sm onion finely chopped – ½ can canned milk – 1 tbl butter – 1 can tomato soup – 1 tbl flour – 1 can tomatoes – 1/8 tsp pepper – 1 tsp salt – 1 c grated cheese – 1 c cooked macaroni. Combine meat, onion, salt, egg and pepper, milk, mix with fork. Make into sm patties. Brown in butter, place in glass baking dish. Spread macaroni on around the meat patties. Pour soup and tomatoes in skillet and heat. Pour over meat and macaroni. Sprinkle with cheese. Bake 30 minutes at 350*.
Jan-nita
ST Helens, OR

Dinner in a Dish

4 tbl lard – 1 c chopped onion – 2 eggs – 1 lb hamb – 1 ½ tsp salt – ¼ tsp pepper – 2 green peppers sliced – 4 med sliced tomatoes – 4 c corn – ½ c cracker crumbs. Put lard in skillet, fry peppers and onion for 5 minute. Add meat and seasoning. Cook till done. Remove from heat add slightly beaten eggs to corn. Put 1 c of the corn in baking dish and ½ of the meat mixture and layer of tomatoes. Repeat cover with crumbs. Dot generously with butter. Bake at 350* for 35 minutes.
Jan-nita
ST Helens, OR

Dinner in a Skillet

1 ½ lb hamb – 1 c chopped onions – 1/3 c chopped green pepper – 1 can tomato soup -3 tbl oleo – 2 c cooked noodles – ½ c grated cheese – 1 tsp prepared mustard. Brown meat, onion and green pepper in oleo. Add remaining ingredients. Simmer 25 to 30 minutes.
Jan-nita
ST Helens, OR

Dory's Pastries

2 lbs hamb – 2 to 3 potatoes pared and sliced – 1 onion sliced – 4 strips of bacon. Mix up a batch of your favorite biscuit dough. Divide into 4 parts. Divide the hamb into 4 portions. Roll out biscuit dough like you would pie crust. Place meat on one side; lay sliced potatoes on top of hamb. Lay onion and seal. Pierce the top with fork. Bake 375* for 30 to 40 minutes on cookie sheet.
Jan
Scappoose, OR

Egg Portugal

1 ½ lb sausage links cut each one in fours – 4 eggs – 10 slices white bread – 2 ¼ c milk – 1 ¼ c grated cheddar cheese – ¾ tsp dry mustard – 1 can mushroom soup – ¼ c vermouth wine – green peppers – onion – brown sausage halfway done. Cube bread put over bread, put sausage, cheese on top of bread. Cover overnight in morning top with soup and wine mixed together. Bake at 350* for 45 minutes or until set.
Edie
Hillsboro, OR

Electric Skillet Hot Dish

Layer in order in electric skillet. hamb – shredded raw cabbage – shredded carrots, diced onions, can of cream of mushroom soup. Cook at 350* covered till lid rattles than turn to 200* for ½ hour. Top with shredded cheese.
Thelma
Richardton, ND

Flank Steak Hawaii Style

1 ½ lb flank steak – 2/3 c oil – 2 tbl honey – 1/3 c soy sauce – 1 tsp ginger – 2 tbl brown sugar – 2 cloves – minced garlic – 6 green onion chopped also tops – 2 tbl red wine vinegar. Place steak in flat shallow dish. Combine rest of ingredients in a bowl, mix well to dissolve sugar and pour over meat and refrigerate. Turn meat 2 or 3 times during the marinating time 6 to 8 hours. When ready to grill or broil drain the marinate from the meat and reserve. Grill or broil the steak 5 to 8 minutes on each side depending on doneness basting a little of marinate while cooking. To serve the steak slice in very thin slices. Save marinate heat to boiling cool & refrigerate. It should be heated to boiling again before using. It will keep for 2 weeks. reboiling is very important.
Betty
Hilo, HI

German Super

5 to 6 potatoes scrubbed not peeled – ¼ c chopped onion – ¼ tsp garlic powder – ½ tsp salt – 1/3 tsp pepper – 3 c cubed Hillshire sausage – 1 c (7 oz) saukraut. Cut potatoes into thumb size pieces, add onion, garlic powder, salt & pepper. Brown in sm amount of oil for 25 minutes till tender. Add sausage and heat. Drain sauerkraut and spread on top. Do not stir. Cover and heat real good.
Lavonne
Emmett, ID

Hamb and Krout

Mix hamb like you do for stuffed peppers – cook rice first. Put layers of sauerkraut on bottom of dish than meat balls and than a layer of krout. Top with bacon. Bake at 350* for 40 minutes.
Anggie
Richardton, ND

Hamb Casserole

4 c potatoes – 1 c celery – 1 onion – salt and pepper – 1 lb hamb – 1 can tomato soup – ¼ c water. Use raw sliced potatoes, line bottom of greased pan with them. Salt & pepper each layer as long as veg last. Press hamb over all. Add water and soup. Cover and bake at 350* for 45 minutes. If it seems dry add a little more water.
Ona
Parkston, SD

Hamb Cheese Bake

2 tbl chopped celery – oleo – ½ tsp salt – 8 slices white bread – ½ lb hamb – 1 egg – dash pepper – ¾ c milk – 1 tbl mustard – 1 c shredded cheese – ½ tsp salt – 1/8 tsp dry mustard. In oven 350* toast bread, butter both sides, cook and stir meat, onion and celery. Prepare mustard and ½ tsp salt till meat is browned and onion tender. Alternate layers of toast, meat mixture and cheese in greased pan 9x9x2. Mix remaining ingredients pour over layers in pan baked uncovered 30 to 35 minutes.
Mary
Portland, OR

Hamb Hot Dish

Brown 1 ½ lb hamb – 1 onion – 1 green pepper. Mix 1 pkg frozen mixed veg or 1 can – 2 tbl butter – 1 can chicken rice soup – 2 cans mushroom soup – 1 ½ c water – 1 ½ c celery – 4 tbl soy sauce – 1 can chow main noodles. Mix meat into the next ingredients except chow main noodles. Bake at 350* for ¾ of an hour, add 2 c of chow main noodles. Bake another 15 minutes.
Marge
Richardton, ND

Hamb Hot Dish

2 lb hamb – 2 or 3 cans of cream of chicken soup – 6 med size carrots (sliced) – 6 potatoes (sliced). Fry meat till brown. Clean and boil carrots till tender. Peel and slice potatoes. (Enough for your own family). Put add in a roaster and mix well. Bake till potatoes are tender. Bake at 350*
Gladys
Northfield, MN

Hamb Stroganoff

½ c chopped onion – 1 lb hamb – 2 tsp salt – 1 can (8 oz) mushrooms -1 c sour cream – ¼ c oil – 2 tbl flour – 1/8 tsp pepper – 1 can cream of chicken soup – noodles. sauté onions in butter, add meat and brown. Add flour, salt, pepper and mushrooms. Cook 5 min. Add soup and simmer 10 min. Stir in sour cream, heat through but do not boil. Serve over noodles.
Lori
Golva, ND

Hamb Turnovers

Sauté. ½ c chopped onions – ½ c green peppers in – 2 tbl butter. Add 1 lb hamb – ½ tsp garlic salt – ½ tsp sugar – 1 tsp salt – ¼ tsp pepper. Cook for 3 minutes and add 1 c tomato sauce to ½ c sour cream – prepare biscuit mix and bake at 400* for 20 minutes. Serve with cheese sauce.
Gladys
Northfield, MN

Hawaiian Style Spareribs

2 sides spareribs – 3 tbl brown sugar – 2 tbl cornstarch – ½ c ketch up – ¼ tsp salt – ¼ c vinegar – 1 tbl soy sauce – 1 can (9 oz) crushed pineapple undrained. combine sugar, cornstarch and salt. Stir in vinegar, ketch up, pineapple juice and soy sauce. Cook till slightly thickened about 5 minutes stirring constantly. Arrange 1 layer ribs in pan. Cover with part of pineapple mixture. Add the layer of ribs and top with rest of sauce. Cover pan tightly and bake at 350* for 1 ½ to 2 hours.
Jan-nita
ST Helens, OR

Homemade Sausage

5 lb hamb – 5 tsp tender quick salt – 2 ½ tsp garlic salt – 2 ½ tsp mustard seed – 1 ½ tsp pepper – ½ tsp red pepper – 1 tsp liquid smoke. Mix together all ingredients and refrigerate 24 hour. Than mix again and put back in refrigerate for 24 hours. Bake at 150* for 8 hours. (Form into preferred size stick before baking)
Jerry
Mantevedio, MN

Hot Dish

Grease casserole layer in order. 1 lb hamb – sliced onion – sliced raw potatoes – cream style corn (1 can). Bake at 325* till potatoes are done.
Gladys
Northfield, MN

Impossible Pie

Mix the following ingredients. ¾ c bisquick – 3 eggs – 1 ½ c milk-1 lb cooked hamb – salt and pepper to taste. Pour in greased 2 qt casserole dish. Bake at 350* for 25 to 35 minutes. Top with cheese and tomatoes. Bake till cheese is melted about 5 minutes.
Tracy
Forest Grove, OR

Italian Delight

½ lb noodles boiled and drained – 1 lb ham browned – 1 clove garlic chopped – some green pepper – 1 onion chopped fine and browned with meat – 1 can tomato soup – ½ can water – ½ c cream style corn – 1 can mushroom soup – 1 tbl Worcestershire sauce – salt & pepper to taste – ½ lb nippy cheese grated (opt). When beef and onion have been browned lightly. Combine all ingredients, except cheese in casserole. Bake 35 to 45 minutes in 350* oven. Sprinkle with the cheese 10 minutes before done if you desire.
Kay
Apache Junction, AZ

Lasagna

2 lb hamb (browned) – 2 tbl sugar – 2 tbl parsley – 3 (8 oz) cans tomato sauce. Cook together simmer while cooking 2 (8 oz) pkg lasagna noodles -.3 lbs mozzarella cheese grated. mix 2 lb cottage cheese with ¾ c parmesan cheese – 1 tbl parsley – 1 tsp oregano - when noodles are tender using a 10x13 cake pan or 6 sm 4x4 pans – put layer of noodles, sauce, cottage cheese, mozzarella cheese, repeat one more time ending with mozzarella cheese. Bake at 350* until done (about 1 hour or until top browned) if using sm pans wrap in tinfoil and freeze.
Wilma Coates
Emmett, ID

Lasagna Ala-Marie

½ pkg lasagna cremates – 1 lb hamb – 1 med onion chopped – 1 tsp Italian seasoning – 1 tsp salt – ¼ tsp garlic salt – ¼ tsp pepper-2 cans (15 oz) tomato sauce – 4 c mozzarella cheese grated. Brown hamb and onions, drain, stir in seasoning and tomato sauce. Simmer 20 minutes. Prepare cremates according to direction, drain. Put one layer cremates in greased 9x13 pan. Put ½ of meat, 1/3 of the cheese. Repeat layers with cheese on top. Bake for 30 minutes. Let stand 10 minutes before cutting to serve.
Viola Coates
Emmett, ID

Lone Star Chili

1 lb ground beef – 1 diced onion – 1 tbl diced fresh jalapeno pepper – 1 (15 oz) can kidney beans with liquid – (14.5 oz) can peeled diced tomatoes – (8 oz) can tomato sauce – 1 c water – 1 tbl apple cider vinegar – 1 tsp salt – 1 tsp chili powder – ¼ tsp garlic powder – 1 ba7 leaf --- brown ground beef in a large saucepan over med heat. Drain fat. Add onion and pepper and sauté for about two min. Add remaining ingredients and simmer for 1 hour, stirring occasionally. Serve one cup in a bowl with the optional cheese, diced onion and whole jalapeño garnish on top. Garnish with your choice – grated cheddar cheese – diced onion – canned whole jalapeno – or chili peppers.
Dean Lebreton
Eagle, ID

Low Calorie Hot Dish

1 head cabbage cut into 8 wedges – ¼ c rice – 1 c chopped onions -1 c hamb browned (I use a lb of hamb) – 1 can or pint tomatoes – 1 c hot water – 2 tsp salt – ¼ tsp pepper. Place cabbage in greased casserole, cover with onion, meat and rice. Mix together tomatoes, water, salt and pepper and pour over all. Bake 1 ½ hour at 350*.
Ona
Parkston, SD

Macaroni Hot Dish

2 c uncooked macaroni – 4 hard boiled eggs – 6 oz dried beef – 2 cans mushroom soup – 2 c milk – 1 c chopped onions – ½ lb shredded cheese. Mix together refrigerate overnight – bake 1 ½ hours, cover first 45 minutes then uncover for a few minutes. (I use ham or chopped spam with the diced beef.)
Ona
Parkston, SD

Meal in one Casserole

1 lb hamb – 2 c raw potatoes sliced – 1 tbl butter – ½ c chopped onion – 1 c sliced carrots – ½ c uncooked rice – ¼ c chopped green peppers – 2 c tomatoes – 1 ½ tsp salt – ¼ tsp pepper – 1 c hot water. Brown meat in butter, place in casserole and add rest of ingredients in layers, potatoes, onion, carrots, rice, green peppers, tomatoes. Season with salt and pepper. Pour over all the water, cover and bake at 325* for 2 hour. Add more water if needed.
Vicky
Del Rio, TX

Meat Balls

1 lb hamb – 1/8 tsp pepper – ½ tsp salt – 1 tbl cornstartch – ¼ c cream or canned milk – 1 tsp nutmeg. Mix all together. Roll into small balls about the size of small egg. Fry in skillet till brown, cover with water, let boil a few minutes. Make thickening with heaping tbl cornstarch and add to meat.
Cora
Sentinel Butte, ND

Meat Loaf

2 lbs hamb – 2 eggs – 1 tsp accent – 1 ½ bread crumbs – ½ c warm water – 1 pkg onion soup mix. Beat thoroughly. Put in loaf pan, cover with strips of bacon and pour over one 8 oz can of tomato sauce. Bake at 350* for 1 hour.
Anna
Yankton, SD

Meat Loaf

1 egg – 1 ½ lb hamb – 1 c quick oatmeal – ½ tsp pepper – 1 c milk – 1 c chopped onion – 2 tsp salt – 1 tsp chili powder – 1 tbl ketch up – 1 tbl Worcestershire sauce. Heat oven to 350*. Butter a 6 c loaf pan. Mix all ingredients thoroughly. Pack in pan, bake for 1 hour.
Ruth
North Platte, NE

Microwave Meat Loaf

2 lb hamb – 1 egg – ¼ c quick oatmeal – ¼ c milk – 2 tbl chopped onions or ½ pkg onion soup mix – 2 tbl brown sugar – 1 tsp dry mustard – dash of allspice and nutmeg – less than 1/8 tsp of salt and pepper. Combine all in lg bowl, mix well shape into covered casserole. Microwave 8 to 10 minutes on high power, than top with the following sauce. 2/3 c ketch up – 2 tbl brown sugar – 1 ½ tsp dry mustard, turn and microwave again for 6 minutes on full power.
Debbie
Rock Rapids, IA

My Favorite Meatballs

2 lb hamb – 1/8 tsp pepper – ½ tsp salt – 1 tbl cornstarch – 1 tsp nutmeg – ¼ c any kind of cream or canned milk. Mix all together. Roll into small balls about the size of a small egg. Brown and cover with water and let boil a few min. Make a thickening with cornstarch and add to meat. You can use half hamb and half plain ground pork.
Cora
Sentinel Butte, ND

Norgwigian Meatballs

3 lb hamb – ½ lb pork ground fine – 1 egg – 1 tsp minced onion – 1 tsp salt – ½ tsp each of cloves, allspice, thyme, pepper, bread and milk mixture made with the cup of milk, boiled and cooled. 2 Slices each of white and dark bread. Mix meats, egg and onion well, add bread and milk mixture and seasonings. Mix well. Form into small balls. Remove meat from pan, add 2 tbl flour to drippings, stir well. Add about 3 c liquid, of broth water. Cook to gravy consistency, return meat balls to gravy. Bake at 300* for 45 to 60 minutes. (I just heat in the pan and don't return to oven).
Marcello
McCook, NE

Old Fashion Beef Veg Soup

3 lbs soup bone – 3 qts water – 2 tbl salt – 2 tsp Worcestershire sauce – ¼ tsp pepper – 1 med onion chopped – 1/3 c barley – 1 c peas -1 c chopped celery – 1 c sliced carrots – 1 c shredded cabbage – 1 turnip peeled and cubed – 3 ½ c tomatoes – 3 tsp parsley flakes. Place beef, water, salt, Worcestershire and pepper in a big pot. Cover and simmer 2 ½ to 3 hours. Remove bone, cut off meat into pieces and return to pot, add remaining ingredients. Simmer about 45 minutes. Can also add rutabaga, a little ketch up and soup mix.
Barbara
Cornelius, OR

Oven Swiss Steak

1 ½ lb round steak – ¼ c flour – 1 tsp salt – 1 (16 oz) can stewed tomatoes – ½ c chopped celery – ½ c chopped carrots – 2 tbl Worcestershire sauce – ¼ c shredded cheese. Cut meat into 4 portions. Mix flour and salt, pound into meat. Set aside rest of flour. Brown meat in small amount of shortening. Place meat in pan. Blend in the rest of the flour with dripping in pan. Add remaining ingredients except cheese. Cook stirring constantly till mixture boils. Pour over meat. Cover and bake at 350* for 2 hours or till tinder. Top with cheese. Return to oven for a few minutes.
Marit
Los Angelas, CA

Paprikash

3 to 4 lg onion chopped pretty fine – 2 tbl lard – sauté onions till done. Add 1 tbl paprika or more. Add cubed beef or chicken and let simmer for a few min. Add 4 c water, salt to taste. When meat is almost done, add 4 potatoes or ½ c rice. Cook until well done. Than drop dumplings into soup.
Sandi
Dwight, ND

Pepper Steak

Thinly slice 1 ½ to 2 lb flank steak diagonally. Brown with 1 chopped onion in 2 tbl oil. Stir in mixture of 1 pkg brown gravy mix, 1 ¼ c water and 1 tbl soy sauce. Stir until thickened. Cover and simmer 30 minutes. Add 2 lg green peppers cut into thin strips. Large tomato cut into wedges. Simmer 10 minutes. Serve over rice.
Joanne
New Tanzelwell, TN

Pepper Steak

2 lbs round or sirloin steak – 2 tbl shortening – 1 ½ c water – ¼ c soy sauce – 2 med onions – 2 green pepper – 2 tbl cornstarch fluffy cooked rice – can also add tomato – ½ tsp ginger – clove of garlic. Cut meat into small cubes. Brown in the shortening about 5 min or until tender. Add soy sauce and water. Simmer for 10 min. Add onions that are cut in length wise strips. Simmer 5 minutes. Add green peppers cut length wise in stripe and add garlic cook till tinder. Add tomatoes last cut into pieces. Thicken meat with cornstarch. Serve over rice.
Penny
Portland, OR

Pepper Steak

1 ½ lb boneless chuck – 2 tbl shortening – 1 ½ c water – 3 tbl soy sauce – ¼ c wishbone Russian dressing – 2 med green pepper thin strips – 2 onions thinly sliced. Cut meat into thin strips. Heat shortening in skillet and brown neat. Add water, dressing and soy sauce. Simmer and brown meat. Simmer covered for 30 min. Add green peppers & onions cook till tender.
Mary
Portland, OR

Pizza Cups

¾ lb hamb – ½ can (6 oz) tomato paste – 1 tbl instant minced onion – ½ tsp salt – 1 tsp Italian seasoning – 1 can (10 oz) refrigerate biscuits – ½ to ¾ c shredded mozzarella or cheddar cheese. Brown and drain beef, stir in tomato paste, onion and seasoning mixture will be thick. Cook over low heat for 5 minutes. Place biscuits in a greased muffin pan. Pressing to cover bottom and sides. Spoon about ¼ c meat mixture into biscuits lined cups and sprinkle with cheese. Bake at 400* for 12 minutes or till golden brown.
Virgina Quenzer
Emmett, ID

Porcupine Meat Balls

(microwave) 1 lb hamb – ¼ c minced onion – 1 egg – 1 c instant rice uncooked – ½ tsp salt – 1 can (16 0z) tomato sauce divided – ¼ tsp pepper – 1 ½ tsp dry mustard – combine beef, onion, rice, ½ of the tomato sauce, egg, salt and pepper mix well. Shape into 12 balls place in round 2 qt shallow casserole. Combine remaining tomato sauce, parsley flakes and mustard. Cover with wax paper, cook 4 minutes on high. Rearrange meat balls. Cover and cook 4 to 6 minutes or till rice is tender and meat is firm.
Virgina Quenzer
Emmett, ID

Porcupine Meatballs

1 ½ lb hamb – ½ tsp pepper – 1 tsp salt – 1 tbl minced onion – ½ c rice. Mix well and shape into balls. Put in skillet; add 1 can tomato soup and ½ can water. Let boil, put meat balls into soup, cover and let simmer
Juile
Sioux Falls, SD

Pronto Pups

½ c cornmeal – ½ c flour – 1 tsp salt – ½ tsp pepper – 1 egg – ½ c milk – 2 tbl oil – 12 wieners. sift dry ingredients. Add egg, milk, and oil. Beat till smooth. Dip wieners into batter, drain. Fry at 375* in deep fat 2 or 3 minutes till golden brown.
Delphine
Belfield, ND

Round Steak W/ Mushroom Sauce

Cut 2 to 3 lbs round steak into 3 inch pieces. Dip in 1 c flour with 1 tsp salt and ¼ tsp pepper. Brown in hot fat and put in a casserole, add 1 can cream of mushroom soup and 1 can of milk. Bake at 350* for 1 hour.
Doris
Beaverton, OR

Round Up Beef Rolls

Filling. 2 lbs hamb – 2 tbl oil – ¼ tsp pepper – ¾ c minced onion – ½ c finely chopped celery – 1 can (15 oz) tomato sauce. Cook meat, onion and celery in oil till brown. Add tomato sauce, salt and pepper. Cook slowly till thick. Dough. 3 c flour – ¼ tsp salt – 6 tbl oil – 4 tsp baking powder – ¼ tsp marjoram – 1/8 tsp sage – ½ c tomato juice – ½ c water. Sift dry ingredients. Cut in oil till course like cornmeal. Combine juice and water add to the flour, turn onto lightly floured board and knead 3 to 4 times. Roll into 9x13 inch rectangle. Spread with meat mixture and roll up like a jelly roll. Bake at 375* for 30 to 35 minutes. Prepare the following sauce and serve over rolls, 1 c mushroom soup – 1/3 c milk – ½ shredded cheese. Combine in pan and cook slowly till cheese melts.
Gladys
Northfield, MN

Runza

½ lb hamb – 1 chopped onion – 2 tbl oleo – 2 c chopped cabbage – ½ tsp salt – 1/8 tsp pepper. Brown meat and onion. Wilt cabbage in oleo. Add to meat with salt and pepper. Roll bread dough very thin into 6 or 7 squares. Place about 3 tbl of meat in center, pinch edge together and place smooth side up on greased baking sheet. Let rise. Bake at 350* for 20 minutes.
Carline
Emmett, ID

Salisbury Steak

1 can golden mushroom soup – 1 ½ lb hamb – ½ c dry bread or cracker crumbs – ½ tsp salt – 1/8 tsp pepper – 1 onion finely chopped – 1/3 c water – 1 egg slightly beaten. Combine ¼ of the soup with the rest of the ingredients except water. Mix well. Shape into 6 patties and arrange in a single layer in 9x13 pan. Bake uncovered for 30 minutes at 350*. Combine remaining soup with water. Spoon over patties. Return to oven and bake for 10 minutes longer or till gravy is hot. can garnish with mushroom sliced.
Darlene
Yankton, SD

Sausage Brunch

¾ lb pork sausage – 6 eggs beaten – ¼ tsp salt – 1 ½ c milk – 1 c shredded cheese – dash pepper – 2 slices bread cubed ½ inch thick – ¾ tsp dry mustard. Fry sausage till browned, drain well. Combine eggs, milk, bread, cheese, mustard, salt & pepper add sausage. Pour into an 8 inch pan cover and refrig several hours or overnight. Bake at 350* for 45 min or till nearly set in center. Let stand 10 min before serving.
Trula
Portland, OR

7 Course Dinner

4 c diced raw potatoes – 1 c diced celery – 2 c sliced raw carrots – 1 can peas and juice – layer of onions – 1 lb hamb browned – 1 can tomato soup. Put in layers in pan, season and cover with strip of bacon. Bake at 350* till veg are done about 1 hour.
Lucille
Shakopee, MN

Six Layer Dish

Sliced potatoes – hamb – onions – sliced carrots – ½ c raw rice – 1 can tomatoes – salt & pepper. Place layers in casserole dish in order listed. Over top layer place can of tomatoes or 1 can tomato soup plus 1 can water. Season each layer with salt & pepper. Bake at 350* for 1 ½ to 2 hours.
Viola
Bryant, SD

Short Ribs & Baked Beans

2 c white beans – 2 lg onions – salt & pepper – 1 ham bone – 1 onion sliced – 1 bottle (7 oz) ketch up – 3 lbs short ribs cut up. Wash & soak beans overnight. Using the water beans were soaked in, combine beans and the 2 onions, salt, pepper and ham bones. Simmer 1 ½ to 2 hours or till beans are almost done or tender. Remove from heat drain all but ½ c of liquid. Refrigerate remaining liquid for later use in soup or gravies. Place beans in casserole and add sliced onion and ketch up and mix well. Brown ribs and place on top beans and bake 2 ½ to 3 hours. Checking coaxially to make sure they don't bake dry.
Cindy
Stanford, CT

Sloppy Joes

2 lb hamb – ½ cup chopped onion – ½ cup catsup – 1 tsp mustard – ½ tsp salt- ¼ tsp pepper – 1 can chicken & rice soup. Mix together and let simmer. Serve over buns. For large family gatherings. 10 lbs hamb – 2 ½ cups chopped onion – 2 ½ cups catsup – 5 tsp mustard – 2 tsp salt – 1 tsp pepper – 6 cans of the soup.
Randy Wilson
Emmett, ID

Stuffed Cabbage Rolls

12 lb cabbage leaves – 1 ¼ lb hamb – 2 tsp salt – ½ tsp pepper – 1 c cooked rice – 1 sum chopped onion – 1 egg -1 table brown sugar – ½ tsp thyme – 2 table oil – 2 cans (8 oz) tomato sauce – ¼ c water – 1 table vinegar. Cover leaves with boiling water and let stand 5 minutes or till limp. Drain. Combine next 7 ingredients omitting the sugar. Place equal portions of meat in center of each leaf. Fold sides of each leaf over meat. Roll up and fasten with tooth picks. Brown in hot oil in a lg skillet. Simmer covered 1 hour basting occasionally.
Ada
North Platte, NE

Stuffed Spareribs

2 sides ribs – 3 tbl fat – ½ tsp sage – ¾ c chopped onions – ¾ c chopped celery – 4 ½ c soft bread crumbs – ¾ tsp salt – 5 tbl milk – 1/3 c finely chopped parsley. Salt and pepper ribs cook onion and celery, add to crumbs and seasonings moisten with milk. Mix and stuff the ribs, roll up. Bake uncovered at 350* till done.
Anggie
Richardton, ND

Swedish Meatballs

2 lb hamb – 1 lb lean pork – 1 egg beaten – 1 sm onion chopped – 1 tsp sugar – 1 c milk – 1 c fresh bread crumbs or mashed potatoes 1 ½ tsp salt – ½ tsp nutmeg – ½ tsp pepper – ½ tsp mace – pinch of ginger – 6 tbl flour – 3 c water or beef broth. You can also use allspice. Mix all together, brown till almost done. Make gravy out of broth and pour over meatballs.
Freda
Hillsboro, OR

Swedish Meatballs

2 tbl butter – ½ c chopped onion – 1/8 tsp pepper – dash nutmeg – 3 slices bread – 1 ½ lb hamb – ¾ tsp salt. Mix all together, than flour and brown. mix 3 beef bouillon cubes or beef base - 2 c boiling water – 1 c cream – 3 table flour – pour over meat and bake at 350* for about 1 hour.
Lucille
Spokopee, MN

Sweet & Sour Meatballs

1 ½ to 2 lb hamb – salt and pepper – 2 slices bread soak in water. Mix all well and make 1 inch balls. Roll in flour. Brown well in hot oil. Remove from pan. Drain off most of the fat. Sauce. 1 can undrained chunk pineapple – ½ c ketch up – 1/3 c vinegar – 1 c brown sugar – add any or all green peppers – almonds, celery and water chestnuts. Mix together and put in pan. Simmer 20 minutes. Add meat balls, cook till done. Thicken with 1 tbl cornstarch and ¼ c water.
Barbie
Wilsonville, OR

Sweet and Sour Meatballs

1 to 1 ½ lb hamb – 2/3 c dark karo syrup – 2/3 c water – 1/3 c vinegar – 2/3 c sugar. Make meatballs and brown in a skillet make a sauce form remaining ingredients. Blend and pour over meat balls and simmer till the meatballs are well done. Mix 2 tbl cornstarch with 1/3 c water. Add to the skillet mixture and cook, stirring till thickened and cooked. Serves 6 to 8.
Tasha Murray
Middleton, ID

Sweet and Sour Meatballs

2 to 3 lb hamb – add garlic powder – salt – oregano – basil – parsley to taste. Brown and set aside. In a saucepan add equal parts of welches grape jelly (a big jar) and 2 small Heinz chili sauce. Simmer till well mixed. Put meat balls and the sauce into crock pot. Simmer for 2 to 3 hour. Serve over rice.
Becky
Gaston, OR

Sweet and Sour Meatballs

1 ½ lb hamb – 2 cans tomato soup – ½ c vinegar – 5 tbl brown sugar – 1 green onion – 1 green pepper. Form into 1 inch balls, brown thoroughly and add all remaining ingredients. Simmer for 1 hour and 30 min. Stir occasionally. Serve over mashed potatoes. Can also use rice.
Thelma
Claskanine, OR

Sweet and Sour Meatballs

1 ½ lb hamb – 2 cans tomato soup – 5 tbl brown sugar – ½ c vinegar – 1 green pepper. Form meat into 1 inch balls brown thoroughly. Add remaining ingredients; simmer for 1 hour and 30 minutes. Stir occasionally. Serve over rice or mashed potatoes.
Thelma
Rainer, OR

Taco Rolls

Brown hamb and onions drain. Add taco mix and cool real good. Cut bread dough into squares. Add 1 (2 lb). Mixture to each rolled out square of dough and fold over. Lay in oiled pan. Put directly in oven at 350* for about 15 to 20 min. I use frozen bread.
Polly
Canby, OR

Toasty Cheese Bake

2 tbl chopped celery - 8 sliced white bread – oleo – ½ tsp salt – ½ lb hamb – ¼ c chopped onions – 1 egg – dash pepper – ¾ c milk – 1 tbl mustard – 1 c shredded cheese – ½ tsp salt – 1/8 tsp dry mustard. Heat oven 350*. Toast bread, butter both sides, cook and stir meat, onion, celery, prepared mustard and ½ tsp salt till meat is browned and onion tender. Alternate layers of toast, meat and cheese in greased baking pan 9x9x2. Mix rest or ingredients. Pour over layers. Bake uncovered 30 to 35 minutes.
Mary
Portland, OR

Top Stove Meat Loaf

1 lb hamb – sliced onion – 1 egg beaten – salt & pepper to taste – 1 tbl salad oil (important to use salad oil) – 2 sliced of bread cubed – milk to moisten. Place in oiled pan the meat balls at med heat, flatten with spatula and cover for 15 minutes turn to brown. When browned pour off liquid turn and brown on other side. Top with cheese if desired. Cover till melted. More beef and onion can be used. But the salad oil is very important.
Janet
Beaverton, OR

2 Bean Dish

1 lb hamb crumbled – ½ c chopped celery – ½ c chopped green pepper. sauté meat. Combine peppers, onion and celery and sauté. Put in casserole. Add 1 can kidney beans and 1 can lima beans. Pour all the liquid off beans. Mix together and add the following. 2 tbl vinegar – ¼ tsp dry mustard – 1 tbl brown sugar – ¾ c ketch up. Stir well. Bake 1 hour at 350* for about 25 minutes.
Jan-nita
ST Helens, OR

Upside Down Pizza

1 lb hamb – 1 med onion – med green pepper – 1 c +2 tbl flour (divided) – 2 tbl basil leaves – 2 tbl oregano leaves – 1 tbl minced garlic – salt and pepper to taste – 1 (15 oz) can of tomato sauce – 2 c shredded cheddar cheese + ½ c – 2 eggs – 1 c milk – 1 tbl veg oil – 1 can mushrooms. In sauce pan, cook the hamb, onions and green peppers until meat is no longer pink. Drain. Stir in 2 tbl flour, basil, oregano, garlic and salt and pepper. Mix well add tomato sauce and mushrooms. Bring to boil and cook for 2 minutes. Transfer to an ungreased 13x9x2 inch baking dish. Sprinkle on 2 cups cheese. Place remaining flour in a mixing bow. Beat in the eggs, milk, oil and salt until smooth. Stir in ½ c cheese. Pour over top. Bake uncovered at 425* for 25 to 30 minutes.
Pearl Cavender
Keizer, OR

Veg Soup W/Dumplings

2 lb beef stew meat – 1 tsp salt – pepper to taste – ½ tsp ginger – 1 c peas – onion – 1 c diced carrots – 1 c celery – 1 c raw potatoes. Bring meat to boil in lg pan of cold water, bring to a quick boil than allow to simmer 2 to 2 ½ hours strain broth. Add veg bring to a boil and drop in dumpling. Cover tightly and simmer for 5 min. Dumplings. 1 egg – ½ c milk – 1 c flour – ½ tsp salt. Beat egg add rest of ingredients and beat again. Drop by spoon.
Bertha
Moorehead, MN

Waikiki Meatballs

1 ½ lb hamb – 2/3 c cracker crumbs – 1/3 c minced onion – 1 egg – 1 ½ tsp ginger – ¼ c milk. Make into balls and brown. Cook until almost done. 1 Can pineapple tidbits with juice – 1/3 c vinegar – ½ c brown sugar – 2 tbl cornstarch. Cook until hamb is done. Serve over rice or mashed potatoes.
Wilma Coates
Emmett, ID

Zippy BBQ Beef Strips

3 lbs beef round steak – cut in ¾ inch strips – ¾ c water – 1 ½ c bbq sauce – ¼ c flour – ½ lb fresh mushrooms (sliced) – 2 tsp salt – ½ tsp pepper – ¼ c oil – ½ c chopped onions – 12 hamb buns. Partially freeze round steak and cut into strips ¾ inch thick about 3 in long. Combine flour, salt, and pepper. Dredge strips of beef in seasoned flour and lightly brown in cooking oil. Pour off drippings. Add onions, and water. Cover tightly and cook slowly 30 min. add BBQ sauce and sliced mushrooms. Cover and cook slowly 3o minutes more. Stirring occasionally. Serve over hamb buns.
Pearl Cavender
Keizer, OR

Apple Doodles

2 2/3 c flour – 2 tsp baking powder – ¼ tsp salt – ½ tsp nutmeg – ½ c sugar – ½ tsp cinnamon – ½ c butter softened – ½ c brown sugar -1 tsp vanilla – 2 tbl sugar. Stir together flour, baking powder, salt, cin and nutmeg. Cream butter, ½ c sugar and brown sugar. Add eggs and vanilla. Mix thoroughly. Combine flour mixture and sugar mixture. Add apples. Combine remaining sugar and cin. Shape dough into balls roll in sugar and cin. Bake on greased cookie sheet at 350* for 12 to 15 min. or until brown. Makes 4 ½ to 5 dozen.
Wilma Coates
Emmett, ID

Baking Powder Biscuits

2 c flour – 4 tsp baking powder – ½ tsp cream of tarter – ½ tsp salt – 2 tbl sugar – ½ c shortening – 1 egg – 2/3 c milk. Mix all together and roll out and cut with cutter. Bake at 350* for 10 to 15 minutes.
Lola
Lake Preston, SD

Belgium Waffle Mix

1 pkg dry yeast – 2 c lukewarm milk – 1 tsp vanilla – ½ tsp salt -4 eggs separated – 2 ½ c flour – 1 tbl sugar – ½ c melted butter. Dissolve yeast in milk. Beat egg yolks. Add yeast and vanilla. Add dry ingredients and melted butter. Fold in stiffly beaten egg whites. Let stand in warm place for 45 min. Use ¼ c per waffle. Sprinkle with powdered sugar.
Martha
Hebron, ND

Biscuit Supreme

Blend well. 2 c flour – ½ tsp salt – 4 tsp baking powder – 2 tsp sugar – ½ tsp cream of tarter. Cut in – ½ c shortening – add 2/3 c milk. Bake at 400* 10 to 15 minutes.
Violet
Hillsboro, OR

Bread

2 pkg yeast dissolved in ½ c warm water and ½ tsp sugar – 1 qt milk – 3 eggs – 3 tsp salt – 1 c sugar – 1 c oil – 11 to 13 c flour. Mix and let rise to double knead once and let rise again. Put in pan, rise and bake at 350* about 30 minutes or more
Sherri
Abaredeen, SD

Butterhorns

mix together – 1 c butter – 4 c flour – ½ tsp salt – 3 tbl sugar – dissolve 2 pkg yeast in ½ c warm water and 1 c warm milk. Add 3 beaten eggs. Add to flour mixture. Cover and refrigerate overnight. In morning roll out like pie crust (thin) sprinkle with sugar and cin. Roll up and slice like cinn rolls. Pat in pan and flatten with hand. Let rise 20 min. Bake 350* 10 to 12 minutes. Ice then sprinkle with nuts.
Polly
Canby, OR

Butterhorns

In the evening before dissolve 1 pkg dry yeast in 1 c warm milk. Work like pie crust. 4 c flour – ½ c sugar – ½ tsp salt and 2/3 c butter, then add 2 eggs and the yeast dissolved in milk. Mix well. Cover and place in a cold place or in ice box overnight. In morning cut dough into 4 parts, roll out rounds and brush very lightly with melted butter and cut into 8 pieces roll up and let rise. Bake at 350* until lightly brown.
Fierda
Watertown, SD

Buttermilk Pancakes

1 egg – 1 ½ c buttermilk – 1 c flour – ½ tsp soda – 1 tsp sugar – 1 tsp baking powder – 2 tbl oil – 1 scant tsp salt.
Thelma
Richardton, ND

Butterscotch Rounds

¼ c butter – ½ c brown sugar – ½ c pecans – 1 pkg yeast – ½ c hot tap water – 1/3 c sugar – 1 tsp soda – 1 c sourcream – 1 egg – 2 1/3 c flour – melt 2 tbl butter in each of two 8 ro 9 inch layer pans. Sprinkle ¼ c brown sugar and ¼ c pecan halves over butter. In large bowl dissolved yeast in hot water. Add 1 1/3 c of the flour and the remaining ingredients. Blend ½ min on low speed, scraping bowl constantly. Beat 2 min. High speed scraping bowl occas. stir in remaining flour. Drop batter by tbl over this mixture in pan. Let rise in warm place for 50 min. Dough will double. Bake at 350* for 25 to 30 min. Till golden brown, immediately invert pans into serving plates. Let pans remain a min so butterscotch drizzles down over the rolls.
Wilma Coates
Emmett. ID

Cake Do-nuts

Beat 3 eggs – 1 1/3 c sugar – 1 ½ c milk – 1/3 c plus 2 tbl melted butter – 4 c flour or more – 5 tsp baking powder – 1 tsp nutmeg -dash of salt. Mix all together and deep fry in hot oil.
Edith
Lake Preston, SD

Carmel Rolls

2 pkg yeast – 1 c water – 1 tbl sugar – let set till yeast works (5 min) – 2 c scalded milk – ¾ c sugar – 1 tbl salt – 3 heaping tbl shortening. Mix all together, let cool. (Just warm) put 3 c flour in bottom of a bowl, add all the liquid ingredients, and mix until well blended with beater. Add 3 eggs one at a time. Add approx. 3 more cups flour till dough is a good texture. Let rise 1 hour. Knead out and rise 1 hour and stretch or roll on bread board. Mix enough butter and brown sugar to spread on top and roll up and cut rolls. In a large pan put ¾ c brown sugar and 1 c cream. Place rolls on top. Bake at 375 for 25 minutes.
Olive
Sentinel Butte, ND

Carrot Bread

1 c grated carrots – 1 c boiling water – 2 tbl butter melted – 1 c brown sugar – 2 beaten eggs – 1 tsp baking soda – 1 c whole wheat flour – 1 tsp salt – 1 c chopped nuts. Pour boiling water over carrots and set aside. Cream together sugar and butter, add beaten eggs. Sift together dry ingredients. Add carrot mixture to creamed mixture, then add dry ingredients and stir in the nuts. Pour into loaf pan and bake 35 to 40 minutes at 350*. If you use smaller loaf pans bake a shorter time.
Pearl Cavender
Keizer, OR

Carrot Pineapple Bread

3 eggs beaten – 1 c oil – 2 c grated raw carrots – 1 tsp salt – 1 (8 oz) can pineapple undrained – 1 tsp cinnamon – 1 ½ tsp soda – 2 c sugar – 1 c nuts – 2 tsp vanilla – 3 c flour. Mix together. Bake at 350* for 4o or more minutes. 3 to 4 loaves according to size.
Mabel
Scappoose, OR

Corn Bread

2 eggs – 1 c sugar – 1 c cornmeal – ½ tsp salt – ¼ c butter – 2 c milk – 3 tsp baking powder – 2 c flour. Mix together and bake in greased iron skillet. Bake at 425* for 20 to 25 minutes.
Mabel
Scappoose, OR

Corn Waffles

1 c cornmeal – ½ tsp baking powder heaped – ¼ tsp soda – 1 tbl oil -1 egg beaten – pinch salt – 1 c buttermilk. Mix all ingredients together and bake. low cholesterol
Ellenore
Rockaway Beach, OR

Crepes

2 eggs – 1 c milk – 1 c flour – 1 tbl veg oil – beat eggs and blend with the rest of ingredients till batter is smooth and just thick enough to coat a spoon. If to thick add a little more milk. Cover and let stand at least ½ hour. Heat a 6 inch frying pan. Oil lightly. Pour in just enough batter to form a very thin layer, tilting pan so batter spreads evenly. Cook on one side turn and brown other side. Repeat till batter is gone. Steak with a layer of wax paper between each one. Keep warm till serving. Fill with fresh fruit.
Wilma Coates
Emmett, ID

Crescent Rolls Spread

2 cans of crescent rolls – chopped vegetables (Cali flour, broccoli, radishes Andy then you wish) – 2 packages of cream cheese – spread dough throughout pan. Bake till done per directions. Spread cream cheese on cooked rolls after cool. Sprinkle vegetables on top. Cut into finger food sizes.
Lesile Garringer
Emmett, ID

Crullers (Norwegian)

2/3 c sugar – ½ c shortening – 4 eggs – 1/3 c milk – ½ tsp salt – 3 ½ c flour – 3 tsp baking powder – ¼ tsp nutmeg. Cream shortening and sugar, add well beaten eggs and milk. Sift dry ingredients and add to eggs. Turn out on floured board and roll ¼ inch thick. Cut in strips, twist or form in knots. Fry in deep fat 365*. Drain on brown paper. Roll in powdered sugar.
Sonja
ST Helens, OR

Denver Dinner Omelet

4 eggs separated – dash pepper – 4 tbl veg oil – 1 (10 oz) pkg cauliflower frozen in cheese sauce – ½ c chopped ham – 1 tbl finely chopped onion – 2 tbl chopped celery - 2 tbl chopped green pepper. Oven at 325*. Beat egg whites till stiff. Beat egg yolks and pepper till thick and lemon colored. Fold in whites. Heat oil over med heat. Tilt pan to coat with oil. Spoon in egg mixture spreading evenly over bottom of pan. Reduce heat to low. Cook uncovered till puffy and light brown on bottom about 5 minutes. Prepare cauliflower as directed on pkg. Bake omelet for 15 to 18 minutes or till knife comes out clean. Slide omelet onto dish and sprinkle ham and onion on it. Spoon cauliflower, sauce, some more ham and green pepper. Serve right away.
Mary
Wibaux, MT

Dollar Cocktail Buns

1 pkg yeast – 1 c warm water – 1 tsp salt – 3 tbl melted shortening – 3 tbl sugar – 1 egg beaten – reserve 1 tbl for brushing buns – 3 to 3 ¼ c flour. Soften yeast in water. Stir in sugar, salt, shortening and eggs. Gradually add flour to make a stiff dough, cover and refrigerate at least 1 hour. Make buns size of a silver dollar. Place on greased baking sheet. Brush with reserved egg and a tsp of water. Cover and rise in warm place until double. Bake at 400* for 10 to 12 minutes or until golden brown.
Glenda
ST Helens, OR

Do-nuts

10 eggs – 1 c cream – 2 tsp soda – 1 tsp salt – 11 c flour – 4 c sugar – 1 qt buttermilk – 4 tsp baking powder – 2 tsp nutmeg. Drop for doughnut maker or cutter into hot grease. Lay doughnuts on paper towels to cool. Makes 8 dozen.
Sandra
Beach, ND

Easy Cinnamon Rolls

Rhodes frozen rolls (18) – chopped nuts – 1 sm pkg butterscotch pudding (not instant) – ½ c brown sugar – 1 tsp cinnamon – 6 tbl butter. Grease and bundt pan. Sprinkle bottom with chopped nuts, add rolls. Arrange in pan. In small bowl mix together, butterscotch pudding, brown sugar and cinnamon. Sprinkle over top of rolls. Add butter cut into pats on top of rolls. Put in cold oven and let rise overnight. In morning, remove pan from oven and pre heat oven to 350*. Bake for 20 to 25 minutes. Invert on plate and enjoy.
Beverly Crandall
Keizer, OR

Favorite Muffins

1 egg – ½ c sugar – ½ c milk – 2 tsp baking powder – ¼ c salad oil – ½ tsp salt – 1 ½ c flour. Heat oven to 400*. Grease bottom of muffin cups. Beat egg, stir in milk and oil. Mix remaining ingred. just until flour is moistened. Batter should be lumpy. Fill muffin cups 1/3 full. Bake 20 to 25 min. or until golden brown (½ full drop 1 tsp jelly in center then put a little more batter on top.)
Norma McBeth
Dallas, OR

Fresh Raw Apple Bread

2 c flour – 1 tsp soda – ½ tsp salt – ½ c shortening – 1 c sugar – 2 eggs – 2 c raw apple (chopped) – 1 ½ tbl milk – ½ tsp vanilla – 1 c chopped nuts – 3 tbl sugar – 1 tsp cinnamon. Sift together the flour, soda, salt. Set aside. Cream together the shortening sugar and eggs. Add the dry ingredients and mix well. Add apples, milk, vanilla and nuts. Pour into a greased loaf pan. Mix 3 tbl sugar and 1 tbl cinnamon and sprinkle over batter. Bake at 350* for 1 hour.
Linda
Sentinel Butte, ND

Golden Corn Bread

1 c cornmeal – ¼ c sugar – ½ tsp salt – 1 c milk – 1 c flour – 4 tsp baking powder – 1 egg – ¼ c shortening. Mix dry ingredients together. Add rest of ingredients. Mix with beater till smooth. Bake in 8x8 inch pan. Greased at 425* for 20 to 25 minutes.
Lila
Deset, SD

Golden Puffs

2 c flour – ¼ c sugar – 3 tsp baking powder – 1 tsp salt – 1 tsp nutmeg – ¼ c oil – ¾ c milk – 1 egg. Heat fat 3 to 4 inches to 375*. Mix all ingredients, beat till smooth. Roll in sugar and cinnamon mixture.
Lorrine
Richardton, ND

Hawaiian Omelet

4 eggs separated – 12 soda crackers rolled fine – ½ c milk – 1 ½ c crushed pineapple – 2 tbl butter – 3 tbl grated cheese. Beat egg yolks, add milk and crackers. Fold in beaten egg whites. Pour into skillet in which butter was melted. Cover and cook until bottom is brown. While eggs are cooking let pineapple simmer to thicken juice. Pour hot pineapple on half of omelet fold over and transfer to hot platter. Sprinkle with grated cheese and put under broiler for a minute to melt cheese. Serve at once.
Mary
Portland, OR

Krumkakea

6 eggs – 1 c sugar – 1 c butter – 2 c flour – beat eggs till light, adding sugar gradually. Add melted butter and flour a little at a time. Bake on iron or skillet and roll quickly or form into a patty shell. Fill with fruit and top with whip cream.
Elsie
Jamestown, ND

Hungarian Butterhorns

4 c flour – ½ tsp salt – 1 tsp vanilla – 3 egg yolks – 1 c butter – 1 c sour cream – 1 pkg yeast (cake). Sift flour, add salt. Crumble yeast into flour. Cut the butter into the flour mixture. Add beaten yolks, sour cream and vanilla mix. Divide the dough into 8 parts. Place into plastic bag and chill while preparing filling. Beat the egg whites till stiff. Add 1 c sugar grad. Fold in 1 c nuts and 1 tsp vanilla. Dredge board with powdered sugar. Roll out dough the size of apple tin and cut into wedges. Spread 1 tsp filling on each wedge and roll toward center. Mold into a crescent shape and bake at 400* 15 to 18 minutes on greased cookie sheet. When cool sift powdered sugar over top. Makes 64 rolls.
Lilo
Hebron, ND

Lefse

5 lg potatoes – ½ c cream – 1 tsp salt – 3 tbl butter – ½ c flour for each cup of mashed potatoes. Boil potatoes and drain off the water. Mash very fine. Add cream butter and salt. Beat until light and let cool. Add flour. Take a portion of dough and roll as for pie crust. Roll as thin as possible and as large as your pancake griddle. Bake on a moderately hot griddle until light brown turning frequently to prevent scorching. Butter as you pile on plate.
Harriet
Hebron, SD

Missouri Bisquick Mix

9 c flour – 1 c + 2 tbl dry milk – 4 tsp salt – 1/3 c baking powder – 1 ¾ c shortening. Sift all ingredients 3 times – cut shortening into mixture till it looks course like cornmeal. Makes 13 c mix. Store in covered coffee tin. Use as a biscuit mix on any biscuit recipes.
Sharon
Desmet, SD

Never Fail Bread

3 pkg yeast – ½ c warm water – 5 c warm water – ½ c sugar – 4 tsp salt – 8 c flour -1/3 c shortening – 7 c flour. Dissolve yeast in ½ c warm water. Set aside for 5 to 10 minutes. In large bowl, add 5 c warm water, sugar and salt. Stir till dissolved. Add yeast mixture. Add 8 c flour and mix well. Knead till smooth. Grease top of bread and cover bowl. Let rise till double in bulk. Bake bread at 375* for 50 minutes. Makes 6 loaves bread or 4 loaves and 2 pie tins of buns.
Darlene
Lake Preston, SD

No Fail Do-nuts

1 c sugar – 2 eggs – 1 c milk – 2 c flour – 1 tsp salt – 3 tsp baking powder – nutmeg to taste – pinch of ginger. Beat eggs well; add sugar, milk, nutmeg, ginger, flour, baking powder and salt. Add more flour to make dough easy to handle (3 c). Roll out to ½ inch thick and fry in hot oil.
Ruth
Owatowa, MN

No Fry Do-nuts

2 pkg yeast – scald 1 ½ c milk (cool to luke warm) – ½ c sugar – 1 tsp salt – 2 eggs – ½ c shortening – ¼ c warm water – 4 ½ c flour – 1 tsp nutmeg – 1 tsp cinnamon – ¼ c melted butter. Dissolve yeast in warm water. Add milk, sugar, salt, cin, nutmeg, eggs, shortening and 2 c of the flour. Blend 1 min at low speed on mixer. Stir in remaining flour. Cover. Let rise till dough doubles in bulk about 50 to 60 min. Turn onto floured board. Roll to ½ inch thick. Cut with cutter. Lift with turner onto greased baking pan 2 inches apart. Cover and let rise till doubled. Bake 8 to 10 min in 425* oven. Immediately brush with melted butter and sprinkle with sugar. Makes 1 ½ to 2 doz donuts.
Faye
Montgomery, AL

No Knead Refrig Rolls

2 pkg dry yeast – ½ c sugar – 2 tsp salt – 1 egg – 2 c warm water – 6 ½ to 7 c flour – ½ c shortening. Preheat oven to 400*. Dissolve yeast in water; add sugar, salt and ½ of the flour. Beat for 2 min. Add egg and shortening. Gradually beat remaining flour till smooth. Cover with damp cloth and refrig. punch down when rises. Bake at 400* for 15 minutes.
Charlotte
Lake Preston, SD

Onion Twists

2 ¼ c bisquick mix – 2/3 c milk – 1 tbl onion powder – 2 tbl oil – 1 egg beaten – coarse salt. Mix bisquick mix, milk, onion powder and oil. Beat 20 strokes. Gently smooth dough into ball on floured board. Knead 5 times. Divide dough into 32 equal parts. Roll each part into pencil like strip, about 12 inches long. Twist into pretzel shape on ungreased cookie sheet. Brush all twists with egg, sprinkle with salt. Bake till golden brown. 425* 10 minutes.
Joice
Hillsboro, OR

Peppernuts

3 c flour – 2 tsp baking powder – ½ c shortening – 1 c sugar – 1 c milk – 1 tsp peppermint extract. Mix in the order given. Roll dough into strips, as thick as wanted. Lay several strips, on bread board, cut across into pieces, about the size of a hazelnut. If soft peppernuts are wanted, place them close together on baking sheet. Bake at 500* a few minutes. They are done when they begin to turn slightly brown. After they have cooled, break them into suitable sized pieces and shake in a bag of powdered sugar. This gives them a festive appearance. Store in a covered container. Olga Peters
Salem, OR

Pineapple Nut Bread

¾ c brown sugar – 2 eggs – 2 tsp salt – 8 ½ oz can crushed pineapple – 1 tsp cinnamon – 3 tbl butter – 2 c flour – ½ tsp soda -¾ c chopped nuts – 2 tbl sugar. Cream brown sugar butter, eggs till fluffy. Measure dry ingredients. Stir ½ of the flour mixture into the creamed sugar. Add fruit & juice. Then remaining flour. Blend in nuts. Pour in a greased 9x5 pan. Sprinkle cin and sugar mixture over top. Bake 350* 60 to 70 min. Linda
Lake Preston, SD

Platter (Swedish)

3 eggs – 3 c milk – 1 c flour – 2 tbl sugar – 4 tbl melted butter – ½ tsp salt. Beat yolks of eggs and add milk. Combine with rest of ingredients and beat (until batter is smooth) Let stand 2 to 3 hours, than fold in stiff beaten egg whites. Butter griddle be sure pan is very hot. Brown on both sides. Roll and serve hot. Spread jam or fruit maybe used.
Sonja
ST Helens, OR

Plinsa (German)

6 lg grated raw potatoes – 1 egg – 1 tsp baking powder – ¼ c flour – 2 tsp salt – use about 1 tbl lard and fry.
Helen
Leola, SD

Potet Kager (Norwegian)

1 qt raw potatoes grated – 4 eggs – ½ c milk – 2 tsp salt – ½ tsp baking powder – ½ c flour – separate yolks from whites of eggs. Combine all ingredients except the egg whites and mix well. Beat whites of eggs until stiff and fold into potatoes. Fry on buttered griddle.
Edith
Lake Preston, SD

Pumpkin and Cream Cheese Muffins

8 oz cream cheese – 3 eggs – 2 ½ c sugar – 2 ½ c flour – ¼ c pecans, (roughly chopped) – 3 tsp cinnamon – ½ tsp salt – 2 tsp baking powder – ¼ tsp soda – 1 ¼ c solid packed pumpkin – 1/3 c vegetable oil – ½ tsp vanilla . Heat oven to 375*. Lightly coat two 12 cup standard muffin tins with oil and set aside. Mix the cream cheese, 1 egg, and 3 tbl sugar in a small bowl and set aside. Toss 5 tbl sugar, ½ c flour, pecans, butter, and ½ tsp cinn together in a medium bowl and set aside. Combine the remaining sugar, flour, salt, baking powder, baking soda, and remaining cinnamon in a large bowl. Lightly beat the remaining eggs, pumpkin, oil and vanilla together in a medium bowl. Make a well in the center of the flour mixture into the well. mix with a fork just until moisten in. Evenly divide half of the batter among the muffin cups. Place two teaspoonfuls of the cream cheese filling in the center of each cup and fill with the remaining batter. Sprinkle some of the pecan mixture over the top of each muffin and bake until golden and a tester, inserted into the muffin center, comes out clean --- 20 to 25 minutes. Cool on wire rack.
Susan Standley
Emmett, ID

Quick & Easy Bubble Bread

2 pkgs buttermilk biscuits (refrig ones) – 1 c brown sugar – 1 tbl cinnamon – ¼ c water – 1 c chopped nuts or raisins – ½ c butter – cut biscuits into quarters and set aside. Combine in pan brown sugar, water and butter and bring to a full boil. Add cinnamon and nuts. Fold in biscuits. Pour into a one piece tube pan or bunt pan. Bake at 350* for 20 minutes. Remove from oven and put on plate.
Irene
Forrest Grove, OR

Quick Raised Do-nuts

1 c luke warm water – 3 tbl sugar – 1 egg – 3 tbl melted shortening – 1 pkg yeast – 1 tsp salt – 3 c flour. Dissolve yeast in water and sugar. Add rest of ingredients and knead. Roll out and cut in 1 inch strips and twist or make figure 8's. Place on table and let rise ½ hour. Fry in hot oil. Cool slightly. Glaze with 1 lb powdered sugar – 1 tsp corn starch and ¼ c butter – 1 tsp vanilla – hot water.
Lorrine
Richardton, ND

Raised Do-nuts

2 pkg yeast – ½ c warm water (mix). add to the following – ½ c sugar – 4 c milk – 1/3 c oil – 1 tsp salt – 12 ½ c flour to make dough. Bake at 375* for 15 minutes or deep fry.
Jackie
Sentinel Butte, ND

Rolls

1 c warm water – 1 pkg yeast – ½ c sugar – ¼ tsp salt – ½ cube butter – 1 ½ c warm milk – approx 6 c flour. Combine and follow in order. Let rise to dough and put in rolls. Put in greased pan and let rise again. Bake at 350* for 20 min.
Vivian
Hillsboro, OR

Rogmundar (Swedish)

6 raw potatoes – 2 eggs well beaten – 1/8 tsp pepper – 1 tsp salt -3 tbl melted butter – 4 tbl flour – ¼ tsp baking powder. Peel potatoes and soak several hours in cold water. Than grate and drain off liquid that forms. Combine with rest of the ingredients. Drop by spoonfuls on hot buttered griddle. Spread to form cake. Brown on both sides. Do not stack cakes. Serve at once.
Sonja
ST Helens, OR

Rosettas

1 c flour – 1 c milk – 2 eggs – 1 tsp sugar. Beat eggs slightly. Add sugar, milk and flour. Mixing till smooth. Fry in deep fat on iron. Cooling the iron each time while sugaring rosettes just baked. Having iron to warm makes rosettes greasy.
Emma
Grand Forks, ND

Rosettas

3 eggs – 1 tbl sugar – 1 tbl oil – ½ tsp salt – 1 ½ c flour – 1 ½ c milk -1 tsp lemon extract. Beat eggs slightly, add sugar, salt, and oil. Beat a little more. Add flour and milk alternally. Let set for several hours before frying.
Emma
Richardton, ND

Slitch Kechula (German)

4 eggs beaten – 1 c sugar (cream these two) add 1 c cream – ½ c milk – 2 tsp baking powder – 2 tsp vanilla – pinch of salt – enough flour to make a dough. Cut dough into squares with 2 slits and deep fry about 400* sugar with powdered sugar when eating them.
Dorothea
Elgin, ND

2 Hour Rolls

Cream ½ c sugar and ½ c shortening. Add 1 c boiling water and beat. Add 2 beaten eggs. Dissolve 2 pkg yeast in 1 c warm water and mix in 1 tbl salt. Add to sugar mixture and add 6 c flour and mix all together. Let rise 1 hour. Shape rolls in shape desired and let rise another hour and bake at 400* 15 minutes or till lightly browned.
Lavonne
Brookings, SD

Waffles

2 eggs – 2 c milk – 2 c flour – 1 tsp soda – ½ tsp salt – ¼ c shortening. Mix and pour into preheated waffle iron.
Wilma Coates
Emmett, ID

White Bread

1 c warm water – 2 pkg yeast – 3 tbl sugar (set for 5 min) 3 c warm water – 3 tbl sugar – 4 tsp salt – 6 tbl oil enough flour to make dough. Make into buns or bread. Bake at 350* until golden brown.
Wilma Coates
Emmett, ID

Zucchini Bread

3 c flour – 1 tsp soda – ¼ tsp baking powder – 2 c sugar – 1 c oil (must be oil) – 1 c chopped nuts – 1 tsp salt – 3 tsp vanilla – 3 tsp cin. – 3 eggs beaten – 3 c grated zucchini (not peeled). Sift together flour, sugar, soda, cin & baking powder. Beat eggs, add sugar, van and oil. Mix well. Stir zucchini. Add dry ingredients and blend. Stir in nuts. (I think the sugar shouldn't be with the flour. I think she copied the receipt wrong) Bake in 2 bread pans at 350* 1 hour.
Lucille
Shakappee, MN

Zucchini Nut Bread

3 eggs – 1 c oil – 1 c sugar – 1/3 c molasses – 2 tsp van. – 2 c flour – ½ c whole wheat flour – 1 tsp salt – 1 tsp soda – ½ tsp baking powder – 2 tsp cinnamon – 2 c shredded zucchini – 1 c raisins – 1 c chopped nuts 350*. Divide the batter between 2 greased and floured 5x9 pans. (loaf). Bake 1 hour or until toothpick comes out clean.
Olga Peters
Salem, OR

Zueiback (German)

2 c milk (scalded) – ¾ c shortening – ¼ c sugar – 1 tbl salt . Dissolve above ingredients in the scalded milk. 2 cakes of yeast dissolved in ½ cup warm water. Add enough flour to make soft dough. (Not sticky when handled) let rise in warm place until dough doubles. Then make your balls in the shape of an 8. Let rise and bake in 400* oven.
Olga Peters
Salem, OR

Blueberry Rhubarb Jam

Cook – 6 c rhubarb – 5 c sugar till done. Add 1 can blueberries pie filling – 2 sm or 1 lg rasp Jell-O. Cook to boiling point and put in freezer jars. Cool and then freeze.
Lee Johnson
Emmett, ID

Boghs Sweet Pickles

Fill jar with small cukes – add 1 tbl salt – 1 tbl pickling spices -1 tbl horseradish – 2 tsp alum – 1 c vinegar – fill jar with cold water and seal. Let stand several months. When jar is opened pour off liquid, slice pickles length wise add 1 or 2 c sugar and let stand 24 hours.
Mary
Portland, OR

Bread and Butter Pickles

12 med cucumbers – 8 med onions peeled – 4 green peppers. ¾ c cooking salt – 6 ½ qts water – 7 c sugar – 6 c vinegar – 3 tbl celery seed – ¼ c white mustard seed – 1 tsp turmic. Wash cukes, onions and green peppers sliced thin, soak several hours or overnight in brine made by dissolving the salt in 6 qts water drain and wash well and drain again before cooking. Combine sugar, vinegar, remaining ½ qt water and spices in large kettle, bring to a boil, boil 3 min. Add veg boil 20 minutes. Fill jars and seal at once.
Jan-nita
ST Helens, OR

Bread and Butter Pickles

25 to 30 med size cucumbers – 6 lg white onions – 3 lg red or green peppers – 12 c salt – 5 c vinegar – 5 c sugar – 2 tbl mustard seed – 1 tbl celery seed – 2 ½ tsp turmeric – ½ tsp cloves. Wash cukes and slice about 1/16 inch thick. Chop onions and peppers, combine with cukes and salt. Let stand overnight or at least 3 hours, drain. Combine vinegar, sugar and spices in lg kettle and bring to a boil. Cukes should be just transparent. Pack while hot and put into jars and seal.
Ellenore
Rock Away Beach, OR

Bread and Butter Pickles

1 c salt – 1 gal water put cukes sliced and soak 2 hours. Make sure water covers cukes. Mix and bring to a boil. 1 qt vinegar-1 tbl mustard seed – 1 tbl turmeric – 1 tbl celery seed – 1 cinnamon sticks (break in small pieces)- 4 c sugar – sliced onions. Put pickles and onions in mixture and cook till pickles turn light in color. Put in jars use a slotted spoon or fork, bring brine back to a boil. Pour over pickles and seal.
Becky
Gaston, OR

Bread and Butter Pickles

6 qts sliced cucumbers – 1 c salt – cover with water and let stand for 3 hours then drain. Mix together the following ingredients – 6 c vinegar – 6 c sugar – ½ c mustard seed – 1 tbl celery seed. Heat together and bring to a boil. Pour over cukes and heat. (Not to boil) put in jars and seal.
Mary
Portland, OR

Canned Apples for Pies

Blend 4 ½ c sugar – 1 c cornstarch – 2 tbl cinnamon – 1 tsp salt -1 tsp nutmeg – 1 tsp lemon juice. Add 10 c water, stir until bubbly and thickened add lemon juice. Put sliced apples in hot jars and pour syrup over and seal. Process 20 minutes for qts and 15 minutes for pints, in hot water bat
Phylis
ST Helens, OR

Canned Choke Cherry Jelly

5 c cherry juice – 1 pkg sure jell – 7 c sugar – ¼ tsp almond extract. Bring juice and sure gel to a boil. Immediately add sugar and bring to a hard boil, time for 5 minutes. Add extract to finish jelly and put into jars and seal with wax.
Anggie
Richardton, ND

Canned Choke Cherry Syrup

2 c cherry juice – ½ c white syrup – 2 ½ c sugar – bring to a boil, turn to simmer and cook 15 minutes. Pour into jars and seal.
Sandie
Dwight, ND

Canned Frozen Cream Corn

9 c corn cut off cob (don't blanch) 3 ½ c water – ¼ c sugar – 1 tsp canning salt – boil 3 minutes. Cool completely. Put in containers and freeze. When using, you can add a little cream to make cream style.
Thelma
Richardton, ND

Canning Garden Relish

chop the following – 2 c green tomatoes – 2 c green peppers – 2 c med cucumbers – 2 c onions. Soak these ingredients overnight in cold water to cover. Adding ¾ c salt to each 1 ½ qt of water. In morning drain off brine. Add 2 c diced celery and 2 c diced carrots cook tender and drain. Mix 4 c sugar – 4 c vinegar and 2 tbl regular mustard and boil 1 minute. Add the prepared veg and boil 3 min longer. Pour into jars and seal at once.
Gladys
Northfield, MN

Canned Pickled Beets

2 c vinegar – 2 c sugar – 1 c water – 1 tsp pickling spice – salt and pepper. Cook beets and take off jackets. Boil above juice first and than put beets in and bring to a boil again and put into hot jars and seal. Makes 4 qts.
Barbara
Cornelius, OR

Canning Refrigerator Pickles

4 c sugar – 4 c vinegar – ½ c pickling salt – 1/3 tsp turmeric – 1 1/3 tsp celery salt – 3 onions sliced – cucumbers sliced thin. Mix sugar, vinegar and spice together. Stir good to dissolve salt and sugar. Do not heat, this syrup stays cold. Wash and sterilize 3 qt jars. Slice onions and cukes into each jar to ½ inch from top. Pour syrup over each to fill jar. Screw on lids. Refrigerate at least 5 days before using. Keep in refrigerate up to 10 months.
Alyce
Lake Preston, SD

Canned Ripe Cucumber Relish

4 c chopped cucumbers ripe – 2 c chopped onion – 1 green pepper -1 red sweet pepper both chopped – 1 tsp salt – 2 tsp mustard seed -2 tsp celery seed – 1 c vinegar – 4 c sugar. Wash and chop all veg set in salt water for 1 hour and drain. boil vinegar, sugar, and seasonings to a boil (hard rolling one) add veg and let come to a boil (hard rolling) again. Put in jars (hot) and seal.
Olive
Sentinel Butte, ND

Canned Rhubarb Apple Sauce

16 c Rhubarb – 4 lbs golden delicious apples (about 12) 1 ½ to 2 c sugar. Trim rhubarb, cut in ½ inch slices. Core and cut apples in quarters. Peeling is not necessary. In lg pot combine rhubarb, apples and sugar, stir gently. Cook over low heat stirring frequently until juice forms and sugar dissolved. Increase heat to med. stir till mixture comes to a boil, simmer till rhubarb and apples are tender about 30 minutes. Put in jars and process in a boiling water bath 20 minutes. About 8 pints.
Barbara
Corneluis, OR

Canned Sauerkraut

Shred good sound heads of cabbage. Packed solid in hot jars. Add 1 tbl salt and ½ tbl vinegar. In each qt fill with boiling water and seal. Let set for 6 weeks before using.
Shirley
Lake Preston, SD

Canned Tomato Soup

18 to 20 lbs ripe tomatoes – 1 Bunch celery chopped – 6 onions chopped (med size) boil hard till soft. Strain through strainer then add 1 c sugar – 2 c flour – 6 tsp salt – 1 c butter – ½ tsp cayenne pepper. Boil all together, till flour is done. Put into jars and cold pack to seal lids.
Paula Starcher
Emmett, ID

Canned Zucchini Relish

8 c chopped zucchini – 4 green peppers chopped – 4 red peppers -chopped – 4 lg onions chopped – 1/3 tsp salt over all for ½ hour, drain and wash. Add 3 c vinegar – 5 c sugar – 1 tsp cinnamon – 1 tsp tumeric – 1 tsp celery seed. Bring to a boil. Seal in pints.
Jeanine
Emmett, ID

Cranberry Relish

1 Bag (1 lb) cranberries – 1 orange – 1 apple – 1-2 cups sugar depends on taste and tartness of cranberries. Chop (food processor to chop) into relish, refrigerate and serve.
Randy Wilson
Emmett, ID

Cucumber Pickles

13 c water – ½ c salt – 1 c sugar – 2 c white vinegar – dill and garlic cloves – boil 15 minutes. Pack cucumbers small or med in hot jars and put syrup over cukes. Put in canner and bring to a boil, leave in canner till cold before taking out.
Jan-nita
ST Helens, OR

Dill Pickles

2 qts cucumbers – 4 to 8 dill heads – 3 cloves or garlic cut fine-1 c vinegar – 3 c water – ¼ c canning salt. Bring to a boil and pour over cukes. Seal while hot.
Marie Workenton
Brookings, OR

Granma Pickles

3 doz cucumbers peel and cut in chunks – 1 qt onions sliced -soak in week brine for 3 hours and drain. Mix 1 qt vinegar – 2 c sugar – ½ tsp turmeric. Put pickling spices in a bag add pickles let simmer till cucumbers are yellow. Put in hot jars and seal.
Mary
Portland, OR

Green Beans or Wax Beans

1 gal. Beans cover with water – ½ c vinegar – ¼ c pickling salt -¼ c sugar. Boil add for 30 minutes. Pack in hot jars and seal. Before using drain and rinse real good. Prepare any way you want.
Elsie
Richardton, ND

Green Tomato Preserves

For each pound of green tomatoes add – ¾ pint sugar – 1 tbl lemon juice – 10 cloves – 1/8 tsp mace – ¼ tsp each of ginger and cinnamon. Let sugar stand on tomatoes 1 hour then add spice and boil till clear. Seal.
Dora Crandall
Eugene, OR

Jalapeno Jelly

Liquify in blender: 1 can jalapeno with seeds (1/2) – 2 small 4oz – ¼ cup vinegar – 1 large green pepper. Cook stir and skim. Add 6 cups of sugar to above mixture – 1 cup vinegar. Add 6 oz certo to above and boil one minute (certo comes in a 6 oz bottle). Add 3-4 drops green food coloring. Cool, put in small jars. Serve on a brick of Philadelphia cream cheese with triskets/crackers. Makes 6 ½ pints.
Randy Wilson
Emmett, ID

Rhubarb Strawberry Jell-o Jam

5 c cut up rhubarb – 3 c sugar – Cover rhubarb with sugar and let set overnight. In morning boil 10 minutes and take off heat and dissolve 1 pkg small box Jell-O to mixture. Put in jars and seal.
Mabel
Scappoose, OR

Salsa (Canned)

30 med tomatoes – ½ to ¾ c vinegar – 10 Cheyenne peppers – 1 tbl salt – 5 lg onions – 1 tbl pepper – 1 tbl garlic salt – 1 bulb garlic 6 green peppers – 2 tbl seasoning salt – 15 tomatillas – 2 cans tomato paste. Chop tomatoes, tomatillsa. Add 2 cans tomato paste, set aside. Chop peppers, onions and garlic fine. Cook ½ hour in ½ c water. Drain liquid. Add tomatoes and tomatillas and tomato paste, add seasonings and cook for 5 minutes put in jars and cook in canner for 20 to 30 minutes.
Pearl Cavender
Keizer, OR

Tomato Catsup

Peel and slice a peck of ripe tomatoes, boil thoroughly. Drain off juice; boil tomatoes slowly for 4 hour. add two tbl salt – 1 tbl black pepper – 1 ½ tsp cayenne – 1 tbl mustard – boil 1 hour. When cool add 1 pint vinegar and seal.
Dora Crandall
Eugene, OR

BBQ Pheasant

2 pheasants cut up. Lay pieces in pan and add small amount of water. Slice lg onion over top and bake covered for ½ hour on each side at 350*. Drain water off and cover with the following sauce; ¼ tsp Tabasco sauce – 1/3 c oil – 1/3 c vinegar – 2 tsp dry mustard – ½ c brown sugar – 1 c ketch up – dash liquid smoke – salt & pepper. Bake ½ hour more on each side with out covering.
Margie
Lake Preston, SD

Broccoli Chicken Casserole

4 chicken breast cooked and boned – 1 pkg or bunch broccoli cooked and drained – 2 can cream of chicken soup – 1 tbl lemon juice – 1 c mayo – ½ tsp curry powder – 1 tbl melted butter – ½ c sharp cheddar cheese grated – ½ c toasted bread crumbs or almonds. Place broccoli in bottom of casserole. Lay chicken on top. Mix soup, mayo, lemon juice and curry powder. Pour over breasts. Sprinkle cheese on top. Bake at 350* for 45 minutes, or till chicken is tender. Remove from oven and sprinkle crumbs that have been mixed with butter on top. Place back in oven for 15 minutes to brown.
Ellenore
Rockaway Beach, OR

Chicken Adabo

8 – 10 chicken thighs – ½ c soy sauce – 2 tbsp vinegar – ½ tsp black pepper – water to cover: in large pot cook about 45 min or until chicken is done. Serve with steam rice. Use juice from chicken to pour over rice.
Barbara Jeans
Emmett, ID

Chicken Casciatore

2 c hot water – 1 pkg chicken rice soup mix – 1 c canned pizza sauce. Mix well, cook over med heat until thoroughly heated. Add ¼ tsp garlic powder and 2 tbl sweet pepper flakes. Pour soup mixture in a 2 ½ qt casserole. Place skin side up over soup mixture cut up chicken. Bake at 350* for 1 hour or till done. Do not turn. Put in a cake pan or roaster but be sure chicken is all coated with the pizza sauce before baking.
Barbara
Tualaton, OR

Chicken Coating

1 c pancake mix – 1 c potato flakes or buds – ¼ tsp pepper – 1 tsp salt – 1 ½ tsp Chile powder. Dip chicken into milk and then into the above mixture. Place on a cookie sheet. Melt ½ c oleo and pour over chicken. Bake for 1 hour at 375*
Jan-nita
ST Helens, OR

Chicken and Dumplings

Heat; 2 (11 oz) cans of chicken soup to boil in a large kettle. Drop by spoonfuls of biscuit dough cover tightly steam with out lifting cover for 15 minutes. A hurry up meal.
Barbara
Cornelius, OR

Chicken Hot Dish

1 ½ c diced meat cooked – 1 ½ c chopped celery – ½ c chopped green pepper – ½ c green onion chopped – ½ c toasted almonds -1 tsp salt – dash pepper – 3 tbl lemon juice – ¾ c mayo – 1 c grated cheese- 1 can water chestnuts. Bake at 450* for 15 minutes.
Dorthea
Coolidge, AZ

Chicken Hot Dish

2 c uncooked macaroni – 2 c chicken cooked – sm onion – 4 c milk -4 c cracker crumbs – 1 c melted butter – ¾ c cheese cut up – 1 can cream of mushroom soup – 1 can cream of celery soup – 1 can cream of chicken soup. Mix all together and bake at 350* for 1 hour.
Dorthea
Coolidge, AZ

Chicken Tortilla Casserole

4 Chicken breast – boil till done, skin, bone & cut up. Cut up in 1 inch sq's. 5 flour tortillas. Grate 1 c cheddar cheese - 1 c Monterey jack cheese – 1 can cream of chicken soup – 5 green onions – ½ can green chilies (opt) diced – ½ c milk. In a buttered casserole pour ½ c broth – ½ chicken – ½ c soup mixture – ½ of tortillas – repeat ending with cheese. Cover & refirg 1 hour or overnight. Bake at 350* for 1 hour.
Joane
Lake Preston, SD

Coating for Oven Fried Chicken

Flour, cornmeal, salt, poultry seasoning, pepper, thyme, garlic powder and rosemary. Mix together and coat chicken. Place on parchment paper and bake till done.
Vance
Forrest Grove, OR

Crunchy Chicken Bake

1 envelope cream of chicken soup – 1/3 c hot water – 1 chicken breast – ¾ c crushed herb seasoned stuffing. Mix – 1 tbl oleo melted. Blend cut of soup with water. Dip chicken in soup mixture then in crumbs. Place in pan and drizzle with butter. Bake at 375* for 45 minutes or till tender.
Jackie
Sentinel Butte, ND

Crispy Chicken Stir Fry

½ tsp pepper – 1 c bisquick – ¼ c oil – 2 c diced uncooked chicken breasts – 2 eggs slightly beaten – 1 green pepper cut in thin strips – 3 carrots cut diagonally in ½ inch pieces – 1 onion sliced in rings separate – 1 can (20 oz) pineapple chunks drained. Mix bisquick and pepper in a bag, stir chicken in eggs. Remove with slotted spoon. Shake in the bisquick till coated. Heat 1 tbl oil in skillet or wok on med high heat, stir fry carrots 2 min. Add green peppers cook again. (2 minutes) Remove and add rest of oil, stir fry chicken until golden brown. Add veg and stir fry till warm. Stir in pineapple.
Sandy
ST Helens, OR

Curried Chicken Breasts

2 pkg chicken gravy mix – 1 tbl curry powder – 1 c water – 6 chicken breast – salt – pepper – paprika. Mix gravy, curry and water in baking dish. Put chicken in brown and serve bag, season with salt, pepper & paprika. Put gravy mix over chicken . Place the chicken in single layer in bag. Close bag with nylon tie, make 6 inch slits in top of bag. Bake at 350* for 45 minutes or till tender.
Mary
Portland, OR

Curried Chicken with Rice

¾ c corn flakes crumbs – 1 tsp salt – ¾ tsp curry powder – ¼ c sherry – 3 chicken breast halved and boned – ½ c raisins – ½ c mayo – 1 (6 oz) pkg long grain wild rice. In a pie pan combine crumbs, salt and curry powder. Coat chicken with mayo, roll in crumbs. Place in lightly greased pan, tucking edge under. Bake at 350* for 1 hour. Combine sherry and raisins and let stand while chicken is baking. Drain reserving sherry. Prepare rice on pkg using the reserved sherry as part of liquid. At serving time stir raisins into cooked rice, place chicken on top of rice.
Vivian
Nova Scotia, Canada

Fried Pheasant

4 tbl flour – ¼ c fat – ½ c cream – ¼ tsp pepper – ½ tsp salt – pheasant. Clean and wash bird, cut into pieces. Dredge with the dry ingredients and brown on both sides in hot fat. Pour cream over the browned meat. Cover and cook slowly for 1 hour.
Kay
Meridian, MS

Glorified Chicken

2 ½ to 3 lbs broiler fryer chicken cut up – 1 tbl oleo melted – 1 can cream of broccoli soup. In baking pan arrange chicken skin side up. Drizzle with oleo. Bake at 375* for 40 minutes. Spoon soup over chicken. Bake 20 minutes more or till tender.
Joan
New Tazewell, TN

Herb Chicken Casserole

1 (3 lb) chicken – ¾ stick of oleo – ½ c chopped celery – ½ tsp salt – 1 can cream of chicken soup – 1 c or more milk – ½ c slivered almonds – ½ c chopped onion – 1 c cream of mushroom soup – 1 pkg stove top dressing – ¾ of a can chow mein noodles. Boil meat in salted water till well done. Remove from bones and chop meat into pieces. Put in large baking dish. Add chow mein noodles. sauté onion and celery in butter. Add the soup and milk. Mix together and pour over chicken and noodles. Heat almonds in ¼ c butter, add to dressing mix and put on top. Bake for 1 hour or till lightly browned.
Melba
ST Helens, OR

Hot Chicken or Turkey Hot Dish

1 ½ c diced cooked meat – 1 ½ c chopped celery – ½ c chopped green pepper – ½ c green onions – ½ c toasted almonds – 1 tsp salt – dash pepper – 3 tbl lemon juice – ¾ c mayo – 1 c grated cheese – 1 c water chestnuts. Mix well together and bake at 450* for 15 minutes.
Dorthea
Coolidge, AZ

Lemon Chicken

¼ c flour – chicken – 1 ¼ tsp salt – 2 tbl oil – 3 tbl ketch up – 1 (6 oz) can frozen lemonade thawed – 3 tbl brown sugar – 1 tbl vinegar. Coat chicken with flour and salt. Brown in oil. Add remaining ingredients and pour over chicken in crock pot. For 3 to 4 hours on high.
Sandy
Puyallup, WA

Oriental Chicken Wings

1 (8 oz) bottle Catalina dressing – ¼ c soy sauce – ¼ tsp ginger – 1 ½ doz chicken wings cut jointed tips off. Combine dressing, soy sauce and ginger. Pour over wings. Cover. Marinate several hours or overnight. Drain. Reserving marinate. Place on broiler pan, broil 15 to 20 minutes turning once brush occasionally with marinate.
Mary
Portland, OR

Pola Delle Case

3 boned chicken breasts – mix together below. 1 c bread crumbs ¼ tsp garlic – 1 tbl minced parsley. dip in flour, salt and pepper-then in egg and cream mixture. Coat with the crumb mixture. Brown in 4 tbl butter. Turn heat down and add ½ c white wine. Cover and cook 15 minutes. Add 3 tbl marsola and cook 10 minutes more. sauce; 3 tbl butter – ½ lb mushrooms -1/4 c green onion – 2 tsp parsley – melt 2 tbl butter and 2 tbl flour – ½ c cream – ½ tsp salt and cook till thicken. Add ½ c sour cream and add onions and mushrooms and pour over chicken and serve.
Laurie
Corvallis, OR

Savory Cresent Squares

1 (3 oz) cream cheese softened – ¼ tsp salt – 3 tbl oleo melted – 2 c cooked cubed chicken – 1/8 tsp pepper – 2 tbl milk – chopped onion – 1/8 oz can refrigerator quick cresent rolls – 1 tbl chives – ¾ c crushed seasoned croutons. Blend cheese and 2 tbl oleo till smooth. Add salt, pepper, onions, chives, milk and chicken. Mix well. Separate rolls into rectangles. Firmly press perforations to seal. Spoon ½ c mixture into center of rectangle. Pull 4 corners of dough to top center of mixture twist slightly and seal edges. Brush top with 1 tbl oleo dipped in crouton crumbs. Bake at 350* on ungreased sheet for 20 to 25 minutes till golden brown.
Gladys
Northfield, MN

Shake and Bake for Chicken

4 c crushed corn flakes – 1 tsp salt – 1 tsp pepper – 1 tsp paprika – 1 tsp poultry seasoning – ¼ c flour. Mix well and store in air tight container. Keeps indefinitely. No refrig needed. Coat pieces of chicken. Place on baking sheet or broiler. Bake 30 minutes at 400*. Turn down heat to 350* and bake 30 minutes longer till done.
Eva
Glova, ND

Sweet and Sour Nuggets

1 box chicken nuggets – ½ of a big can pineapple juice – 1 tbl sugar – 1 jar mar chino cherries. Add cherry juice, pineapple juice and sugar and cornstartsch just enough to thicken on low heat. Add green peppers, onion, pineapple, cherries and tomato. Simmer for a few minutes. Pour over nuggets and simmer till nuggets are done.
Sandy
Vancover, WA

Soy Sauce Wings

¾ c soy sauce – ½ c oil – salt – pepper – green onion. Soak wings in mixture for 1 to 1 ½ hour. Turn several times. Place chicken in baking pan, use ½ of the sauce for baking. Bake at 350* for 45 minutes to 1 hours.
Leola
Rapid City, SD

Turkey and Wild Rice Divine

1 c wild rice – 1/3 c white rice – ¼ c butter – ½ c chopped onion – 1/3 c flour – 1 c cream – 1 c broth - 4 c turkey chopped – ¼ c silvered almonds – sm jar pimentos chopped – salt – pepper – 1 sm can mushroom stems and pieces. Sauté onions in butter, add flour, make a white sauce of flour, cream broth, salt and pepper to taste. Combine rice's and cook till done. Drain. combine all other ingredients with the rice's, pour white sauce over, mix well. Bake at 3508 for 30 to 40 minutes. You may need more white sauce than this makes. I usually make a bigger recipe of this.
Mixkey
Killdeer, ND

Turkie Loaf

½ c cooked rice – 1 c boiling water – salt – 3 eggs yolks – 1 ½ c milk – 1/8 c chopped onions – celery – 4 c diced cooked turkie or chicken – 3 oz soft bread cubes – 3 egg whites. Cook rice in boiling water. Blend egg yolks and milk, mix all together the rest of ingredients except whites. Beat whites till stiff and fold into turkie mixture. Bake in greased pan at 375* for 50 minutes. Serve with gravy.
Mabel
Scappoose, OR

Turkey Squares

3 c chopped left over turkie – 2 c bread crumbs – ¼ c chopped onion – ¼ tsp poultry seasoning – 1 can cream of mushroom soup -1 c cooked rice – 1/3 c diced celery – 4 eggs well beaten – 2 c turkie broth – combine all except soup. Bake at 350* for 1 hour. Serve with heated mushroom soup over top. Heat with a little milk so its like a gravy.

Wilma Coates
Emmett, ID

Baked Ham

1 ham – 1 c brown sugar – 2 tbl cinnamon – 1 tsp pepper – 4 c flour – 2 tbl ground cloves – 2 tbl dry mustard, pineapple juice, trim some of the fat from ham. Combine flour, sugar, and spices. Add enough juice to make dough, which can be easily handled about a cup. Roll out into an oval lg enough to cover top and sides of ham part way down. Place ham in cold over then turn on at 325* and bake about 3 ½ to 4 hours. Basting ham with juice every 30 minutes. Remove from oven at end of baking time lift off jacket from meat, sprinkle ham with brown sugar and return to oven to brown.
Mary
Jesup, GA

Barbecue Pork

1 c diced left over pork – ½ c ketch up – 2 tbl brown sugar – 2 tbl vinegar – 1 tbl Worcestershire sauce. Heat all ingredients together and serve on split bun.
Jan-nita
ST Helens, OR

BBQ Pork Chops

1 tbl four – ¼ tsp cloves – ¼ c ketch up – 1 tsp dry mustard – ½ tsp celery seed – salt and pepper. Place chops in large cake pan and sprinkle with salt and pepper. Blend dry ingredients. Add ketch up. Mix and add 1 c water, stir. Pour over chops and bake at 350* for 1 hour.
Viola
Bryant, SD

Breakfast Brunch Casserole

Grease a 9x13 pan. 1 lb ham cubed – 1 can mushrooms – 3 to 4 green onions chopped – 1 green pepper chopped – 2 c grated cheddar cheese – layer in order. Mix with beater – 18 eggs – ½ pt sour cream – 2 tsp salt – ½ tsp pepper. Pour this mixture over the rest of ingredients. Bake at 350* for 45 minutes to 1 hour or till knife inserted comes out clean.
Carlyon
ST Helens, OR

Cantonese Meatballs

1 lb pork sausage – 1/3 c milk – ¼ tsp sage – 1 egg slightly beaten – ½ c fine soda crackers crumbs. Beat all ingred in bowl. Shape into balls. Brown slowly for about 10 minutes. Pour off fat – ¼ c water – 1 tbl vinegar – ¼ c ketch up – 1 tbl soy sauce – 2 tbl brown sugar. Mix all ingredients together. Pour over meatballs and heat about 15 minutes or till heated through. You can add drained pineapple. Chunks.
Gladys
Portland, OR

Coke Pork Chops

8 pork chops – 1 c catsup – 1 c coke – 1 c brown sugar. Mix together catsup and coke. Pour over pork chops. Sprinkle the brown sugar over all. Bake uncovered for 1 ½ hour on 350*. Turn ½ way through baking time.
Pearl Cavender
Keizer, OR

Corn Dogs

2/3 c corn meal – 1/3 c flour – 1 tsp salt – ½ c milk – 1 egg beaten - veg oil – 8 to 10 wieners. Mix well. Insert wooden skewer in one end of wiener, coat with some additional flour, dip in mixture. Fry in deep fat fryer at 375* till golden brown.
Jackie
Sentinel Butte, ND

Easter Ham

1 fully cooked ham with bone 10 to 12 lbs – 1 (12 oz) lemon soda pop – ½ c brown sugar – 1 tbl mustard – ½ c pineapple juice – cloves – mar chino cherries. Place ham fat side up on a rack. Pour ½ of soda over ham. Bake ham at 325* at 15 minutes per lb. Remove 30 minutes before cooking time is up. Carefully remove rind and score ham fat. Combine brown sugar and mustard spread over ham. Put ½ cherry on top holding in place with a clove. Combine rest of soda and pineapple juice. Drizzle some over ham. Bake 30 minutes longer. Frequently basting with juice.
Millie
Port Arthur, TX

Ham and Potato A gratin

Mix in a greased 10x6 baking dish – 3 c cut up cooked potatoes – 2 c cooked ham cut up. Pat into a heavy skillet – 1 1/3 c milk. - cheese cut into pieces about 1 ½ c – 2 tsp dry mustard – 2 tsp Worcestershire sauce – ½ tsp salt – ¼ tsp paprika. Stir over med heat till cheese melts. Do not boil. Pour over ham and potatoes. Bake at 350* for 15 min. Top with 3 ½ oz can French onion rings. Bake 10 minutes longer.
Dorethea
Cooliage, AZ

Ham & Potato Casserole

3 tbl butter -3 tbl flour – 1 ½ c milk – 1 tsp salt & pepper – 1 c cooked diced ham – ½ c grated cheddar cheese – 2 c cooked potatoes – 6 sm whole onions – ¼ c butter. Melt 3 tbl butter, blend flour and add milk stirring constantly. Cook till thickened, boiling about 3 min. Add seasonings & cheese. Cook slowly till cheese melts. Add ham, potatoes and onions. Pour mixture in a greased casserole. Sprinkle with crumbs. Lightly browned.
Lavonne
Emmett, ID

Ham Loaf

1 can (20 oz) pineapple slices drained – ¼ c raisins (save juice from pineapple) – 2 lbs ground cooked ham – 2 eggs slightly beaten – 2 c soft bread cubes – ½ c minced celery – ¼ c milk – 1 ½ tsp dry mustard – dash pepper – 1 tbl brown sugar – 1 tbl oleo – 1 tbl cornstarch. oven 350*. Pat pineapple dry with paper. Sprinkle brown sugar over bottom of a 9x9 pan, line bottom and sides of pan with pineapple. Press meat mixture into pan. Bake 1 ½ hour. set aside 5 minutes. Unfold onto serving platter mean while combine juice and remaining ingredients cook till thickened and smooth over meat.
Sally
Gray, KY

Ham Luau

2 lbs ham slices – 1 can sliced pineapple – ½ c brown sugar – 1 egg -1 tsp dry mustard – 1/8 tsp ground cloves – ¼ c melted oleo – 4 c croutons – foil. Snip fat on ham, place in pan lined with foil. Drain pineapple reserving syrup. Mix together sugar, mustard and cloves. Stir in about 2 tbl pineapple juice. Brush ½ of mixture over ham cover with foil. Bake at 325* for 50 minutes. Beat together ½ juice, egg and melted butter and toss gently with croutons. Shape into balls turn ham and brush with brown sugar mixture. Arrange pineapple slice and wrap around ham. Place a crouton ball on each slice of ham. Return to oven and bake for 30 minutes.
Tina
Hilo, HI

Ham Stew

½ " thick slice o ham – 4 med potatoes – 4 carrots – 1 sm onion -1 tsp salt – pepper to taste – 1 (1 lb) can baked beans in tomato sauce – 1 can tomato soup (undiluted) cube ham, potatoes, carrots and onion. Put in crock pot with water to cover. Add baked beans and tomato soup. Cook on high for 4 hours stirring once. (Not quite as much water as it says. Easy on the pepper)
Wilma Coates
Emmett, ID

Hawaiian Pork Chops

4 to 6 pork chops – ½ c shortening – 1 can (6 oz) frozen pineapple juice thawed – 1 tsp sugar – ¼ tsp cinnamon – 1 tsp cornstarch – 4 to 6 pineapple slices – ¼ c flour – ¾ c water – 1 tsp lemon juice – ¼ tsp nutmeg – 1 tbl cold water. Trim fat off chops. Sprinkle with salt then coat with flour, brown on both sides in the shortening. Drain excess fat. Add pineapple juice ¾ c water, sugar, lemon juice and spices. Simmer over low heat for 30 min. combine cornstarch & cold water. Add to chops. Cook & stir till sauce thickens. Top each chop with pineapple slices. Cook for 5 minutes longer.
Jan-nita
ST Helens, OR

Hawaiian Pork Lula

drain; 1 can (20 oz) pineapple slices reserve juice – measure ¼ c pineapple juice, add water to remaining juice to make 1 ¾ c set aside for stuffing. Moisten 6 chops with the ¼ c juice. Empty 1 envelope of shake and bake for pork in shaker bag, add ½ tsp around ginger, coat chops in the mixture. Arrange chops in a single layer or rack in a shallow pan. Place 1 pineapple slices on each one. Dice remaining pineapple set aside. Bake chops at 425* for 25 minutes. Meanwhile heat the 1 ¾ c juice and water, place contents of very season from stove top dressing mix for pork and ¼ butter in a qt baking dish. Add the hot liquid and stir to blend and partially melt butter. Add the stuffing bread, stir to moisten. Add diced pineapple. Bake uncovered with chops for 15 to 25 minutes or till done.
Tina
Hilo, HI

Pigs Knuckles and Sauerkraut

3 lb pig hocks – 2 lbs sauerkraut. Put first 2 ingredients in kettle or Dutch oven and add 6 c water. Bring to a boil and simmer covered, 3 ½ hours or till meat is tender. Add salt. Make a dumpling batter. Sift together 2 c flour – 2 tsp baking powder – 1 tsp salt. Cut in 1 tbl shortening. Mixing with fork stir in ¾ c milk to form soft dough. Drop on meat and cover and cook till dumplings are done about 15 minutes.
Grandma
Gray, KY

Pork Chops and Rice

6 chops – oleo – salt and pepper – onion slices – rice – 1 can tomato soup – 1 can tomato paste – 3 c boiling water. Brown chops in a small amount of oleo, arrange chops in pan or casserole. Season, place onion slices on each chop. Place 2 tbl rice on each chop. Pour soup over rice, add tomato paste, and season again. Add boiling water, cover. Bake at 325* for 1 ½ hours. Add a little more water as needed if to dry.
Glenda
ST Helens, OR

Pork Chop Creole

4 pork chops – salt – 4 green pepper rings – pepper – 4 onion slices -1 can tomato soup. Brown chops, drain off fat. Sprinkle chops with salt and pepper place a onion ring and pepper ring on each chop. Pour soup over meat and cover. Cook over low heat for 45 minutes.
Iris
Beaverton, OR

Pork Chops, Potatoes & Dumplings

Brown chops and bake use drippings and slice raw potatoes, onion, salt & peppers and fry till a little brown. Add water to cover potatoes. Use frozen bread dough thawed and let rise to half size, pinch off and lay on top of potatoes. Cover and leave covered for about 30 minutes or till you can hear potatoes frying.
Mary Jean
Richardton, ND

Potet Suppe (Potato Soup)

7 slices bacon diced – ½ c minced onion – 5 c diced potatoes – 4 c milk – celery salt. Fry bacon till nearly done. Add onion and cook until clear. Add potatoes, cover tightly and cook 10 minutes than add milk. Bring to a boil and add small dumplings. Add seasoning and continue cooking over low heat for 20 minutes.
Sonja
ST Helens, OR

Rice Casserole

Finely chopped 2 c celery – 1 lg onion – ½ green pepper – 1 pkg dry chicken noodle soup mix – ½ c uncooked rice – 3 c boiling water – 1 lb sausage – 1 oz pimiento – ½ c water chestnuts. Put water, rice and soup mix in casserole in a 350* oven for ½ hour. Brown sausage, drain off all fat except 2 tbl. sauté celery, onion and green pepper in fat and add to rice mixture in oven. Add pimento (opt) and water chestnuts. Bake 1 ½ hour more.
Mabel
Scappoose, OR

Rice Pork Chop Bake

onion diced – diced celery – diced green pepper – 1 can cream mushroom soup – 1 can cream chicken soup – 6 pork chops – raw rice – 1 can celery soup cream – 2 cans water. Sauté onion, green pepper and celery in pan. Add raw rice and soup, water. Place chops on top. Bake at 350* till done about 2 hours. Can turn oven down after 45 minutes to 325*
Twila
Oldham, SD

Roast Pork

4 lb pork loin or boneless pork shoulder roast – ¾ c brown sugar – paprika – 4 slices pineapple. Season meat with salt & pepper. Place in roasting pan. Bake at 350* about 40 min per lb. Remove for oven. Sprinkle brown sugar over top of roast. Arrange pin over fat portion of meat. Pour juice over meat. Sprinkle lightly with paprika. Return to oven till pin pieces are lightly browned. Drippings maybe thicken for gravy.
Anne
Brown Creek, MI

Sausage & Rice

Brown 1 lg pkg of sausage in skillet slowly – chop 1 green pepper – 1 onion – 3 stalks celery – add veg to sausage and cook 10 to 15 min. add 1 c cream of chicken soup – 1 can cream of mushroom soup dilute each can with 1 can water and 1 c uncooked rice. Pour into lg baking dish. Bake at 350* for 1 hour. Stir gently at half hour.
Gloria
Portland, OR

Stenekjam Brunch

6 slices buttered bread cubed – ¾ lb grated cheese – 4 egg well beaten – 2 c milk – ½ tsp salt – ½ tsp dry mustard – 1 can mushroom bits and stems – 1 c cubed ham. Place bread in buttered 9x12 inch pan. Layer cheese ham and mushrooms. Pour ¾ of liquid overall (egg & milk). Refrigerate overnight. Top with remaining liquid and some bread cubes. Bake 40 min at 325*. Let stand 10 minutes before serving.
Mabel
Scappoose, OR

Stuffed Pork Chops W/Honey Glaze

1 (6 oz) dressing mix with herbs – butter and wild rice – 1/3 c chopped celery – ¼ c oleo – ¼ c chopped onions – 1 ½ c boiling water – 1/3 c raisins – 1 c chopped apples – 6 to 8 (1 ½ inch thick) pork loin chops cut with packets – 1 c honey – 1 tbl packed brown sugar – 1 tbl soy sauce; Combine dressing, celery, onion, water and oleo. Mix well till most of liquid is absorbed. Stir in raisins and apples. Spoon stuffing loosely into pockets of chops. Place chops in single layer in lg baking dish. Chops should not be touching. Combine honey, brown sugar, and soy sauce. Bake chops uncovered at 350* for 45 to 50 minutes. Baste frequently with honey glaze. if more glaze is needed double recipe. Bake remaining stuffing in a lightly greased casserole. Bake it at 350* for 25 to 30 minutes.
Lavonne
Emmett, ID

Sweet & Sour Pork

2 lb spare ribs browned – 1 lb chopped onion – 1 green pepper chopped – ½ c vinegar – 1 ¼ c brown sugar – 4 tbl soy sauce – 4 tbl flour – 4 tbl water. Spread meat in pan, over the top, put onions and green peppers. Mix rest of ingredients pour over top. Cover and bake 2 hour. at 350*
Doris
Scappoose, OR

Sweet and Sour Pork

2 lg green pepper – ¼ c oil – 1 ½ lb pork – 4 tbl flour – pinch pepper -2 tsp soy sauce – 1 c bouillon cube of chicken or beef – ½ c sugar -4 slices pineapple rings or chunks – 1/8 c vinegar - 2 ½ tsp corn-starch. Cut pork in small portions and shake in bag with the flour and pepper. Put oil in pan and brown pork well on all sides. Pour out all but 1 tbl of the oil. Cut peppers in med pieces and the pineapple and add to pork. Add 1/3 c of the bouillon broth. Cover and cook over low heat for 10 min. Blend together the cornstarch, vinegar, sugar and 2 1/3 c broths. Add and stir till it thickens. Serve over rice.
Dottie
Beaverton, OR

Verenike

1 c water – 1 egg white – salt & pepper to taste – flour to make soft dough. Filling; 1 egg yolk – salt and pepper to taste – 2 ½ c cottage cheese (dry curd) roll out dough to about 1/8 inch thick. Place about 1 heaping tbl in one corner. Fold over boiling water and cook ten minutes. Gravy; fried ham with canned milk no thickening.
Olga Peters
Salem, OR

Weiner Boats

1 can mushroom soup or cream of chicken – 8 wieners – ½ c milk -2 pkg frozen green beans cooked drain can use fresh or canned beans – 4 slices cheese cut in strips – 4 slices partially cooked bacon cut in half. in baking dish stir soup till smooth, blend in milk, stir in beans. Slit wieners lengthwise stuff, with cheese. Arrange on top of beans. Top with bacon. Bake at 350* for 25 minutes.
Iris
Beaverton, OR

Weiner Hot Dish

5 diced med potatoes – 12 wieners diced – 1 can whole kernel corn – ¼ c green peppers chopped – ¼ c onion chopped – 1 can cream of chicken soup – precook potatoes, place in casserole add diced wieners, pepper and onion. Drain corn and add soup. Mix all ingredients. Bake at 350* for ½ hour.
Vicky
Del Rio, TX

BBQ Salmon

6 salmon fillet or salmon steaks spoon barbecue sauce on top of each steak. Light if you don't like a lot of sauce. Heavier for a lot of sauce. Bake at 350* for 30 minutes or until salmon flakes easily with a fork. Serve.
Pearl Cavender
Keizer, OR

Clam Chowder

12 lg clams – 6 c water – 3 tbl butter – 3 garlic cloves sliced – 2 med onions sliced – ½ tsp pepper – 3 tsp dried basil – 2 med carrots scraped – 1 lg potato – 1 lg parsnip scraped – 1 tsp dried thyme – 6 tbl heavy cream. Wash clams out, steam in a large pot. In another lg pan melt butter; add the garlic 1 min later. Add onions and fry 3 min. Until onions are translucent not brown. Add pepper and basil. Stir in with wooden spoon. Chop the clams and add to onions and fry 4 minutes longer, add 1/3 of the clam liquid, bring to a boil reduce heat to a bubbling simmer. Coarsely chop veg and add rest of liquid, bring to a boil, reduce heat, simmer for an hour. Take chowder off and add cream.
Geneva
Island City, OR

Crab Meat Luncheon

2 (6 oz) pkg frozen crabmeat (thawed) – I use fake crab – 1 (8 oz) pkg cream cheese softened – 3 tbl mayo – 2 tbl onion chopped – lemon juice to taste – dash Worcestershire sauce – dash Tabasco (opt) – 8 French rolls – 2 lg ripe tomatoes sliced – 8 slices amercing cheese – the night before serving. Mix together the crab, cheese, mayo and seasonings. Refrig. To prepare for serving, butter rolls lightly. Divide crab mixture evenly on top. Top with a slice of cheese & tom. Bake 350* till hot. 25 to 30 minutes or cheese melts.
Marit
Los Angeles, CA

Crab Stir Fry

1 pkg fake crab or fresh crab – soy sauce (opt) – 1 pkg (10 oz) frozen oriental style veg with seasoning – 1/8 tsp each, garlic powder and ground ginger. Combine crab, veg, garlic and ginger. Heat veg according to pkg. Stir and fry till all is well heated.
Jimmy
Hillsboro, OR

Crispy Cat Fish

½ tsp salt – ¼ tsp pepper – 1 c cornmeal – oil – 6 catfish fillets – 1 c milk – ¼ tsp paprika; Combine salt, pepper, cornmeal. Dip fish in milk, roll in cornmeal mixture. Pour oil in heavy skillet to a depth of one inch. Heat oil to 375*. Fry fish few pieces at a time until golden brown and fish flakes easily with fork. Drain on paper towel. Sprinkle with paprika.
Alice
Coolidage, AZ

Filling for Zucchini Bread

Tuna fish; 2 cans – sweet pickle juice – mayo – salt and pepper. Mix all together. Egg filling, 4 hard boiled eggs (mashed) mustard, vinegar, salt and pepper. Mix all together. Cut zucchini bread length wise. On bottom layer put the tuna then bread, then egg filling then bread, pour cheese whiz on the top and cut into finger sandwiches.
Shirley
Warren, OR

Frying Mixture for Fish & Meat

3 c wheat checks cereal – 3 c wheat rice cereal – ½ c bisquick – ½ c potato flakes – ¼ c powdered milk – paprika. Grind cereal and mix all together. Roll fish, chicken or pork chops in egg then in mixture. Put 4 tbl of oleo in a cookie sheet and put fish or other meat single layer and bake at 350*. Fish about 12 minutes one each side.
Bernice
Lake Preston, OR

Quick Salmon Casserole

1 can salmon – 1 can cream of celery or mushroom soup – 6 hard boiled eggs –
¼ c finely minced onions – ½ c mayo – ½ tsp salt – ¼ tsp pepper – 1 c crushed
potato chips. Combine all ingredients, except eggs and chips. Chop egg and fold
into mixture. Pile lightly into greased casserole. Top with chips. Sprinkle with
paprika. Bake at 400* for 25 minutes.
Thresa
Roy, OR

Salmon Patties

2 c cracker crumbs – 3 eggs slightly beaten – ½ tsp salt – 1 tsp butter – 1 can
salmon – ¾ c milk – ¼ tsp pepper. Combine like meatloaf patties and brown in
a fry pan for a short time on each side till brown.
Gail
Hetland, SD

Salmon Steaks

6 (1 inch) salmon steaks – 1/3 c butter – ½ tsp salt – grated onion – ¼ tsp paprika
– 1 tsp Worcestershire – place salmon on shallow greased pan. Melt oleo in pan
and mix with salt, paprika and Worcestershire. Pour over salmon and sprinkle
with onion. Bake at 350* for 25 to 30 minutes.
Dottie
Beaverton, OR

Scalloped Salmon

1 lb Can salmon – 1 ¼ c milk – 2 tbl flour – 2 tbl butter – ¼ tsp salt – ½ c
buttered bread crumbs. Prepare a sauce with milk, flour and butter. Place a layer
of salmon in bottom of buttered baking dish. Add a layer of crumbs. Pour some
of the sauce over them. Add another layer in the same manner top with crumbs.
Bake at 350* until sauce bubbles and crumbs are brown.
Gertie
Beach, ND

Tuna Bake

1 can green peas or beans – 4 tbl butter – 1 ½ c diced potatoes – 1 c diced carrots – ½ c chopped onions – 4 tbl flour – milk – 1 tsp salt – 1/8 tsp pepper – 2 can tuna. Drain peas, reserve liquid. Cook potatoes, carrots and onion in this liquid 8 to 10 minutes. Drain and save liquid. Melt butter in pan stir in flour to make a smooth paste. Add milk to veg liquid to make 2 c. Add to butter mixture. Cook over low heat. Stir till mixture thickens. Add seasonings. Combine veg and tuna in buttered 2 qt casserole. Pour sauce over all. Bake at 325* for 1 hour covered.
Gladys
Northfield, MN

Tuna Casserole

1 can mushroom soup – 1 c water – put in butter casserole and stir together. 1 can tuna water packed – 1 c coarsely cut celery – 1 c coarsely cut onion – 1 sm can Chinese noodles – reserve enough noodles for the top – 1/3 c cashew nuts. Mix all together in the casserole and top with Chinese noodles. Bake 350* for 45 minutes.
Mabel
Scappoose, OR

Tuna Casserole

1 c macaroni – 1 c tuna – 1 c string beans – 1 c cream of mushroom soup – mix all together. Top with cheese slices. Bake at 350* for ½ hour.
Vickie
Del Rio, TX

Tuna Rice Casserole

1 ½ c uncooked rice – 2 cans tuna undrained – 1 can cream mushroom soup – ½ c milk – ¼ c grated cheese – 1 tsp Worcestershire sauce. Cook rice, mix soup, milk and Worcestershire sauce. Add rice and tuna. Sprinkle with cheese and bake at 350* for 30 minutes covered.
Dottie
Beaverton, OR

Tuna Loaf

preheat oven to 370* - 1 slice bread or 4 soda crackers – 1 egg slightly beaten – 6 ½ oz can tuna – ½ c milk – 1 tsp onion flakes – ½ tsp prepared mustard – 1 tsp chicken broth and seasoning mix – ½ tsp pepper. Mix well and pour into casserole and bake 45 minutes.
Virginia Quenzer
Emmett, ID

Tuna Noodle Casserole

3 c noodles – ½ c mayo – 1/3 c chopped onions – ½ c milk – 1 can cream of celery soup – ½ c slivered almonds – 1 can tuna drained – 1 c sliced celery – ½ tsp salt – ¼ chopped green pepper – 4 oz sharp shredded cheese. Cook noodles and drain. Combine with tuna, mayo, celery, onion, green pepper and salt. Blend soup with milk and heat thoroughly. Add cheese, heat and stir till cheese melts. Add to noodles. Turn into 2 qt casserole. Top with almonds. Bake uncovered at 425* for 20 minutes
Linda
Desmet, SD

Tuna Pie

4 c noodles cooked and drained – 1 (8 oz) cheese whiz spread – 1 (6 ½ oz) can tuna fish drained – 3 eggs slightly beaten – ½ c celery sliced – ¼ c chopped pimentos (opt) – ½ tsp onion salt. Combine ingredients, mix well. Spoon into greased 9 inch pie pan. Cover loosely. Bake 325* for 35 minutes uncovered let stand 5 minutes before serving.
Jan-nita
ST Helens, OR

Baked Tamale Pie

1 lb hamb – 1 c chopped onion – 2 tbl oil – 1 can (16 oz) tomatoes – 1 can corn – 1 pkg (6 oz) cornbread stuffing mix – ½ c water – ½ c green pepper chopped – 1 can (3 ½ oz) black pitted olives – 1 c shredded cheddar cheese. Brown meat in oil. Add onion and green pepper, cook till tender drain. Stir in tomatoes, corn, olives and chili powder to taste. Cover and simmer 10 min. Prepare dressing as directed on pkg. Using 1 ½ c water. Stir ½ of the cheese into meat mixture. Pour into 2 ½ qt casserole. Spoon stuffing around edge of dish and sprinkle remaining cheese on top. Bake uncovered at 400* for 30 minutes until hot and bubbly. Garnish with more olives.
Polly
Canby, OR

BBQ Pork

2 lbs pork butt – 1 clove garlic minced – about ¼ inch – slice of fresh ginger root mashed (can use ground ginger) – 2 tsp sugar - 1 tsp salt – 2 tsp sherry – 3 tbl soy sauce – 2 tbl honey – ½ tsp Chinese 5 spice – ¼ tsp red food coloring (I use 1 tsp ginger when i make this) Cut meat into ½ or ¾ inch strips. Combine the garlic, ginger, sugar, salt, soy sauce, honey, 5 spice and food coloring, pour over the meat and marinate & roast in oven 325* for 1 ½ hours. Basting frequently.
Cho
San Franisco,CA

BBQ Pork (Chinese Style)

1 tbl sugar – salt to taste – ¼ tsp Chinese 5 spices – 3 tbl white syrup – 2 tbl soy sauce – 1/3 c cooking wine – red food coloring. Marinate meat for 30 minutes to 1 hour. Cut pork roast in strips. Oven 350*. Put frying pan or cake pan with water under meat. Hang meat on a cloths hanger on rack in oven for 35 to 45 minutes. Check every 15 minutes and brush marinate mixture over top of pork.
Sherry
Portland, OR

Beef Enchiladas

2 lbs beef chuck steak or top sirloin (cut in chucks) - 1 can enchilada sauce (milk) – 1 can green chilies – 1 pkg brown gravy mix – chopped green onions, olives, tomatoes, grated cheese (cheddar). Cook meat until tender. Add sauce, green chilies and gravy mix. Simmer about 15 to 20 minutes. Put meat mixture down the middle of flour taco shell. Roll around the meat and lay seam side down in casserole dish. Pour remaining meat sauce over tortilla shells, topping with grated cheese. Bake 350* for 30 to 45 minutes. Top with chopped onions, olives and tomatoes.
Wilma Coates
Emmett, ID

Beef Pea Pod Chow Yak

½ lb beef flank steak thinly sliced – 1 tsp finely chopped or minced ginger – ½ tsp sugar – 1 tsp soy sauce – ½ tsp cornstarch -6 tbl oil divided – 1 c chopped onions – 1 c sliced celery – 1 can bamboo shoots – 1 can water chestnuts sliced – ½ c chicken broth or water – ½ tsp salt – ½ tsp sugar – ½ tsp cornstarch dissolved in 2 tsp water. Marinate beef in ginger, soy sauce and cornstarch for 20 minutes. Heat wok until smoke rises. Add 3 tbl oil and swirl it around. sauté beef till half cooked. Remove meat from wok. Heat remaining oil and stir fry onions, celery, chestnuts, shoots and pea pods for 1 minute. Add bok-choy and stir, add mushrooms and stir in. Return meat to pan and thicken with the cornstarch mixed with water. Serve over rice or serve alone.
Jimmy
Hillsboro, OR

Chicken Enchiladas

Serves 4 prep time 50 min

4 chicken breast – 4 green onions sliced – 2 tbsp fresh cilantro chopped – 1 jalapeno seeded & minced – 3 cans green enchilada sauce – 8 corn tortillas – 1 c reduced fat cheddar cheese shredded – 2 c lettuce shredded – ½ c light sour cream – 1 tomato diced – 1 can olives sliced – cook chicken – shred - add 1 can of enchilada sauce . Cook stirring occasionally until heated. Add 2 remaining can enchilada sauces in bowl micro 2 min. dip each tortilla then fill with chicken mixture. Roll up & place in dish pour remaining sauce over enchiladas. Sprinkle with cheese. Bake until cheese is melted (15 min) top with lettuce, tomato, olives, sour cream. 9x13 dish lightly coat spray.
Stephanie Crays
Emmett, ID

Chicken Fricassee with Parsley Dumplings

3 lbs chicken (cut up) – 1 can cream of chicken soup – salt, pepper and paprika to taste – 1 c milk – arrange chicken skin side up in a baking dish. Sprinkle with salt, pepper and paprika. Cover with wax paper and microwave on high 10 min. Mix soup and milk. Spoon over chicken pieces cover with wax paper and microwave on high until done. 8 to 12 minutes longer. Drop dumplings by spoonful around edge of dish (I make a double batch and put dumplings all over) Microwave uncovered on high 7 minutes. Parsley Dumplings. 2 c buttermilk baking mix – 2 tsp parsley – 2/3 c milk – ¼ tsp poultry seasoning.
Pearl Cavender
Keizer, OR

Chinese Casserole

2 ½ c chow mein noodles – 1 can tomato soup – 1 can water – 1 can sliced water chestnuts – 1 c sliced mushrooms – ½ c cashews broken – 1 can Chinese veg – 1 can cream mushroom soup – 1 c diced onion – 2 tbl soy sauce – 1 c chopped celery – 2 lb lean hamb. Brown meat mixture with rest of ingredients and bake in well greased pan. 350* for 1 hour.
Helen
Pacifica, CA

Chinese Chicken Wings

Wings (cut tip off) – sprinkle with garlic salt – beat 2 eggs – 1 c flour (dip in egg mixture and roll in flour) brown in oil – then heat ¾ c sugar – ¼ c pineapple juice – ¾ c catsup – ½ c vinegar – ½ tsp salt – 1 tsp accent – 1 tsp soy sauce – pour over wings. Bake 350* ½ hour.
Pearl Cavender
Keizer, OR

Chinese Dish

1 lg onion – ½ green pepper – 3 stalks celery – 1 lb hamb – 1 small can bamboo shoots – 1 can water chestnuts – 1 can mushrooms or fresh ones – 1 can bean sprouts or fresh ones. Cut onions and celery in lg chunks, dice green pepper. Start all the above to cook till limp. Add meat cook till meat is done. Add 1 ½ c water with 2 bouillon beef cubes, pour over vegs and meat. Add mushrooms. cook 15 minutes on low. Add bamboo shoots, water chestnuts mix 3 tbl cornstarch with a little water. Add to mixture make just a little thick, add sprouts, heat. Serve over rice or chow mein noodles.
Mary
Portland, OR

Chinese Tuna Casserole

2 cans tuna – ½ c or more each of celery, onions chopped – 1 can cream mushroom soup – 1 lg can chow mein dried noodles – 1 can water chestnuts – chopped cashews. Mix all together, put in casserole and top with potato chips. Bake at 325* for about ½ hour or till golden brown.
Dorletta
Corvallis, OR

Chinese Meat Balls

1 lb hamb – 1 c small cubed bread – 1 egg slightly beaten – ½ tsp salt – ¼ c finely chopped onions – ¼ tsp allspice – ¼ tsp ginger – 1 can (12 oz) pineapple chunks unsweetened – 1 can (10 ½ oz) beef broth – 1/3 sliced water chestnuts – 2 tbl cornstarch – cooked rice – 1 sm green pepper cut into thin strips. Mix meat, bread, egg, onion, salt & 1/8 tsp allspice. Drain pineapple reserve juice. Shape meatballs around pineapple chunks. Brown meat balls, pour off fat. Add broth ½ c pineapple juice, water chestnuts, ginger and rest of the allspice and pineapple chunks. Cover over low heat 20 minutes. Combine rest of juice and cornstarch, slowly stir into sauce. Add green pepper, stir occasionally till sauce thickens and pepper is done. Serve with rice.
Jimmy
Hillsboro, OR

Crispy Wan Tans

1 pkg Wan tan wrappers – ¾ lb ground pork – ¼ c finely chopped green onions – 1 tbl soy sauce – 8 oz can water chestnuts finely chopped – 1 tsp salt – 1 tsp cornstarch – ¾ tsp ginger. Mix all together and put in wrappers and deep fry.
Jimmy
Hillsboro, OR

Egg Foo Young

1 c chopped onions – 1 c finely chopped celery – 3 tbl oil – 1 c (6 oz) crab meat – 8 eggs slightly beaten. Fry onions and celery in oil in skillet till tender and barely browned. Add crab stir and add eggs sprinkle with 1 tsp glutamate (opt) fry like one lg or several cakes on very low heat turning over when brown on one side. Serve with soy sauce. Make large or 8 small cakes.
Sherry
Portland, OR

Fajitas

½ c oil – 2 tbl red wine – ½ c lime juice – 1/3 c finely chopped onions – 1 tsp sugar – ½ tsp thyme – ½ tsp oregano – ½ tsp pepper -¼ tsp cumin – 3 garlic cloves minced – 2 lbs round steak – 10 flour tortillas. Combine first 10 ingredients and mix well, trim fat and remove bone. Pound to ¼ thicknesses. Add steak to marinate, turn to coat, cover and refrigerate 8 hours or overnight. Remove meat and drain. Grill steak over med coals 4 to 6 minutes on each side or to doneness you want. Slice meat diagonally into thin slices. Heat tortillas. Wrap around meat and choose of toppings. pincanti sauce, guacamole, chopped tomatoes, chopped onions or sour cream.
Jan-nita
ST Helens, OR

Mexican Hot Dish

1; 2 c pinto or kidney beans cooked – 2 table oil – ½ c chopped onion – 1 tsp salt – ¼ tsp garlic powder – 1 tsp chili powder – 3 tbl water – 2 tbl tomato paste – ¼ c sliced ripe olives – ½ c fresh corn – ½ chopped green pepper – ¼ c chopped parsley – ½ c chopped celery. # 2; 2 ½ c cold water – 1 ½ c cornmeal – 1 tsp salt – ½ tsp chili powder – ½ c or more grated cheddar cheese. Grind or mash beans mix tom paste in water. In skillet sauté onion in oil and combine all of # 1. Heat over med heat. If beans are all ready hot no more than 5 min. needed all seasonings to taste. Combine # 2 except cheese. Cook over med heat till corn meal thickens and comes to a boil. Grease 8x8 Pan and spread 2/3 of #p 2 cornmeal over bottom of pan. Than pour bean mixture over cornmeal and spread remaining cornmeal on top. Sprinkle with cheese. Bake at 350* for ½ hour. Boots
Warren, OR

Mexican Hot Dogs

Wieners – chili – flour tortilla – grated cheese, heat meat and chili before assembling. Put a hot dog and a large spoonful of chili and some grated cheese in the center of a tortilla. Fold as you would for a burrito. Place on a large cookie sheet and heat in the oven at 350* for a few minutes.
Shirley
Glova, ND

Sweet and Sour Pork

1 lb pork chops – 1 tsp sherry – ¼ tsp salt – cornstarch – 2 med carrots cut small – 1 egg a 3 c onions cut small – ¼ c ketch up -¼ tsp pepper – 1 tbl flour – oil – 1 sm can mushrooms – 1 clove garlic sliced – 1 tsp soy sauce – ¼ c each vinegar, and sugar. Cut meat in bite size pieces, sprinkle with sherry, salt and pepper. Beat egg slightly and mix with flour & cornstarch (1 tbl) coat meat with the batter. Remove pieces one at a time and drop into 5 c of oil heated to 375* on frying thermentor. fry about 1/3 at a time till lightly browned and cooked through. Remove and drain. Mix 1 ½ tbl cornstarchs - ¾ c water and remaining ingredients, ketch up, soy sauce and vinegar and sugar. Heat 5 tbl oil in skillet and add this mixture and cook stirring till thick. Add pork and veg. Mix & heat gently.
Jimmy
Hillsboro, OR

Sweet and Sour Pork

1 lb lean pork shoulder or fat – salt – pepper – 2 green peppers -3 tbl chopped onions – 4 slices pineapple reserve juice – 3 tbl cornstarch – ½ c pineapple syrup – 1 c bouillon broth – ¼ c vinegar – ¼ c sugar – 4 c boiled rice – 2 tsp soy sauce; heat a little fat and brown the pork thoroughly, which has been cut into 1 inch cubes, sprinkle well with salt and pepper. Add bouillon and cook covered over low heat for 20 minutes. Cut green pepper into 1 inch strips and add. Also add onions and pineapple sliced cut into 8 pieces. Cook another 10 minutes. Blend cornstarch with sugar, vinegar, soy sauce and pineapple juice add to mixture. Stir constantly till thickened. Cook 5 minutes longer and add extra salt and pepper if necessary. Serve over rice.
Jan-nita
ST Helens, OR

Sweet and Sour Ribs

2 lb spare or country ribs browned – 1 green pepper chopped – 1 ¼ c brown sugar – 4 tbl flour – 1 lg onion chopped – ½ c vinegar – 4 tbl soy sauce – 4 tbl water. Spread meat in casserole – over top put chopped onions and green peppers. Mix rest of ingredients together and pour over top. Cover and bake 2 hours at 350*. Doris
Scappoose, OR

Taco Crepes

1 c flour -3 eggs – ½ c cornmeal – ¼ tsp salt – 1 ½ c milk. filling 1 ½ lb ground beef – 1 can cream style corn – 1 onion (chopped) – 2 8 oz) cans tomato sauce – finely chopped chili peppers to taste -1 pkg taco seasoning mix – 1 can refried beans – garnish; 4 oz shredded cheddar cheese – 1/3 c black olives. Use ¼ c crepe mixture and fry in sm amount of oil in small skillet. Tilt the skillet to make thin crepes. Fry only till very lightly browned. Turn. Simmer filling while making crepe. Roll up and place in 9x13 inch pan. Pour any remaining filling over top. Top with cheese and olives. Bake 375* 20 to 45 minutes.
Pearl Cavender
Keizer, OR

Taco Grande

1 pound ground turkey – 1 package (1 oz) taco seasoning mix – water – 1 jar (16 oz) salsa – 8 (6-7 inch) flour tortillas – 2 cups (8 oz) shredded co-jack cheese – 1 green onion – 4 cups shredded lettuce – ½ cup sour cream –preheat oven to 350* . Spray bottom and side of deep dish baker with vegetable oil. Place turkey in 10" frying pan. Cook and stir over medium heat 8-10 minutes or until turkey is no longer pink. Breaking turkey into small crumbles. Add taco mix and amount of water directed on package. Continue cooking according to package directions. Remove pan from heat. Stir in 1 cup of the salsa. Arrange 4 tortillas in bottom and up side of baker. (Tortillas will overlap on bottom of baker but not all of the area on the side of the baker will be covered) Spoon turkey mixture evenly over tortillas. Sprinkle with 1 cup of the cheese. Slice green onion. Sprinkle half of the onion over cheese. Top with remaining 4 tortillas, overlapping tortillas slightly to create a scalloped edge effect. Press tortillas down over filling. Spread remaining salsa over tortillas. Sprinkle with remaining cheese and onion. Bake 30 minutes. Let stand 5 minutes. Cut into wedges over lettuce and top with sour cream.
Ryan
Emmett, ID

Taco Rolls

Make your own bread or use frozen bread. Roll out and put following mixture on each triangle. Meat mixture; hamb, onions, browned lightly (not done) drain. Add taco seasoning, cheddar cheese and mozzarella cheese grated. Bake at 350* for 20 minutes.
Polly
Canby, OR

Tamale Bake

9x13 pan – 1 ½ lbs hamb – ½ c chopped onions – 1 can tomatoes – can corn – 1 tbl salt – 1 tbl chili powder – ¼ tsp pepper – ¼ c cornmeal. Brown onions, and hamb till brown. Stir in tomatoes, corn, salt, chili powder and pepper. Stir ½ c cornmeal mixed with 1 c water. Cover and simmer 10 minutes. Add olives chopped put in pan mix to the meat and veg meanwhile heat 1 ½ c milk – 1 tsp salt – 2 tbl butter. Slowly stir in cornmeal, cook till thickened, remove from heat add eggs and pour over the above mixture. Bake at 375* for 30 to 40 minutes.
Viola Coates
Emmett, ID

Tamale Pie

1 can (15 oz) creamed corn – 1 can (15 oz) whole corn – 2 sm can (8 oz) tomato sauce – 1 can chopped (4 ½ oz) olives or pitted or halves olives – 3 tbs oil – 1 lb chicken, or ground beef or left over meat – 6 tbs chili powder – 1 tsp salt – 3 lg dry onions – 2 cups polenta – 2 cups milk – 4 eggs soak 2 cups polenta and 2 cups milk overnight. In large pan put oil, add chopped onions, sauté until onions are clear, add ground beef, and cook until done. Add corn, tomato sauce, olives, mix well. Dilute chili powder with water to make soft paste. Add into the pan. Add polenta and mix thoroughly. Lastly add eggs, one at a time. Mix than pour into ungreased 2 large casseroles. Bake 50 to 60 minutes at 350* oven. Penny Campbell
Emmett, ID

Turkie Sukiyake

3 tbl oil – ¼ c soy sauce – 1 c diced green peppers – 1 c sliced celery – 1 c diced green onions – 2 c cooked diced turkie. Heat oil, add vegs. Cook stirring over med heat 5 minutes or till vegs are tender but not mushy. Add turkey and soy sauce stir till mixed and heated thru. Serve over rice.
Polly
Canby, OR

Walking Tacos

1 lb hamb browned – ½ bottle taco sauce – 8 oz sour cream – 1 can refried beans – 1 pkg taco seasoning. Mix well put on plate cover with the topping of your choice like onion, tomatoes, cheese, lettuce, taco chips or shell.
Ella
Dickinson, ND

Wan Tans

Grind 1 head Chinese cabbage – 1 bunch green onions – pork roast (no fat). Add 5 Chinese spice or accent spice – 1 egg and cornstarch to hold together, mix all. Put a tbl of mixture on egg roll or wan tan skins and roll up and deep fry. Sauce dip – 1 can (5 ¼ oz) tomato juice – ½ c sugar – vinegar – boil. Thicken with cornstarch and a dash of lemon juice. Can put in green peppers – diced celery and pineapple in dip to.
Sherry
Portland, OR

BBQ Sauce

5 tbl butter – 12 oz bottle chili sauce – 1 c packed brown sugar -1 ¼ tsp salt – 5 tbl Worcestershire sauce – 2 ½ c ketchup – 1 c diced onion – 1 tbl mustard – dash garlic salt – dash charcoal broiling flavoring. Use cooked roast so its tender and pulls apart. Pour the sauce over beef and serve on hamb buns.
Marie
Beach, ND

BBQ Sauce

½ c chopped onions – ½ clove – minced garlic – ½ tsp chili powder -1 tbl Worcestershire sauce – ½ tsp salt – 2 tbl oil – 2 tbl vinegar -¾ c water – ¾ c ketch up – ¼ tsp pepper. Brown onions in oil till lightly browned. Add remaining ingredients, cover and simmer about 20 minutes. If to thick add a small amount of water. Use immediately or keep in a covered container in refrig till needed. Serve hot.
Mabel
Scappoose, OR

BBQ Sauce

½ c brown sugar – 2 c ketch up – 1 c sugar – ¼ c Worcestershire sauce – chili powder – 1 med onion chopped – 1 lemon. Bring to boil lemon and onion and a ½ c water. Strain and mix rest of ingredients.
Millie
Mott, ND

Broccoli Cheese Dip

½ c butter or oleo – ¼ c chopped onion – 1 3 c chopped celery – 1 pkg frozen chopped broccoli, partially thawed – 1 can (10 oz) mushroom soup – 1 (6 oz) garlic cheese roll (can use American processed cheese) 1 can (4 oz) chopped mushrooms drained. Melt butter in skillet. Sauté onion, celery and broccoli until tender crisp. Combine the remaining ingredients in crock pot. Stir. Cover & simmer on low 1 ½ to 2 hours.
Loretta
Dickinson, ND

Carmel for Rolls

for 24 rolls; never gets hard – 1 ½ c brown sugar - 4 tbl milk – 4 tbl white syrup – 4 tbl oleo – 1 tsp vinegar. Boil 2 minutes and put in bottom of pan. I use 2 9x13 pans.
Lola
Lake Preston, SD

Cheese Ball

2 pkg (8 oz) cream cheese – 2 tbl chopped green onion – ¼ c chopped green peppers – 1 can (8 oz) crushed pin drained. Mix all ingredients together. Divide in half. Roll in 1 ½ c chopped nuts. Makes 2 cheese balls.
Sharon
Cornelius, OR

Clam Dip

8 oz cream cheese – 1 tbl mayo – 1 onion chopped fine – 3 little pods of garlic chopped fine – 1 or 2 cans minced clams – salt and pepper to taste – 3 to 4 stalks celery chopped real fine. Mash cheese with spoon or with beater until creamy for about 5 minutes. Add mayo and whip. Than add rest of ingredients.
Barbara
Cornelius, OR

Cottage Cheese Dip

2 c cottage cheese – 1 tsp seasoned salt – 1 tsp pepper – 1 tsp garlic powder – 1 tbl onion flakes – 1 tsp paprika – 1 tbl chopped chives – 1 tsp Worcestershire sauce – 1 sm can clams with liquid. Mix together and chill.
Opal
Tillamook, OR

Creamy Dip for Vegs

1 c plain low fat yogurt – 2 ½ c mayo – ½ c milk – 1 2 tbl parsley flakes – ¾ tsp garlic powder – ¾ tsp onion powder – 1 ½ tsp salt- 1 tsp pepper. Combine and blend well.
Loretta
Dickinson, ND

Creamy Salsa Dip

1 c Sour cream – 1 c chunky salsa – 1 envelope ranch dressing mix. Combine sour cream, salsa and ranch mix. Mix well, cover and chill at least 1 hour.
Carolyn
ST Helens, OR

Dip for Bread Sticks

8 oz cream cheese softened – 8 oz sour cream – 1 sm jar dried beef chopped – 1 tbl minced dried onion – 1 tbl Worcestershire sauce. Mix well and microwave until bubbly around edge. Chill.
Lori
Golva, ND

French Onion Dip

2 c sour cream – ½ c mayo – 1 pkg onion soup mix – stir 1st two ingredients until smooth. Stir in soup mix. Cover chill, stir before serving.
Joan
New Tazewill, TN

Ham & Cheese Ball

2 cans (6 ½ oz) chopped ham or 2 c ground hamb – 1 pkg (8 oz) cream cheese softened - ½ c real mayo (not salad dressing) – 2 tbl chopped onion (dry is better) – 1 tbl chopped parsley – 1 tsp Tabasco sauce – 1 c chopped walnuts. Mix ham, cheese, mayo, onion, parsley, tabasco sauce together. Chill for 1 hour. Form ball. Roll in nuts. Chill and serve with crackers.
Loretta
Dickinson, ND

Hot Cheese Dip

1 lb sharp Cheddar cheese melt chunks – add 1 can diced green chilies – ½ jar salsa. Keep hot in a fondue pot. Dip is good with corn chips.
Sandy
Puyallup, WA

Pineapple Glaze

1 can (8 oz) crushed pineapple – 1 c packed brown sugar – 1 tbl prepared mustard – 1 tsp dry mustard – juice of one lemon -dash of salt. Drain pineapple and reserve juice. Combine pineapple and rest of ingredients and stir to mix well. Add as much juice as necessary to have mixture of consistency. Brush over meat during last few minutes of BBQ-ing.
Barbara
Cornelius, OR

Taco Cheese Dip

1 lb hamb browned add - ½ bottle taco sauce – 1 pkg taco seasoning – 1 can fried beans. Heat all this. Frito chips. Line plate with chips than meat, sour cream. Top with cheese, onion, lettuce and tomatoes.
Jan-nita
ST Helens, OR

Taco Dip

Heat a can of refried beans, spread on a plate, spread next sour cream. Cut up green onions meat. Shredded lettuce (opt) diced tomato, olives, avocados diced, put grated cheese on top. Use tortilla chips.
Michelle
Deer Island, OR

Tarter Sauce

1 c chopped sweet pickles or relish – 1 sm onion chopped – ¼ tsp lemon juice – 1 dash Tabasco sauce – 1 qt mayo – 1 oz parsley flakes. Mix together.
Elsie
Wilaux, MT

Texas Taco Dip

2 cans beans and jalapeño dip – 3 avocados – 1 can olives chopped cheese grated – 3 tomatoes – 8 oz sour cream – 2 bunches green onions – 1 pkg taco seasoning. Put dip on lg plate, mix sour cream, ½ c mayo and taco seasoning. Pour over dip. Layer avocados soaked in lemon juice, tomatoes, onions, olives, and cover with grated cheese. Can add hamb and green chilies.
Paula Starcher
Emmett, ID

Veg Curry Dip

¾ c mayo – 1 ½ tbl grated onion – 4 ½ tbl ketch up – 1 ½ tbl honey -1 ½ tbl lemon juice – 1 ½ tbl curry. Mix all together and chill
Eunice
Lake Preston, SD

Veg Dip

2/3 c mayo – 2/3 c sour cream – 1 tbl parsley flakes – 1 tbl dry mustard – 1 tbl onion minced – 1 tbl dill weed – 1 tsp seasoned salt.
Martha
Warren, OR

Caribbean Punch

2 cans (46 oz) pineapple juice – 2 qts frozen lemonade – 1 ½ qts orange juice – 1 qt cranberry juice cocktail style – 2 c apple juice – ice cubes and 1 lemon thinly sliced. Mix together. Makes 2 gal.
Loretta
Dickinson, ND

Cocoa Mix

1 pkg powdered milk (8 qt size) – 6 oz jar coffee mate – ½ c powdered sugar – 1 lb box nestles or Hershey quick – mix together above ingredients and its really good. Use hot water to dissolve.
Pearl Cavender
Keizer, OR

Hot Chocolate Mix

1 ½ cups cocoa – 2 cups white sugar – 1 cup powdered sugar – 1 container coffee creamer – 1 4lb can powdered milk. Mix together and put in container.
Randy Wilson
Emmett, ID

Frozen Banana Punch

1 lg frozen orange juice – 1 lg pineapple and grapefruit juice – 2 c sugar – 4 ripe bananas mashed – 6 c water; freeze in ½ gallon milk cartons. Let stand 2 hours before serving. Add 1 bottle of ginger ale. Makes 1 gallon.
Pearl Cavender
Keizer, OR

Punch

6 oz can squire – 12 oz can frozen lemonade – 46 oz can pineapple juice – 3 qt 7 up. Mix all together.
Wainita
Seattle, WA

Punch

2 pkg cherry kool aide – 2 c sugar – 2 qt water – 1 qt 7 up – 1 qt unsweetened pineapple juice – mix everything except 7 up. Chill. Add 7 up before serving.
Wilma Coates
Emmett, ID

Punch

1 pkg cherry kool aide – 1 pkg raspberry kool aide – 2 c sugar – 2 qts water – 1 can (46 0z) pineapple juice – 1 qt ginger ale. Chill. Serve on ice. For green punch use lemon and lime kool aide.
Jan-nita
ST Helens, OR

Wedding Punch

10 mashed ripe bananas – 46 0z pineapple juice – 12 oz undiluted frozen orange juice – 12 oz undiluted frozen lemonade – 8 c water – mix together and freeze in quart containers. When ready to use, add 1 liter 7 up to each quart of semi thawed punch mix.
Beverly Crandall
Keizer, OR

Bath Salts

3 cups Epson salt – 2 cups sea salt – 3 drops fragrance oil (any flavor) – 2-3 drops food coloring. Mix together then put in glass containers. Garnish with raffa, bows and give as gifts.
Randy Wilson
Emmett, ID

Candy Clay

Mix the first four ingredients. Then add sugar and knead. -1/3 c margarine – 1/3 c light corn syrup – ¼ tsp salt – 1 tsp vanilla or peppermint extract – 1 pound confectioners sugar.
Julie Hahn
Salem, OR

Chocolate Play Clay

1 (16 oz) container ready to spread chocolate frosting – 1 c creamy peanut butter – 1 ½ cups Confectioners sugar ---- in a large bowl, combine all the ingredients and mix well. Immediately ready for play! Store in an airtight container in the refrigerator. It should keep for a couple weeks refrigerated. As with all edible clays, if the children are going to taste this clay, they should wash there hands before making it and taste it before they begin playing with it.
Julie Hahn
Salem, OR

Edible Play Dough

1/3 c margarine – 1/3 c light corn syrup – ½ tsp salt – 1 tbsp vanilla extract – 2 pounds confectioners' sugar – food coloring ---- mix all ingredients together. Make shapes, and then eat. This dough can be refirg in a plastic bag or bowl.
Julie Hahn
Salem, OR

Gingerbread Play Dough

1 c flour – ½ c salt – 2 tsp cream of tartar – 1 c water – 1 tsp veg oil – ground cinn & ground ginger ---- mix all and cook in a heavy saucepan over med heat while stirring frequently. When it begins to pull away from the sides of the pan, remove from the heat and knead until smooth. Store in an air tight container.
Julie Hahn
Salem, OR

Glitter Play Dough

1 c flour – 1 tbsp veg oil – 1 c water – ½ c salt – 2 tsp cream of tartar – food coloring – glitter --- mix all ingredients except glitter. Place in a saucepan and heat, stirring constantly, until it forms a ball. Remove from pot, add glitter and need until smooth. Glitter play dough will be good for several weeks stored in a tightly sealed container at room temp. Do not refrigerate.
Julie Hahn
Salem, OR

Group Play dough

9 c flour – 1 c salt – 3 tbl alum – 4 c hot water – ½ c oil – coloring (food coloring or liquid tempura added to water) --- mix dry ingredients together. Add wet ingredients and mix. Then knead. Store in Tupperware container or zip lock bag. Good for several weeks.
Julie Hahn
Salem, OR

Finger Paint

½ c glossy laundry starch – ½ c soap flakes – 1 ½ c boiling water – 1 tbl glycerin – dissolve starch in small amount of cold water to make paste. Add boiling water. Cook mixture until it becomes clear, stirring constantly, about 5 minutes. Remove from heat and add soap flakes. Stir until dissolved. Add glycerin and pour into as many jars as you want colors. Add vegetable colors or calcimine coloring to the mixture in each jar. Does not stain cloths. Washes out.
Pearl Cavender
Keizer, OR

Flavored Play Dough

1 c sifted flour – ½ c salt – 3 tbsl veg oil – 1 small package unsweetened powdered drink mix or kool-aid – 1 c boiling water ---mix flour, salt, oil and drink mix or kool-aid. Add boiling water. Stir together; knead mixture until it forms soft dough. Keep it in a plastic container with a lid between uses, and it lasts forever.
Julie Hahn
Salem, OR

Helpful Hints

To remove grease and grime from the glass of oven doors, place a little baking soda on a damp cloth. Simply wipe grime away.

1 tbl mayo mixed with 1 tbl olive oil, works great for shining leaves of your plants.

Candles kept in the freezer are easier to find in an emergency. They also burn longer and do not drip.

House or window wash – ½ c ammonia – 2 tbl corn starch – 1 c vinegar – up to 1 gal of water.
Olga Peters
Salem, OR

Kool-aid Playdough

2 – 3 sm packages kool-aid – 2 ½ c flour – ½ c salt – 1 tsp alum – 2 c boiling water – 3 tbl oil ---- mix dry ingredients together. Add wet ingredients and mix. Then knead. Store as playdough in zip lock bag. Good for several weeks. Double for classroom.
Julie Hahn
Salem, OR

Lavender Flower Play Dough

3 c flour – 2 c water – ¾ c salt – 3 tbsp oil – 3 tbls cream of tartar – 1/8 c violet powdered tempera paint – 10 – 20 drops lavender flower essential oil - -purple glitter ----- in a large pot, mix together the first five ingredients until smooth. Place the pot over medium heat, stirring constantly until the mixture forms a large ball. While the mixture is still warm, place it on a floured cutting board and knead in additional flour until the dough has a silky texture. Add powdered paint and lavender essential oil and knead thoroughly. Sprinkle with purple glitter and knead again. Store in an airtight container.
Julie Hahn
Salem, OR

Lemon Play Dough

1 ½ c water – 2 tsp liquid food coloring – 2 tbsp cooling oil – 2 c flour – 4 tbsp cream of tartar – 1 or 2 drops lemon oil --- in a large pot, combine water, food coloring and oil. Add flour, salt and cream of tartar. Over medium heat, cook and stir for about five minutes, until a ball of dough forms. Cool the dough for five minutes and then knead it with your hands until smooth. Store in a zip-type bag or an airtight container in the refrigerator when not in use.
Julie Hahn
Salem, OR

Modeling Clay

1 c flour – about ½ c water – 1 c salt - food coloring – 1 tbl alum; add water gradually to just the right consistency tint desired color. No cooking required.
Pearl Cavender
Keizer, OR

Peanut Butter Play Dough

1 c peanut butter – 1 c corn syrup – 1 ¼ c confectioners' sugar---mix all. Model with clean hands on a clean surface. Eat your artwork when finished.
Julie Hahn
Salem, OR

Peppermint Play Dough

2 c flour – 1 c salt – ½ c water – 1 tsp vinegar – food coloring or wonder colors – ¼ tsp peppermint extract --- mix the flour and salt in a large bowl. Slowly add water and vinegar, and stir with a wooden spoon until the mixture is stiff. Knead until pliable. Divide the dough into separate pieces for each color desired. Poke your finger into the center of each section of dough, drop in the food color and peppermint extract, and knead until the color is uniform and the dough is smooth. Store, tightly covered and labeled, in a plastic bag or container in the refrigerator. Play dough will keep for months if you refrigerate it after each use. to use – take out of the refrigerator about 5 minutes before you're ready to play so that the dough will be soft. if you like something you have created, you can leave it to air dry for 24 hours or help it along by placing in a warm oven at 200* for several hours. It should harden enough to paint, shellac, or spray with art fixative.
Julie Hahn
Salem, OR

Play Dough

Mix; 1 ½ c flour – stir in 1 ½ water – ¾ c salts – food coloring – 1 tbl cream of tarter; microwave 5 minutes. Stirring 3 times during the cook time. It is done when it loses its sticky wet look and forms into a ball. Knead and let cool. Store in a closed container. This makes a nice gift.
Pearl Cavender
Keizer, OR

Silly Putty

2 c warm water – 2 c glue (Elmer's) – 3 tsp twenty mule and team borax --- mix 1 c water with glue in container. Stir mix 1 c water with borax in second container. Add food coloring. Stir. Stir glue mixture while adding borax mixture. Stir quickly, and then mix with hands. Mixture may be slimy or sticky at first. This mixture sets up rapidly. Store in a Tupperware container.
Julie Hahn
Salem, OR

Vanilla Play Dough

2 c flour – 1 c salt – 2 tsp cream of tartar – 2 tbl oil – 2 c water – food coloring – vanilla extract ---- measure out the dry ingredients into a large mixing bowl and then stir them together thoroughly. Put the dry ingredients into a saucepan with the oil, water, food coloring and vanilla extract. Stir continuously over low heat until a dough forms. Turn the dough out onto a lightly floured pastry board and knead while the mixture cools. Continue to knead for 5 to 10 min. If the mixture is too dry, occasionally dampen your hands while kneading. If it is too sticky, dust the mixture with a little extra flour. Store play dough in a plastic container with an airtight lid.

Julie Hahn
Salem, OR

Any Fruit Pudding

Melt 1 cube oleo in deep baking dish. In other dish mix. 1 c sugar -1 c sugar – 1 c flour – 2 tsp baking powder – ¾ c milk; pour mixture over milted oleo (do not stir) pour then any fruit as long as it isn't pie filling. Put ¾ c sugar over the fruit. (Do not stir) bake at 350* for about an hour or until done.
Melba
ST Helens, OR

Apple Crisp

6 apples – 2/3 c flour – 1/3 c butter – 1 c brown sugar. Slice apples in bottom of oiled baking dish. Mix flour, sugar and butter real good. Spread over apples. Bake at 375* for 35 minutes.
Jan-nita
ST Helens, OR

Apple Dabble

¼ c oleo – 1 egg – 1 tsp soda – 1 tsp cinnamon – 1 tsp vanilla – 2 c grated tart apples – 1 c sugar – 1 c flour – ¼ tsp salt – ¼ tsp nutmeg – ¼ c chopped nuts. Mix all ingredients. Pour into a greased 9x13 pan. Bake at 350* for 45 minutes. Serve warm with ice cream or whipped cream.
Glenda
ST Helens, OR

Apple Turnovers

Apple mixture; cook 8 apples – 1 c sugar – 1 tsp cinnamon. Mash and spread over dough recipe below. Dough; 2 ½ c flour – 8 tbl lard, salt and enough water to make a med dough. You can use frozen dough round out dough, spread 6 tbl of lard on dough makes layers leave overnight. Add mixture apples. Bake at 350* for about 10 to 15 minutes or till browned.
Hilda
Hebron, ND

Banana Cream Pudding

2/3 c sugar – 2 tbl cornstarch – 1/8 tsp salt – 1 can of milk – 2 tsp vanilla – bananas. Combine sugar, cornstarch and salt. Stir in milk. Cook over low heat till slightly thickened. Remove from heat and add vanilla. Cool. Slice bananas and add to pudding. Or can layer a pan with vanilla cookies and put layer of bananas and than pudding.
Lola
Lake Preston, SD

Berry Cobbler

3 c berries – 2/3 c to 1 c sugar – 2 tbl cold water – ¼ c plus 2 tbl cream or ¼ c milk plus 2 tbl melted butter – ¾ c water – 1 tbl cornstarch – 1 c bisquick. Heat fruit and water. Stir in sugar. Dissolve cornstarch in 2 tbl cold water and blend into fruit. Boil 1 minute. pour into 2 qt dish. Pat with butter, sprinkle with cinnamon. Mix cream and bisquick thoroughly with fork. Drop dough by spoonfuls onto hot fruit. Bake 20 minutes at 350*
Jan-nita
ST Helens, OR

Blueberry Cobbler

Top crust -- 2/3 c sugar – ¼ c flour (I used cake & pastry flour) – ½ tsp ground cinnamon – ¼ tsp ground nutmeg – ½ tsp grated lemon peel – 2 tsp lemon juice – 1/8 tsp salt – 6 cups blueberries – 1 tbsp butter or margarine prepare cobbler or top crust as directed preheat oven to 425* for filling, toss together sugar, flour, cinnamon, nutmeg, lemon peel, lemon juice, salt and blue berries. Place filling in 9 ½ x 1 ½ "deep pie plate. Dot with margarine or butter. Top with crust. Bake 50 min or until golden brown.
Penny Campbell
Emmett, ID

Blueberry Dessert

Make graham cracker or vanilla wafer crust; 20 to 22 crackers crushed about 1 ¼ c – 1 tbl sugar and ¾ stick melted oleo. Press crust into pan. Topping; 2 envelopes of dream whip topping – 1 can blueberries pie filling on crust and than dream whip. Chill overnight.
Gladys
Northfield, MN

Blueberry Dessert Pizza

1 pkg white or yellow cake mix – 1 ¼ c quick oatmeal – 1 egg – ½ c oleo softened – ½ c chopped nuts – ¼ c packed brown sugar – ½ tsp cin. – 21 oz can blueberry filling. Grease 12 inch pizza pan or 9x13 pan. In an lg bowl, combine cake mix. 1 c oats and 6 tbl oleo at low speed until crumble. Reserve 1 c crumbs for topping. To remaining crumbs blend in egg. Press into pan. Bake 12 minutes at 350*. Meanwhile to the 1 c of crumbs add remaining ¼ c oats, - 2 tbl oleo, brown sugar and cinn, beat until well mixed. Remove pan from oven and spread pie filling on it. Sprinkle with crumbs mixture. Return to oven and bake 15 to 20 minutes or until crumbs are like golden brown. Cool completely. Top with whip cream.
Beatrice
Richardton, ND

Bread Pudding

3 c soft bread crumbs or 4 c for a firmer pudding – ½ c sugar – 2 c scalded milk with ½ c butter – 2 eggs slightly beaten – ¼ tsp salt – 1 tsp nutmeg; mix together and put in 1 ½ to 2 qt casserole. Place dish in pan of hot water. Bake at 350* for 40 to 45 minutes. Done when knife inserted comes out clean.
Edith
Lake Preston, SD

Brownies

½ c butter – 2 sq choc – 1 tsp vanilla – ½ c nuts – 1 c sugar – ½ c flour – ½ tsp baking powder. Mix like cookies. Put in a greased pan. Bake at 350* for about 10 to 15 minutes. Cut in sq.
Mary
Portland, OR

Brownies

1 c sugar – 1 stick oleo – 4 eggs – 1 lg can choc syrup – 1 c flour -1 c nuts. bake at 325* for 25 minutes. frosting; 1 ½ c sugar – 6tbl milk – 6 tbl oleo – boil for 3 ½ minutes take from stove add ½ c choc chips and 2 handfuls mini marshmallows.
Lola
Lake Preston, SD

Brownies Zucchini

2 c flour – 1 c sugar – 1 tsp salt – ½ c cocoa – 1 ½ tsp soda – 2 c zucchini - mix then add: ½ c oil – 2 tsp vanilla – ½ c nuts: grease pan and bake @ 350* for 25 min.
Viola Coates
Emmett, ID

Butterscotch Pudding

¾ c brown sugar packed – 3 tbl cornstarch – ½ tsp salt – ¾ c water – 1 ¼ c milk – ¼ c butter; cook until thick, than blend into hot mixture. 2 eggs and 1 tsp vanilla. Boil 1 minute more.
Lola
Lake Preston, SD

Carmel Pecan Squares

1 pkg butter pecan cake mix – ¼ c butter – 3 ½ c chopped pecans – 1 c packed brown sugar – ½ c sugar – 1 c butter – ½ c honey – ¼ c whipping cream. Heat oven to 350*. Place cake mix in lg bowl. Cut in ¼ c butter till mixture resembles coarse crumbs. Press in bottom of ungreased jelly roll pan. Top with pecans halves. In lg heavy pan, combine brown sugar, sugar, 1 c butter and honey. Bring to a full rolling boil over med heat, stirring constantly. Boil 3 min remove from heat. Stir in whip cream until well blended. Pour hot mixture evenly over pecans. I use chopped instead of halves. Bake 17 to 22 min. or until entire surface is bubbly. Cool completely cut into squares or bars.
Claudia
Emmett, ID

Cherry Dessert

6 oz cherry Jell-O – 2 c hot water dissolve. Chill but not set. Add 1 can cherry pie filling – 1 can crushed pineapple drained. Put in cake pan and let set. topping; 1 c sour cream – 8 oz pkg cream cheese – ¼ c sugar – 1 tsp vanilla. Mix and spread on set Jell-O and cherry mixture. Crushed walnuts maybe sprinkled top.
Loretta
Dickenson, ND

Cherry Tarts

¾ c sugar – 2 (8 oz) pkg cream cheese – 1 tsp vanilla – 2 eggs – 1 tsp lemon juice. Mix until smooth. In muffin tin use paper cupcakes cups. Put a vanilla wafer cookie on bottom than put 1 tbl cream cheese mixture on top of cookies. Bake at 350* for 15 minutes. Cool. Put 1 tbl of Cherrie pie filling.
Shelly
Scappoose, OR

Cherry Tarts

Boil 1 c sour cream and add 1 tsp baking soda – 3 tbl butter – 3 tbl sugar, cool. Add 1 egg – 3 c flour – 1 pkg yeast dissolved in ½ c water. Mix and let stand 15 minutes. Roll thin and cut in squares. Fill with cherries or other fruits. Let rise 1 hour. Bake at 350* about 10 minutes and frost.
Joanne
Richardton, ND

Cherry Torte

What you need: 1 c graham crackers crumbs – 1 c flour – ½ c chopped nuts – ½ c sugar – 1 c butter – 8 oz cream cheese softened – 1 c powered sugar - 8 oz container cool whip – 1 can cherry pie filling preheat oven 350*. Mix together first five ingredients. Bake for 10 min. Then press into a 9 by 13 pan leaving a small amount for topping. Mix together – cream cheese and powered sugar. Gently fold in cool whip. Spread mixture over crust after it is cooled. Next spoon the cherry pie filling over cream cheese mixture. Sprinkle remaining topping over top. Refrigerate.
Susan Standley
Emmett, ID

Choc Mint Squares

1 ½ c finely crushed choc wafers – 6 tbl oleo melted – 1 jar (7 oz) marshmallow cream – ½ tsp mint or spearmint extract – few drops green food coloring – ¾ c Hershey bars – 2 c whipping cream. Combine wafers crushed and oleo, press firmly into bottom of pans. Beat the marshmallow cream, extract and food coloring till smooth. Fold in ½ c of candy bars. Whip cream till peaks form and fold in marshmallow mixture. Spread over the wafers and sprinkle candy bars pieces over top. Cover and freeze for at least 6 hours. Take out 10 to 15 minutes before serving.
Shelly
Scappoose, OR

Cin Swirl Bread Pudding

2 c + 3 tbl half & half divided – 4 eggs – ½ c sugar – 1 tsp vanilla extract – ½ c sweetened dried cranberries – ½ c chopped pecans – 1 loaf (16 oz) cinnamon swirl bread – 2/3 c caramel topping from a jar, warmed – whipped cream (opt). Preheat oven to 325* coat 8 "square pan with cooking spray. Whisk 2 c half & half with eggs, sugar and vanilla. Combine cranberries and pecans. Diagonally cut bread slices in half to make triangles. Layer bread and cranberry nut mixture 2 times. Evenly pour egg mixture over bread. Cover with foil, pressing down to make bread even with pan rim. Let stand 10 min. Remove foil. Bake 55 minutes or until cooked and golden brown. Mix Carmel sauce with remaining half and half while warm and pour over top. Serve with whipped cream.
Pearl Cavender
Keizer, OR

Coconut Crumb Desert

2 c flour – 2 c coconut – 1 c butter – ½ c brown sugar. Put all together in a 9x12" pan. Mix and brown, in 350* oven. Stirring often till lightly browned. Cool. Set aside 1 c put rest in bottom of pan. Mix 1 lg vanilla instant pudding – 2 c coconut 1 lg cool whip. Sprinkle remaining 1 c crumbs on top.
Anggie
Richardton, ND

Cool Coconut Dessert

Crust; 1 c flour – 2 tbl sugar – 2/3 c butter – ½ c chopped nuts. Bake at 375* for 10 minutes. Toast 2/3 c coconut while baking crust stirring frequently in oven. Filling; 8 oz cream cheese – 1 c powdered sugar – 1 c cool whip. Beat 2 pkg instant coconut puddings with 3 c milk. Let set a few min and pour over cheese. Add rest of whipped topping and sprinkle with coconut.
Jackie
Sentinal butte, ND

Cream Rice Pudding

3 lg eggs – 1 ½ c sugar – 3 c milk – 2 c cooked rice – 2 tsp vanilla – 1 tsp nutmeg; lightly buttered 1 ½ qt glass baking dish. In lg bowl, lightly beat eggs with sugar. Stir in milk, rice, vanilla. Pour into dish. Place dish in 9" square metal pan. Bake 1 hour 10 minutes. Until knife inserted near center comes out clean. After cool stir and sprinkle with nutmeg.
Wilma Coates
Emmett, ID

Date or Raisin Mumbles

Crust; ¾ c butter melted – 1 c brown sugar – 1 ¾ c flour – ½ tsp salt – ½ tsp soda – 1½ oatmeal; mix butter and sugar, than add dry ingredients then oatmeal. Put 1/3 of the mixture in greased pan 9x13. Press down, than put filling and spread evenly. Filling; 2 ½ c raisins or dates chopped – ½ c sugar - 2 tsp cornstarch – ¾ c water – 3 tbl lemon juice. Cook over low heat until thick at least 5 minutes. Put rest of crumb mixture over dates or raisins evenly. Press down. Bake at 350* for 20 to 30 minutes.
Kay
Apache Junction, AZ

Death by Chocolate

1 box (19.8 oz) fudge brownie mix – 3 pkg (3.5 oz each) instant chocolate pudding – 8 chocolate covered toffee candy bars (1.4 oz heath bars) – 1 container (12 oz) frozen whipped topping thawed. Preheat oven according to brownie package directions. Bake brownies according to package directions; Let cool. Prepare chocolate pudding according to package directions. Break candy bars into small pieces in food processor or by gently tapping the wrapped bars with a hammer. Break up half the brownies into small pieces and place in the bottom of a large glass bowl or trifle dish. Cover with half the pudding, then half the candy, and then half the whipped topping. Repeat layers.
Amber
W. Salem, OR

Dodes Apple Crisp

Combine; 1 c flour – ½ tsp salt – ½ tsp soda – ½ c brown sugar – 1 c oatmeal – ½ c melted oleo. Put ½ of this in greased bottom of pan. Dice 3 ½ c apples put on top of crumbs, dot with butter and 2/3 c sugar and cinnamon. Cover with remaining crumbs. Bake at 350* for 45 minutes or until apples are done.
Eva
Cagarey, Alberta Canada

Double Fudge Brownie Torte

1 pkg brownie mix – ½ c chopped pecans – 1 qt fudge ice cream softened – fudge ice cream topping; prepare brownies mix with the pecans as on pkg. Put in 3 greased and floured 9" cake pans. Bake 10 to 15 minutes. Do not overcook. Cool layers in pan 10 minutes. Remove and cool completely on rack. Place one layer on cake plate. Cover with ½ of the ice cream. Top with 2 nd cake, put rest of ice cream. Work fast. top with 3 rd cake. Cover with foil or plastic wrap. Freeze and store in freezer, until serving time. Remove from freezer 10 to 15 minutes before. Spread a thin amount of fudge topping over the top of cake. Cut in thin slices.
Lavonne
Emmett, ID

Fresh Peach Desert

Crust; ½ c butter – 1 ¾ c flour – ¼ tsp salt – 2 lb sugar. Mix and pat in 9x13 pan. Bake at 350* for 15 minutes. Filling; 2 c sugar – 4 tbl cornstarchs – 2 c water and 2 cut up peaches. Cook till thick. Remove from heat and add 1 pkg peach Jell-O and 1 tbl butter. Cool. Slice 8 peaches over the crust and pour filling over this.
Marly
Lake Preston, SD

French Cherry Dessert

3 egg whites – 1 c sugar – 20 soda crackers crushed – 1 tsp vinegar – 1 tsp baking powder – 1 tsp vanilla – ½ c chopped nuts – 1 pkg dream whip – 8 oz cream cheese – ½ c powdered sugar – 1 ½ tsp vanilla – 1 can cherry pie filling. Beat until stiff peaks. Fold in soda crackers, baking powder, vinegar, vanilla and nuts. Spoon into 9x13 pan, bake at 350* for 20 minutes or until done. Cool. Combine cream cheese, ½ c powdered sugar – 1 ½ tsp vanilla and dream whip and beat until smooth. Spread over egg mixture. Spread pie filling on top. Chill.
Elaine
Lake Preston, SD

Fruit Dessert

do not grease pan; 1 c pie filling – 1 c crushed pineapple undrained – 1 pkg white cake mix – 1 cube oleo soften and sprinkle with nuts. Bake at 300* for 1 hour and 15 minutes.
Doris
Beaverton, OR

German Kucken

dough; 1 c sugar – 2 c warm milk – 3 pkg yeast – 1 tbl salt – 1 c oil -1 c warm water – 3 eggs – 5 c flour; dough is sticky don't add more flour. Roll like pie shell (crust) filling; 2 tsp vanilla – 1 tsp salt – 1 c sugar – 6 eggs – 1 c sour cream. Let dough rise until double in bulk. Roll nuts. Bake at 325* till golden brown.
Dorothea
Coolidge, AZ

Graham Cracker Toffee

Grease lg cookie sheet. Fill cookie sheet with graham crackers cut in half. Boil 1 minute – ½ c butter – ½ c oleo – ½ c sugar – 1 tsp vanilla; then add 1 c sliced almonds. Spoon or pour over crackers; Bake at 325* for 10 minutes. Loosen edges set until firm, cut where lines of crackers are.
Barbara
Emmett, ID

Grandma's Rice Pudding

½ c sugar – 1 tbl flour – 1 tbl cornstarch – ¼ tsp salt – ½ c cold milk – 2 slightly beaten egg yolks. Mix sugar, flour, salt and cornstarch. Stir in cold milk and egg yolks. Add 2 ½ c scalded milk and 1 c cooked rice. Cook in double boiler just till it starts to thicken. Add raisins, vanilla. Fold in beaten egg whites. Pour into 2 qt baking pan. Place in lg pan of boiling water. Bake at 325* for 20 minutes.
Grandma
ST Helens, OR

Homemade Ice Cream

6 eggs beaten – add 1 ½ to 2 c sugar. Beat until thick with electric mixer – 1 tbl vanilla – pinch of salt – 1 qt cream – finish filling ice cream maker with milk.
Marlyn
Lake Preston, SD

Lemon Dessert

20 graham crackers – ½ stick melted butter and a little bit brown sugar – mix for crust and press into square pan. Mix 1 pkg lemon chiffon or instant lemon pudding mix following directions on box. Cool if using the chiffon. If using instant pour over the crumbs. Then add 1 c milk to pkg of instant vanilla pudding mix. Fold in 1 c whipped cream. You can add a ½ can crushed pineapple drained and top with mar chino cherries. Spread over lemon layer and chill 1 hour. Can be made several days ahead.
Jenny
Brookings, SD

Old Fashioned Bread Pudding

Turn on oven to 350*. Cut 5 slices buttered bread into ½ "squares. Place in larger bowl and stir in 4 c milk and 1 c raisins (opt). In med bowl, beat 2 whole eggs and 2 egg yolks slightly. Stir in; ¾ c sugar – 1 tsp nutmeg – 1 ½ tsp vanilla and ½ tsp salt. Combine egg and bread mixture in large bowl. Fold into bread mixture. Pour into greased 2 qt baking dish. Set in pan of hot water. Bake 1 hour and 15 minutes or until knife in center comes out clean. Remove from oven. Cool. Chill. Serve plain or with whipped cream.
Olga Peters
Salem, OR

Overnight Cream Good Dessert

Crush ½ lb of vanilla wafers, put in pan 8x12 (I use a pie tin). Cream ½ c oleo with 1 ½ c powdered sugar add 2 eggs one at a time, beat until smooth and creamy. Drain 9 oz can of crushed pineapple and add to 1 pint of whipped cream. Pour into pan with wafers and sprinkle with more crumbs. Let stand in refrig overnight.
Jenny
Veronia, OR

Pineapple Rice Pudding

4 c cooked rice – ¼ c sugar – 1 tsp vanilla – 1 can (#2) crushed pineapple drained – 1 c heavy whipping cream – ¾ c chopped mar chino cherries drained. Combine rice, pineapple and cherries. Whip cream with sugar and vanilla. Fold into rice. Chill.
Polly
Canby, OR

Peach Pudding

¾ c sugar – ½ tsp salt – 1 c flour – ½ c milk – 4 tbl oleo – 1 tsp baking powder – 2 c peaches drained (save juice). Combine sugar and butter than add other dry ingredients alternating milk. Pour batter over sliced peaches placed in bottom of 8x2 pan. Topping; 1 c sugar – 1 tbl cornstarch – ¼ tsp salt – 1 c peach juice boiling. Mix dry ingredients and sift over batter. Pour 1 c boiling peach juice over this and bake at 350* for 50 to 60 minute. Serve warm.
Melba
ST Helens, OR

Pecan Diamonds

Crust; 1 1/3 cube oleo – 2/3 c sugar – 1/egg plus 1 yolk – 1 tsp-vanilla – dash of salt – 2 tsp baking powder – 3 ¾ c flour; press in a jelly roll pan or cookies sheet with sides. Bake at 325* for 15 minutes. filling; 1 1/3 c oleo – ¾ c honey, melt; add 1 1/3 c brown sugar – ¼ c sugar and boil all for 3 min. Add 3 c pecans and ¼ c cream. Put on top of crust and bake again 30 minutes.
Patty
Emmett, ID

Pistachio Pudding Dessert

Mix; 1 c flour – ½ c butter – 2 tbl sugar – press into 9x13 pan. bake at 375* for 10 to 12 minutes. Beat 2 minutes 1 (8 oz) pkg cream cheese must be soft – 1 c powdered sugar – 13 ½ oz container of cool whip have at room temp. When crust is cold put ½ of this mixture into crust. Mix until thick; 2 (3 oz) pkg instant pistachio pudding – 2 ½ c milk. Spread over cream cheese layer. Spread remaining cream cheese over pudding.
Corrine
Hillsboro, OR

Plum Dessert

Quarter or cut up plums in buttered pan 9x13. Mix flour ½ c and 1 ½ c sugar or more to how sweet you want it. Pat on top of prunes or plums. Take a white cake mix dry and put on top. Melt a cube of butter and dribble over top. Sprinkle with nuts. Bake at 350* for 45 minutes to 1 hour.
Lavonne
Emmett, ID

Popovers

Beat 2 eggs well, beat in 1 c milk, and then 1 c sifted flour, and ½ tsp salt. Beat toughly. Pour into very hot muffin cups of glass, iron or heavy aluminum, with ½ tsp butter in each until one half full. Bake 45 min. Use a very got oven 475* for 15 minutes. Then moderate oven 350* to finish baking.
Olga Peters
Salem, OR

Pluma Mos – German

Makes ½ gal – cook any kind of tart fruit (cherries and plums) 2 qt water to 1 qt fruit. Bring to boil, and mix together ½ c flour -¾ c sugar – 1 c sweet cream. Beat well and add to boiling fruit. Bring to boil. Remove from stove and cool. Maybe eaten hot or cold. Sugar may be added last to prevent curdling.
Olga Peters
Salem, OR

Pumpkin Cobbler

Crust; 2 eggs beaten – ½ c sugar – ½ c milk – 1 (6 oz) pkg pancake flour (3/4 c) – 2 tbl melted oleo – 1 tsp pumpkin spice; filling 2 eggs beaten – ½ can milk – ½ tsp pumpkin spices – 1 can (30 oz) pumpkin pie mix. To make crust, combine eggs, sugar and milk in small deep dish. Add pancake flour and pumpkin spice, mix well. Pour melted oleo in 8x11 pan and spread the crust to cover bottom of pan. Make filling; combine eggs, milk, spices and pumpkin. Mix well and poor over crust. Bake at 325* for 50 to 60 minutes until crust is brown and filling is set. The crust will rise up three filling. Serve plain or with whipped cream.
Lavonne
Emmett, ID

Pumpkin Dessert

Prepare graham cracker crust; 27 crushed cracker – ¼ c sugar -½ c butter melted. Pat into 9x13 pan. Bake at 300* for 7 to 10 min.-cool. Smooth ½ gallon soft vanilla or slice ice cream on crust. Freeze. Mix together. 1 can pumpkin (2 cups) 1 ½ c sugar – ½ tsp salt – 1 tsp cinnamon – ½ tsp ginger – ¼ tsp cloves; prepare 1 pkg dream whip. Fold into pumpkin mixture. Spread over top of ice cream and freeze till ready to eat.
Becky
Gaston, OR

Raspberry Delight Dessert

20 double graham crackers crushed – mix with melted butter and make graham crust; Cream ¾ c butter and 2 c powdered sugar. Beat 2 eggs until thick and lemon colored. Add to butter mixture mix well. Spread this carefully over crust. Grind a layer of walnuts over this. Dissolve 1 pkg raspberry Jell-O in 1 c boiling water and add 2 pkgs frozen raspberries. Chill to quick thick. Spread chilled Jell-O over this. Whip ½ c cream and spread over layer. Lastly sprinkle the top with additional cracker crumbs.
Mickey
Killdeer, ND

Refrigerator Dessert

1 White or strawberry cake mix – 1 pkg cool whip – 1 box strawberry Jell-O (sm) – 1 box (10 oz) frozen strawberries. Bake cake as directed, when cool poke holes into cake. Almost to the bottom 1 ½ to 2 inches apart. Mix Jell-O with a little less water then called for. Then with a spoon pour 1 tbl or more of Jell-O into holes. Top; it is good if it spills around the holes and top as it keeps it moist. Put into refig. Drain strawberries and cool whip. Chill. Spread over cake and refrigerate.
Carmer
Richardton, ND

Rhubarb Crunch

2 c brown sugar – 1 ½ c quick oats – 2 tsp cinnamon – 1 ½ c sugar – 1 c water – 2 c flour – 1 tsp vanilla – 1 c melted oleo – 5 c diced rhubarb – 2 tbl cornstarch; mix brown sugar, flour, oats, oleo & cin. until crumbly. Press half of mixture into greased 9x13 pan, cover with rhubarb. Combine sugar, cornstarch and water, cook till thick. Remove from heat. Add vanilla. Pour over rhubarb sprinkle rest of crumb mixture and pat lightly. Bake at 350* for 45 to 55 minutes. Serve with whip cream.
Marge
Beach, ND

Rhubarb Delite

Crust; 1 c flour – ½ c oleo – pinch of salt – 2 tbl sugar. Blend well and put in 12x12 pan. Bake at 350* for 15 to 20 minutes. filling; 2 ½ c cut rhubarb – 1 c sugar – 3 tbl flour – 3 egg yolks beaten – pinch of salt – 1/3 c canned milk. Mix all together. Cook stirring constantly till thick. Pour onto crust. Top with meringue made from the 3 egg whites and ½ c sugar. Bake at 350* till brown.
Martha
Desmet, SD

Rhubarb Cobbler

1 c sugar and 1 c water make a hot syrup and pour over 4 c rhubarb cut up. Let stand. Cream ½ c butter and 1 c sugar. Add 1 egg – 1 ½ c flour – 1 tsp baking powder – 1 c milk. Put this batter in pan. Pour rhubarb over batter use a 9x13 pan. Bake at 350* for 30 to 50 minutes.
Mabel
Scappoose, OR

Salted Peanut Chews

Crust; 1 ½ c flour – ½ c brown sugar – ½ tsp salt – ½ tsp baking powder – ¼ tsp soda – ¼ c oleo – 1 tsp vanilla - 2 egg yolks slightly beaten; combine ingredients; press into a ungreased 9x13 pan. Bake at 350* for 12 to 15 minutes. Remove from oven and cool. Top with 3 cups miniature marshmallows. Topping; ½ c corn syrup – ¼ c butter – 2 tsp vanilla – 1 (8 oz) pkg peanut butter chips – 2 c rice crispies – 2 c peanuts. Combine syrup, butter, van, and chips in lg sauce pan. Heat until warm and chips are melted. Stir until smooth. Remove from heat and stir in cereal and nuts. Spoon warm topping over marshmallows. Spread evenly. Cool completely. Cut in bars.
Martha
Webster, MN

Spiced Peach Betty

2 c fresh peaches or any fruit – 1 c brown sugar – 1 c flour – 1/8 tsp nutmeg – ¼ tsp cinnamon – ½ c butter – put peaches in greased baking dish. Mix rest of ingredients except butter. Cut in butter. Sprinkle over top. Bake at 350* for 40 minutes.
Anggie
Richardton, ND

Sundae Brownies

Combine; 1 c flour – 1 c sugar – 1 tsp salt – 1 tsp vanilla – ½ tsp baking powder – 2/3 c shortening – 3 eggs – 1 c choc syrup – ¾ c nuts. Beat together all ingredients. Spread in greased cookie sheet. Bake at 350* for 25 to 30 minutes. Choc Sunday frosting; Combine ½ c choc syrup – 2 tbl soft butter – 1 ½ c powdered sugar – ½ tsp vanilla. Spread over brownies. If necessary add a little milk.
Sandy
Dwight, ND

Triple Strawberry Trifle

1 pkg vanilla pudding – 1 ¾ c milk – 1 (4 oz) cool whip thawed – 1 (8") angle food cake in pieces – 1/3 c orange juice – 2 c sliced sweetened strawberries. Prepare pudding mix with milk. I use instant; cover with wax paper and cool to room temp. Fold in 1 c of the whip, cut cake in 1 ½ "cubes. Place in a bowl and

sprinkle with orange juice. Spoon strawberries evenly over cake. Completely chill at least 2 hours. Top with remaining topping and strawberries halved.
Melba
ST Helens, OR

Uncooked Refrigerator Dessert

Cream together thoroughly; 1 lb box of powdered sugar – 1 c butter – add; 1 sq melted choc – 3 beaten egg yolks – 1 tsp vanilla – 1 c chopped nuts. Fold in 3 stiffly beaten egg whites. Line bottom of pan with cup crushed vanilla wafers; also sprinkle some on top of mixture. Let stand in refrig. 2 hours or overnight.
Lorene
Scappoose, OR

Vanbakkets (Cream Puffs)

1 c water – ½ c butter – 1 c flour – 1/8 tsp salt – 4 eggs. Bring water and butter to a boil, add flour sifted with salt. Mix well and cook slowly for 2 minutes. Remove from heat. When cool. Add one egg at a time, beating until smooth. Drop by tsp on greased pan 1 ½ inches apart. Bake at 450* for 20 minutes. Reduce heat to 350* and bake 20 minutes.
Sonja
ST Helens, OR

Apple Bars

Mix like pie crust; 2 ½ c flour – 1 c shortening – 1 tsp sugar – 1 tsp salt; separate 1 egg – put yolk in cup and fill with milk to make 2/3 c. Save white. Add milk to flour mixture. Roll half the dough to fit 9x13 pan or cookie sheet 9x11 with sides. Fit and bring up sides of pan. Sprinkle with 3 handfuls of crushed corn flakes. Slice 6 or so apples on cornflakes. Mix 1 c sugar and 1 tsp cinnamon. Sprinkle over apples. Roll out other half of dough large enough to press top and sides together. Beat egg whites stiff and spread over top of dough. Bake at 350* for 45 minutes. Make a frosting with powdered sugar, cream or hot water and almond extract drizzle over top while still warm.
Kate
Richardton, ND

Babe Ruth Bars

1 c sugar – 1 c brown sugar – 1 ½ c white syrup – 1 c peanut butter – 7 c cornflakes – 1 c Spanish peanuts. Bring sugars and syrup to boiling point. Let boil 1 min. Add peanut butter stirring until blended and then pour over corn flakes and peanuts. Mix well and press into a buttered pan. Topping; melt 1 pkg choc chips – 3 tbl peanut butter – 2 tbl butter. Melt in double boiler over low heat. Spread over candy and cool
Marie Workentin
Brookings, OR

Babe Ruth Bars

1 c sugar – 1 c brown sugar – 1 ½ c corn syrup – 1 c peanut butter – 7 c corn flakes – 1 c Spanish peanuts. Bring to a boil and first 3 ingredients. Boil 1 minute. Remove from heat stir in peanut butter pour over corn flakes and peanuts. Press in cookie sheet. Frosting 1 lg bag choc chips – 2 tbl butter – 3 tbl peanut butter melted.
Anggie
Richardton, ND

Baby Ruth Bars

Bring to boil and dissolve. ½ c white sugar – ½ c brown sugar – 1 c karo syrup – 1 c chunky peanut butter; take off stove and add; 1 c roasted peanuts – 6 c corn flakes; stir well. Press into balls. If you wish you may coat with choc.
Lisa
Emmett, ID

Banana Bars

2 eggs – 2 bananas – ½ c oleo – 1 tsp soda – 2 c flour – 1 ½ c sugar -¾ c buttermilk; bake on cookie sheet at 350* for 15 to 20 minutes frost with powdered sugar frosting.
Dawn
Arlington, SD

Butterscotch Bars

Combine 2 eggs beaten – 1 c sugar – ¾ c oleo – boil slowly for 2 minutes stirring constantly. Add 2 c miniature marshmallows and whip well. Add 2 ½ c graham cracker crumbs – 1 c nuts – 1 c coconut. Press into 9x13 pan. Cool. Melt 12 oz pkg butterscotch chips – 2 tbl peanut butter. Spread over and cool until set.
Eleanore
Sentinal Butte, ND

Butterscotch Cheesecake Bars

12 oz butterscotch chips – 1/3 c butter melted – add 2 c graham crackers – 1 c nuts; press ½ of this in bottom of greased 9x13 pan. Beat until fluffy. 8 oz cream cheese. Beat in 1 (14 oz) can milk – 1 egg and 1 tsp vanilla. Pour on top of crumb mixture, top with remaining crumbs. Bake at 350* for 25 to 30 minutes or until toothpick comes out clean. Chill.
Debbie
Rock Rapids, IA

Choc Cherry Bars

1 pkg fudge cake mix – 1 tsp almond extract – 1 c cherry pie filling – 2 eggs beaten; frosting; 1 c sugar – 5 tbl oleo – 1/3 c milk – 1 c choc chips; in lg bowl combine ingredients, and mix well. Pour into pan and bake 20 to 30 min. 350* Greased and floured pan. Frosting combine sugar – oleo and milk. Boil stirring constantly for 1 min. Remove from heat stir in chips until smooth. Pour over bars.
Gladys
Northfield, MN

Choc Malt Bars

1 oz sq unsweetened choc – ¾ c sugar – 2 eggs – ½ c nestle quick -½ tsp salt – ½ c walnuts – ½ c shortening – ½ tsp van. – 1 c flour -½ tsp baking powder; melt choc cool. Cream together, sugar, vanilla, shortening till fluffy. Beat in eggs. Blend in choc. Sift together dry ingredients, stir into creamed mixture. Stir in nuts. Spread in greased 8x8 pan. Bake at 350* for 20 to 25 minutes -frosting; cream 2 tbl soft oleo – ¼ c nestle quick – dash salt. Beat 1 c powder sugar and enough milk to spread.
Bobbie
Desmet, SD

Chow Mein Bars

¾ c light syrup – ¾ c peanut butter – ½ c sugar; cook these ingred over med heat. Stirring until mixed. Do not boil. Remove from heat. Add 2 c chow mein noodles. Spread in buttered 9x9 " pan. Melt 6 oz choc chips with 1 tbl milk and pour on top.
Vicky
Del Rio, TX

Carrot Bars

4 eggs – 2 c sugar – 1 tsp salt – 2 tsp soda – 1 c oleo – 2 tsp cin – 2 ½ c flour – 3 jars baby food carrots (sm jars) bake at 350* for 15 to 20 minutes.
Lucille
Shakopee, MN

Choc Peanut Bars

Cream together; 1 c brown sugar – 1 c sugar – 2 cubes oleo – 1 tsp vanilla – add and beat 2 eggs. Sift and add 3 c flour – 1 tsp soda – 1 tsp baking powder. 350* Spread in greased pan. Bake until golden brown about 10 to 15 minutes. Cool slightly and spread with peanut butter frosting; frosting; mix well 2 ¾ c powdered sugar - ½ cube oleo – 6 tbl cocoa. Boil ½ c water – 1 tbl white syrup – dash of salt. Add to sugar mixture and beat until shinny. Add vanilla and beat.
Mary
Portland, OR

Cocoa Bars

2 c sugar – 2 c flour – 4 tbl cocoa – 1 tsp cinnamon. Place these ingredients in a bowl set aside. 1 cube oleo – ½ c shortening – 1 c water bring these to a boil (rapid bowl). Pour boiling mixture over dry ingredients in bowl. Mix well. Add 2 eggs – ½ c butter-milk – 1 tsp soda – 1 tsp vanilla. Mix well. Bake on large cookie sheet for 20 minutes at 350*.
Mabel
Scappoose, OR

Coffee Bars

¾ c shortening – 1 ½ c brown sugar – 2 eggs – ¾ c hot coffee – 2 ¼ c flour – ¾ tsp baking powder – ¾ tsp soda – ¾ tsp cinnamon – ¾ c raisins or coconut – 2/3 c nuts; mix all together and spread on a cookie sheet. Bake at 325* for 15 to 20 minutes.
Dorletta
Corvallis, OR

Congo Bars

2/3 c shortening – 2 ½ tsp baking powder – 1 tsp salt – 1 c chopped nuts – 6 oz choc chips – 3 eggs – 1 c sugar – 1 c brown sugar – 1 tsp vanilla – 2 2/3 c flour. Cream shortening, sugar, eggs and vanilla. Add sifted dry ingredients. Stir in nuts. Add chips. Spread in a greased 15x10 pan.
Linda
Lake Preston, SD

Congo Bars

1 c sugar – 1 ¼ c brown sugar – 2/3 c butter – 2 ¼ c flour – ½ tsp salt – tsp baking powder – 1 pkg choc chips; Spread on cookie sheet. Bake at 350* for 15 to 20 minutes. When cool cut into squares.
Mabel
Scappoose, OR

Corn Flake Bar

Melt together; ½ c butter – 1 pkg marshmallows have ready; 4 to 6 c crushed corn flakes – 1 c coconut - ½ c crushed nuts; mix this all together. Press into 9x13 pan. Top with melted Hershey bars or choc chips.
Vicky
Del Rio, TX

Date Nut Bars

½ c oleo – 1 ½ c pitted dates – 1/3 c chopped maraschino cherries – ¾ c sugar – 3 c rice krispies – 1 c chopped pecans or walnuts; measure oleo, dates, cherries and sugar into sauce pan. Cook over med. heat stirring constantly until mixture becomes a soft paste. Remove from heat. Add krispies and nuts. Mix thoroughly. Portion by level measuring tbl onto wax paper or buttered baking sheet. Shape into balls. Let stand till cool.
Dorothy
Vancover, WA

Dream Bars

½ c shortening – ½ tsp salt – ½ c brown sugar – 1c flour. Mix all together. Put into ungreased 9x12 pan. bake 13 minutes or until lightly brown. blend the following and than spread over the top; 1 c brown sugar – 2 tbl flour – ½ tsp baking powder – 1 tsp vanilla – 1 ½ c coconut – 2 eggs beaten – 1/8 tsp salt – ½ c nuts. Bake again at 350* for 15 to 20 minutes. cut while warm
Jan-nita
ST Helens, OR

Frosted Apple Bars

2 ½ c flour – 1 tbl sugar – 1 tsp salt – 1 c shortening – 1 egg yolk. Add milk to yolk to make 2/3 c; mix like pie crust take ½ and put in bar pan. Filling; 6 apples peeled and sliced – 2 tbl flour – 1 ½ c sugar – 1 tsp cinnamon. Mix all this and put on crust, add rest of crust on top of apples. Beat egg whites till frothy and spread on top crust. Bake at 375* for 40 minutes or till apples are done. Frost.
Lucille
Shokoppe, MN

German Cake Bar

1 German cake mix choc – ¾ c melted butter – 3 oz canned milk – mix together. Put half of the batter in 9x13 pan bake 6 min. Melt a pkg of Kraft caramels in the milk (3 more 0z). put over the cake that is baked, add 1 c choc chips on top of the Carmel than add rest of the cake batter and bake 20 min at 350*.
Lola
Lake Preston, SD

Magic Cookie Bars

½ c oleo – 1 ½ c graham cracker crumbs – 1 c canned milk – 1 ½ c flaked coconut – 1 c chopped nuts – 1 c plain m&m's. In 9x13 pan. Melt oleo in 350* oven. Sprinkle over oleo evenly. Top with rest of ingredients. Press down firmly. Bake 25 to 30 minutes until slightly browned. Cool and cut into bars. Store loosely covered at room temp.
Sandy
ST Helens, OR

Melt a-way bars

1 c oleo – 1 c sugar – 1 egg separated – ½ c chopped nuts – 1 tsp vanilla – 2 c flour – ½ c chopped nuts. Combine all ingredients except egg whites and second cup of nuts. Press dough into ungreased jelly roll pan. Brush top of dough with egg white. Sprinkle with ½ c nuts or you can also use sugar and cinnamon.bake at 350* for 25 to 30 minutes.
Polly
Canby, OR

Mixed Nut Bars

1 ½ c flour – ¾ c brown sugar – ½ c butter; mix and pat into 9x13 pan. Bake 10 to 12 minutes. Cool 10 min than pour over crust – 1 (13 oz) can of mixed nuts. Make a syrup of ½ c white syrup – 2 tbl butter – 6 oz pkg of butter scotch chips. Pour this evenly over the crust and nuts. Return to oven and bake another 10 minutes.
Micky
Killdeer, ND

Mound Bars

Put in 9x13 pan. Melt 1 stick oleo and 3 tbl brown sugar and 1 ½ c graham cracker crumbs. Mix together in pan. Bake at 350* for 10 minutes. Spread 1 can canned milk over top then 2 c coconut. Bake at 325* for 15 minutes. Melt 2 c choc chips and spread on top.
Kathy
Dickinson, ND

Nut Goodie Bar

Melt together; 12 oz pkg choc chips – 12 oz pkg butterscotch chips – 1 sq unsweetened choc – 2 c creamy peanut butter. Put half of mixture in a 12x6 or a 10x15 pan. Place in freezer to set. Keep rest in kettle. Filling; 2 sticks oleo – ½ c canned milk – ¼ c dry pudding vanilla mix (not instant). Add 1 tsp maple flavoring. Stir in 2 lb powdered sugar. Spread over choc in pan. Put in freezer to set. Add 1 lb Spanish peanuts to remaining choc in kettle and spread over filling. Put in freezer until set. To cut let stand at room temp 5 to 10 minutes. Cut in sm squares and store in freezer in covered containers.
Beverly
Richardton, ND

Oatmeal Bars

1 ¼ c butter – ¾ c brown sugar – 1 tsp soda – ½ c sugar – 1 tsp cinnamon – 1 egg – ¼ tsp nutmeg – 1 tsp vanilla – 3 c oatmeal – 1 ½ tsp flour. Mix and press dough into bottom of ungreased 13x9 pan. Bake 25 minutes or golden brown. Cool completely before cutting. 350*
Olga Peters
Salem, OR

O-Henery Bars

4 c oatmeal – 1 c brown sugar – 2/3 c melted butter – 1 tsp vanilla – ½ c white sugar; melt butter, add brown sugar, syrup and vanilla. Remove from heat stir in oatmeal. Pat mixture in a buttered and floured 9x13 pan. Bake for 15 minutes. Melt together; 1 (16 oz) pkg choc chips and 2/3 c chunky peanut butter. Spread on oatmeal mixture cool thoroughly.
Anggie
Richardton, ND

Orange Date Bars

Cook till thick; 1 c dates – ½ c sugar – 1 tbl flour – 1 c water. Remove from heat and add 1 c candy orange slices cut up. Nuts maybe added. Cool. Mix in bowl. 1 c brown sugar – ¾ c shortening – 2 tbl milk – 2 eggs – 1 ¾ c flour – 1 tsp soda – pinch of salt – 1 tsp vanilla. Pour 2/3 of batter in greased 9x9" pan. Pour filling on top, then rest of batter. 350* for 30 to 40 minutes.
Joan
Richardton, ND

Pecan Bars

Mix yellow cake mix with – 1 egg and 3 tbl butter till crumbly. Put in the bottom of pan. 9x13. mix 1 can eagle bread milk with ½ c butter – brickle chips – 1 c chopped pecans – 1 beaten egg. Pour this over the crust mixture and bake at 350* for 25 minutes. I also used choc chips and walnuts.
Thelma
Richardton, ND

Peanut Butter Bars

½ c honey – ½ c peanut butter – 1 c powdered milk- mix. Add; nuts, choc chips, raisin or chopped dates. Roll into balls and refrigerate on wax paper. Don't touch sides for an hour or so. Than roll in coconut or graham cracker crumbs.
Charla
Forest Grove, OR

Pineapple Bars

½ c butter – ½ c brown sugar – 1 c flour; cream together, mix until crumbly. Put in cake pan. Bake at 350* for 10 minutes. Cool a little. Mix 2 eggs – 1 c chopped nuts – 1 c brown sugar – ½ tsp salt – 1 tsp vanilla; pour over first mixture bake for 20 minutes cool before frosting. topping; 1 c cream (coffee cream or ½ & ½) – 2 tbl butter – 1 c sugar – 3 tbl cornstarch – 3 egg yolks – 1 sm can crushed pineapple. Boil all together till thick and spread on 2 nd layer.
Mary
Mankato, MN

Poppy Seed Bars

1 box lemon or yellow cake mix – 1 pkg instant lemon or vanilla pudding – 2 tbl poppy seeds – 1 c water – ½ c oil – 4 eggs; mix together, add water and oil. Beat in one egg at a time. Pour into well greased bunt or angle food pan. Bake at 350* for 45 minutes.
Scott
Richardton, ND

Pumpkin Bars

4 eggs – 2 c sugar – 1 c oil – 1 can (15 oz) pumpkin; mix in lg bowl. Sift and add the following to above and stir – 2 c flour – ½ tsp salt – 2 tsp baking powder – 1 tsp soda – ½ tsp cloves – 2 tsp cinnamon – ½ tsp ginger – ½ tsp nutmeg. Mix well and pour into greased floured pan, 12x18 and 1 inch deep. Bake at 350* for 25 to 30 minutes. Frosting; 1 (6 oz) cream cheese – ¼ stick of butter – 1 tsp vanilla – 4 c powdered sugar. Beat cheese, butter, vanilla and cream together until soft. Add sugar until easy to spread.
Betty
Yakima, WA

Raisin Bars

2 c raisins boiled in 2 c water cooled – 2 eggs well beaten – 3 ½ c flour – 2 tsp cinnamon – ½ c nuts – 1 c butter – 1 ½ c sugar – 1 tsp vanilla – 1 tsp soda – add to 1 c raisin juice. Combine butter, sugar. Add eggs, soda and raisin mixture. Add flour, cin, van, raisins and nuts. Bake at 325* for 15 to 20 minutes. Frost while warm.
Bernice
Dismet, SD

Raspberry Jam Bars

½ c butter – 2 eggs separated – ½ tsp salt – ¼ c sugar – 1 ½ c flour. Cream butter with sugar, add egg yolks. Add flour in which salt has been sifted, spread in greased square pan 8x8. Spread with layer of raspberry jam topping. Raspberry jam topping; 2 egg whites – ½ c sugars – 1 tsp vanilla – ¼ c nuts. In separate bowl, beat the egg whites until stiff. Add sugar and vanilla. Spread on top of jam. Sprinkle nuts on top. Bake at 350* for 30 minutes. Cut in squares when cool.
Jackie
Desmet, SD

Russian Bars

6 tbl oleo – ½ c sugar – 1 egg yolk – 1 tbl light cream – ½ tsp vanilla – 1 c flour – 1 tsp baking powder – ½ c apricot preserves – 1 egg white – 1/3 c sugar – 1/3 c nuts – 1 tsp cinnamon; cream butter and ½ c sugar, add egg yolks, cream and vanilla, beat well. Add flour and baking powder. Chill overnight or a couple of hours. Pat into on ungreased cookie sheet. Spread preserves over. Beat egg whites till soft peaks form. Gradually add 1/3 c sugar and cinnamon beating to stiff peaks. Spread over top sprinkle with nuts. Bake 350* for 12 minutes. Cool and cut into bars.
Melba
ST Helens, OR

Sour Cream Raisin Bars

Crust; 1 c brown sugar – 1 ¾ c oatmeal – 1 tsp soda – 1 c oleo – 1 ¾ c flour – ½ tsp salt; mix until chunky. Press half in 9x13 greased and floured Pan. Add filling. Sprinkle rest of crumbs over the top. Bake at 350* for 20 minutes. Filling; 2 c raisins – 1 c sugar – 3 eggs slightly beaten – 2 ½ tbl cornstarch – 1 (12 oz) sour cream – 1 tsp cinnamon. Mix thoroughly. Cook until conspiracy of gravy.
Kate
Arvada, CO

Unbaked Peanut Butter Bars

¾ c sugar – 1 ½ c peanut butter – ¾ c white syrup – 3 c rice krispies – bring syrup and sugar to a boil. Remove from stove. Add peanut butter and rice krispies. Press in a greased 9x13" pan. Cut and serve.
Pearl Cavender
Keizer, OR

Apple Pie

2/3 to ¾ c sugar – 2 tbl flour – ½ tsp cinnamon – 1/4 tsp nutmeg – ½ tsp grated lemon peel – 1 to 2 tsp lemon juice – 6 to 7 cups thinly sliced, peeled and cored cooking apples (2 lbs) – 1 tbl butter or margarine. Mix all but butter. Put in unbaked pie crust. Dot with butter and top with unbaked crust. Cut small slices in top crust and bake at 350* until apples are done.
Penny Campbell
Emmett, ID

Apple Pie One Crust

Peeled apples – 1 1/3 c sugar – 3 tbl flour – ¾ tsp salt – 1/3 c light cream – ¼ tsp cin. Slice apples thin. Combine sugar, flour, salt and cream. Mix well cover apples with cinnamon. Bake at 375* for 1 ½ to 2 hours or until apples are tender. If crust gets to brown cover with foil during the first hour of baking.
Melba
ST. Helens, OR

Blueberry Pie (2 crust)

2 ½ c fresh berries – ½ c flour – dash salt – 1 tbl lemon juice – 1 c sugar – 2 tbl oleo; combine berries, sugar, flour, salt and lemon juice. Fill pie shell. Dot with oleo. Bake at 400* for 45 to 50 minutes.
Polly
Canby, OR

Cherry Pie

1 cup sugar – ¼ c cornstarch – ½ tsp salt – 5 cups pitted fresh tart cherries – 1 tbl butter or margarine, mix every thing except butter. Pour into an unbaked pie crust. Dot with butter and cover with another crust. Bake at 350* till browned.
Penny Campbell
Emmett, ID

Chocolate Pie

Mix 1 c sugar – 3 tbl flour – 3 tbl cocoa; add 1 c boiling water when smooth remove from fire. Add 3 slightly beaten egg yolks and tbl batter. Cook in double boiler 10 to 15 minutes. Cool. Add 1 tsp vanilla. Put in crust.
Melba
ST Helens, OR

Coconut Pie (makes own crust)

4 eggs – 1 ¾ c sugar – 2 c milk – 1 c self rising flour – 1 tsp vanilla -¼ c melted butter – 1 ½ c coconut; combine all ingredients in order. Pour in a greased pie tin. Bake at 350* for 45 minutes, or until golden brown.
Melba
ST Helens, OR

Crazy Apple Crust Pie

1 c flour – 2 tbl sugar – 1 tsp baking powder – ½ tsp salt – ¾ c water – 2/3 c shortening – 1 egg; in sm bowl blend well the above at lowest speed, beat for 2 minutes. Spread batter in 9 or 10 inch pie pan. Carefully spoon the filling below into the center of batter. Do not stir; filling; 1 can pie filling – 1 tbl lemon juice and ½ tsp cinnamon. Bake at 425* for 40 to 45 minutes until crust is golden brown. If using fresh apples or frozen heat a little and thicken with flour and sugar.
Melba
ST Helens, OR

Custard Rhubarb Meringue Pie

Prepare one unbaked crust into 9 or 10" pan – 3 c cut rhubarb – 1 ¼ c sugar – 3 tbsp flour – ¼ tsp salt – 1 c half & half or milk – 3 lg eggs (I use only 2 of the yolks ---3 whites go into the meringue) for meringue – 3 egg whites – ½ tsp vanilla – ¼ tsp cream of tartar, and 6 tbsp sugar. Pie filling beat yolks add sugar, flour, salt then add cream, and rhubarb. (you can warm the rhubarb mixture in microwave oven until it just starts to get a little custard look before putting it into unbaked pie shell. Then reduce time for baking) bake in unbaked pie crust at 425* for 20 minutes, then reduce to 350* and continue baking for 20-30 minutes. Check for done with wet knife blade; it should come out clear form pie filling mixture when done. Then put meringue on top and bake about 10 min more for meringue to brown.
Penny Campbell
Emmett, ID

Fresh Strawberry Cream Pie

Makes 2 pies – ¾ c strawberry syrup – ¼ c water – 3 tbl cornstarch – 1 c sugar; boil until thick may have to add more cornstarch. Cut strawberries in baked shells about 3 pts per crust and then pour sauce over the top of berries, can top with a few more berries.
Luicile
Shakeppe, MN

Hershey Pie

20 marshmallows – 3 sm chocolate bars – ½ c milk – 1 c chopped pecans – 1 c whipped cream – 1 baked pie shell (9") melt first ingredients in double boiler. Cool. Add rest of ingredients and poor into shell. Refrigerate until chilled and firm.
Dorothea
Coolidage, AZ

Juneberry Pie

1 tbl lemon juice – ½ c creams – ¾ c sugar – 1 round tbl flour to each – 2 c berries; mix to frozen or fresh berries and pour into pie shell. Bake at 350* for 45 minutes. If using frozen berries don't thaw them.
Jan-nita
ST Helens, OR

Kentucky Pecan Pie

1 c white syrup – 1 c brown sugar – 1/3 c milted oleo – 1 tsp vanilla – 3 eggs slightly beaten – 1 heaping c pecan halves – salt; combine syrup, sugar, salt butter and vanilla. Mix well. Add slightly beaten eggs, pour into a 9 inch unbaked pie shell. Sprinkle nuts over top. Bake at 350* for 45 minutes.
Nell
Gray, KY

Lattice Topped Blueberry Pie

¾ c sugar – ¼ c flour – 1 tsp each – cin and grated orange peel -4 c fresh or frozen berries thawed if necessary – 2 unbaked pie shell – 2 lb orange juice – 1 tbl oleo; combine sugar, flour, cinnamon and orange peel, lightly toss with berries. Place in pie shell. Sprinkle with orange juice dot top with oleo. Roll out remaining pastry, cut into ½ inch strip orange in lattice pattern on top of pie. Seal and flute. Bake at 425* for 10 minutes lower heat to 350* and bake 35 to 40 minutes or until crust is golden brown and filling begins to bubble.
Vivian
Hillsboro, OR

Lemon Meringue Pie

1 c sugar – 3 tbl cornstarch – ½ tsp salt – 1 c boiling water – 3 egg yolks – 1 lemon rind grated – ½ c lemon juice – 2 tbl butter – baked 9 " shell. Mix sugar, cornstarch, salt, and water stirring constantly until the mixture boils. Reduce heat. Add a small amount of hot mixture to egg yolks, stir in lemon rind and juice and butter return to stove. Boil 1 min and stir constantly. Cool. Beat lightly before pouring into the pie shell. meringue; 3 egg whites – ½ tsp baking powder – dash of cream of tarter and sugar until stiff peaks form. Place on top of filling and bake at 250* for 15 to 20 minutes until meringue is slightly browned.
Edith
Lake Preston, SD

Mock Apple Pie

Pastry for 1 pie crust (9") – 36 Ritz crackers – 2 c water – 2 c sugar – 2 tsp cream of tarter – 2 tbl lemon juice – grated rind of lemon – butter or oleo – cinnamon; roll out bottom crush and fit into pie shell. Bake crackers coarse in pie tin. Combine water, sugar and cream of tarter in pan. Boil gently for 15 minutes. Add lemon juice and rind. Cool pour over crackers dot generously with butter and sprinkle with cinnamon. Cover with crust, trim and flute edge together. Cut slit in top. Bake at 450* for 30 to 35 minutes. (I bake at 425*)
Wilma Coates
Emmett, ID

Mud Pie

22 Oreo cookies – butter brickle ice cream – slivered almonds – ¾ stick butter – fudge topping – choc ice cream – whipped cream. Crust; mash Oreo cookies with ¾ stick butter, pat into pie plate. Fill crust ½ full with butter brickle ice cream. Pour a thin layer of fudge topping on top. Cover with 1 pkg slivered almonds, than fill with choc ice cream. Freeze for 1 to 2 hours. Serve with whip cream.
Connie
Hebron, ND

Mud Pie

Crush 1 ½ lb pkg Oreo cookies – add ¾ c melted butter, press firmly in 2 (9x13) pans. Freeze until firm. Spread ½ gal vanilla ice cream over crushed and refreeze. Spread solid ice cream with a mixture of 8 oz jar of butterscotch syrup. Top with an lg carton of whipped topping and chopped peanuts. Freeze until firm. Serve while frozen.
Debbie
Emmett, ID

One Mix Custard Pie

2 c milk – 2/3 c sugar – 4 eggs – ½ stick oleo – ½ c flour – ¼ tsp salt – 1 tsp vanilla – 1 c coconut. Place all in blender blend 20 seconds. Bake at 350* for 45 minutes. Makes a big pie.
Lillian
Lake Preston, SD

Pecan Pie

4 eggs – 1 lb brown sugar – ¾ c water – ¼ c soft oleo – 1 tsp vanilla – single crust pecan halves. Line pie tin with crust. Combine sugar and water in 2 qt thick sauce pan. Place over moderate heat, stirring until sugar dissolves. Bring to a full boil and cook 3 minutes. Gradually stir hot syrup into the eggs. Blend oleo and vanilla into mixture. Turn filling into pie crust. Nuts on top. Bake 350* 1 hour or until set.
E.M.
Hillsboro, OR

Peanut Strussel Pie

Mix with a fork to make crumbs; 1 ½ c powdered sugar and ½ c peanut butter – 2 baked pie shells. Spread ¾ of the crumbs in bottom of shells. filling; 2 c milk – 5 tbl sugar – dash of salt – 1 ½ tbl butter – heat this and than add the following – 3 tbl cornstarch – 3 egg yolks – and 1 c milk; cool until thick. Add filling to pie crust while hot, top with egg whites beaten stiff. Sprinkle rest of crumbs on top of meringue and bake until well browned about 5 minutes in 425* oven.
E.M.
Hillsboro, OR

Pie Crust

Blend 4 c flour – 1 tbl sugar – 1 ½ tsp salt; mix in 1 ½ c lard – add 1 beaten egg – 1 tbl vinegar and a ½ c cold water. Mix all together.
Violet
Hillsboro, OR

Pie Crust

1 ½ c flour – ½ c shortening – cut together until marble size – 4 tbl water mix and roll. Makes 2 pie crusts.
Wilma Coates
Emmett, ID

Pineapple Cream Pie

¾ c sugar – ¼ c flour – ¼ tsp salt – 2 c milk – 3 egg yolks – 2 tbl oleo – 1 can crushed pineapple – 1 tsp vanilla; combine sugar, flour and salt. Add milk gradually then add slightly beaten egg yolks and oleo. Cook over low heat until thickened. Add pineapple and vanilla. Pour into a 9 inch baked pie shell. Top with meringue. Bake at 325* for 20 to 25 minutes.
Lavonne
Emmett, ID

Rhubarb Custard Pie

1 pie shell – filling; 4 rhubarb cut into ¼ inch slices (if frozen don't drain) – 1 c sugar – 2 tbl flour – 1 ¼ tbl lemon juice – 1/8 tsp salt; combine rhubarb, sugar, flour, lemon juice and salt. Mix well turn into pie shell. Bake at 375* for 25 minutes. Mean while make topping; 3 eggs – 1 c whipping cream – 2 ¼ tbl melted oleo – ½ tsp nutmeg; beat eggs, stir in cream, butter and nutmeg. Pour over hot rhubarb and bake 10 minutes longer until top is golden. Chill in refrigerator at least 2 hours before serving.
Lavonne
Emmett, ID

Rhubarb Meringue Pie

3 egg yolks whipped – 1 to 3 c rhubarb – 1 heaping tbl flour – 1 c cream – 1 c sugar – juice of 1 orange or ¼ c orange juice. Put this mixture in an unbaked pie shell. Bake at 450* for 15 minutes reduce heat to 350* for 30 minutes longer. Remove from oven. Cool and top with the following; ¼ tsp salt – 3 egg whites – ½ tsp vanilla – 6 tbl sugar. Add salt and vanilla to egg whites. Beat to stiff foam add sugar at tbl at a time. Continue beating until mixture forms moist peaks. Spread over pie, bake at 350* for 12 to 15 minutes or until golden brown.
Anggie
Richardton, ND

Rhubarb Pie

3 c cut rhubarb – 3 tbl flour – dash of salt – 1 c sugar – 2 tbl butter – ½ tsp grated orange peal; combine rhubarb, sugar, flour, peel and salt. Fill pie shell. This is a crust pie. Bake at 400* for 40 to 50 minutes.
Polly
Canby, OR

Rocky Road Chiffon Pie

1 pkg chocolate chiffon pie filling mix – 1 c boiling hot milk – ¼ c sugar – 1 c miniature marshmallows – 1/3 c chopped pecans – 1 baked 8" or 9" pie shell, cooled – place mix in small deep mixing bowl (about 1 ½ qt size). Add boiling hot milk, mix well. Beat vigorously with rotary beater, or at high speed of electric mixer, until filling stands in peaks (about 3 to 6 min). Add sugar slowly, while beating beat a minute longer. Fold in marshmallows and pecans. Spoon into pie shell. Chill until set (about 2 hours). Top with whipped cream, if desired. Homogenized or skim milk is recommended.
Pearl Cavender
Keizer, OR

Sour Cream Raisin Pie

1 c cooked raisins – 1 c sugar – 1 tbl flour – 3 egg yolks; use whites for meringue – 1 c canned milk and 2 tbl vinegar; mix vinegar in milk and let stand – 1 tsp nutmeg – 1 tsp cinnamon. Add all too boiling raisins and cook till thick.
Eunice
Lake Preston, SD

Velvet Almond Fudge Pie

1 c blanched slivered almonds – 1 big pkg choc pudding – ¾ c white syrup – ¾ c canned milk – 1 egg slightly beaten – ½ c choc chips melted – 1 unbaked 8 inch pie shell. Chop almonds and toast at 350* for 3 to 5 minutes. Set aside. Blend together until smooth into pudding, syrup, milk, egg and chips. Add almonds and pour into pie shell. Bake at 375* about 45 minutes or until top is firm and begins to crack. Cool at least 4 hours and garnish with whip cream.
Carla
Forest Grove, OR

Almond Butter Cookies

1 c butter – ½ c sugars – 2 c flour – ¼ tsp salt – 1 tsp almond extract – 5 to 6 tsp water. Cream butter and sugar. Add other ingredients. Chill dough 30 minutes. Form one inch balls and roll in sugar. Stamp on cookie, bake at 350* 8 to 10 minutes or until lightly brown.
Carol
Emmett, ID

Applesauce Oatmeal Cookies

2 c honey – 1 c oil – 2 eggs – 3 ½ c flour – 2 tsp nutmeg – 2 tsp cinnamon – 1 tsp salt – 2 c oatmeal – 2 c raisins – 2 c applesauce with 2 tsp soda mixed in. Mix together and drop by spoonfuls onto cookie sheets. Bake at 375* for 10 minutes.
Viola Coates
Emmett, ID

Believe it or not Cookies

2 c peanut butter – 2 c sugar – 1 egg – splash of vanilla – mix everything together, just blended in. Press flat with fork in pan. Bake at 325* for 10 minutes.
Delorse
Richardton, ND

Best Ever Sugar Cookies

1 c sugar – 1 c powdered sugar – 2 eggs – 1 c oleo – 1 c oil – 1 tsp vanilla – 1 tsp soda – 1 tsp cream of tarter – 4 c flour + 2 tbl. Cream sugar, oleo, oil, and vanilla. Sift dry ingredients. Add to creamed mixture. Put it in refrigerator for awhile till it gets firm enough to roll out into balls and flatten with hands and put sugar on them. Bake at 325* for 8 to 10 minutes.
Lola
Lake Preston, SD

Butterbrickle Cookies

1 c sugar – 1 c brown sugar – 1 ½ c shortening – 2 eggs – 1 tsp soda -1 tsp vanilla – 1 tsp cream of tartar – 6 crushed heath candy bars – 4 c flour; mix all together, flatten. Bake 350* for 8 to 10 minutes.
Lucille
Shokopee, MN

Can't Believe they're Cookies

1 egg – 1 c sugar – 1 c chunky peanut butter (candy kisses or choc stars) Combine first 3 ingredients. Drop with tsp on an ungreased cookie sheet. Put a chocolate kiss or star on top of each cookie. Bake at 350* for 10 minutes.
Cindy
Emmett, ID

Chocolate Chip Cookies

2 ¼ c flour – ½ tsp soda – 1 tsp salt – 1 c shortening – ½ c brown sugar – 1 c sugar – 2 eggs – 2 tsp vanilla – 16 oz choc chips – 1 c nuts; mix all ingredients and bake 350* for 10 minutes.
Wilma Coates
Emmett, ID

Chocolate Chip Cookies

1 1/3 c butter – 1 1/3 c shortening – 2 c sugar – 4 eggs – 2 c brown sugar (packed) – 4 tsp vanilla – 2 tsp soda – 2 tsp salt – 7 c flour -2 (16 oz) pkg choc chips. Mix all ingredients. Bake 375* for 8 to 10 minutes.
Trula
Portland, OR

Chocolate Chip Cookies

1 c butter – ¾ c brown sugar – ¾ c sugar – 2 eggs – 2 tbl hot water – 2 ½ c flour – ½ tsp salt – 1 tsp soda – 1 lb milk choc bar -¾ c nuts – 1 tsp vanilla. Drop cookies by spoonfuls onto pan. Bake 7 to 9 minutes at 400*.
Beverly
Beach, ND

Chocolate Chip Pudding Cookies

Mix and set aside; 2 ¼ c flour – 1 tsp baking soda – 1 tsp baking powder – combine and beat until smooth and creamy in separate bowls; 1 c soft butter – ¼ c sugar – ¾ c brown sugar – 1 tsp vanilla – 1 (4 oz) instant vanilla pudding; beat in two eggs, gradually add flour mixture. Then stir in 1 (12 oz) pkg choc chips – 1 c nuts chopped. Batter is stiff. Drop by spoonfuls 2 inches apart onto ungreased cookie sheet. Bake at 375* for 8 to 10 minutes. Make about 6 doz.
Julie
Emmett, ID

Chocolate Crinkles

½ c oil – 12 tsp cocoa – 2 c sugar – 4 eggs – 2 c flour – 2 tsp vanilla – 2 tsp baking powder – ½ tsp salt – 1 c powdered sugar – mix oil, cocoa and sugar. Blend in one egg at a time until well mixed. Add vanilla. Stir flour, baking powdered and salt in oil mixture. Chill overnight. Bake at 350* drop by tsp of dough into powdered sugar and roll. Shape into balls. Place about 2 inches apart on greased sheet. 8 to 10 minutes. (Do not over bake)
Melba
ST Helens, OR

Chocolate Sandwich Cookies

½ c soft butter – 2 c flour – 1 c sugar – ½ tsp baking powder – 1 egg – 1 ½ tsp soda – 1 tsp vanilla – ½ tsp salt – 1 c milk – ½ c cocoa. Beat until smooth, drop on cookie sheet. Bake at 400* for 7 minutes. Cool and fill with – 3 c powdered sugar – ½ tsp vanilla ¾ c shortening – ¼ c milk.
Thelma
Richardton, ND

Christmas Butter Cookies

cream; 1 c butter – 1 c sugar – 1 egg – 1 tbl milk – 1 tsp vanilla. Add; 2 ¾ c flour – 1 tsp baking powder – ¼ tsp salt. Chill. Roll out small portions at a time. Cut with floured cookie cutters. Bake at 350* 8 to 10 minutes. decorate.
Cheryl Hamilton
Emmett, ID

Christmas Cookies

3 ½ c flour – 1 ½ c sugar – 1 c oleo – 1 tsp salt – 1 tsp soda; mix these together like pie crust. Than add the following; 2 beaten eggs – ½ c sour cream and a tsp vanilla. Roll out thin and cut with cookie cutters.
Vivian
Hillsboro, OR

Cocoa Crinkles

¾ c oil – ¾ c cocoa – 2 c sugar – 4 eggs – 2 tsp vanilla – 2 c flour -2 tsp baking powder – ½ tsp salt. Chill overnight. Drop rounded dough balls in ½ c powdered sugar. Bake 10 to 12 minutes at 350*
Joan
Richardton, ND

Coconut Macaroons

2 egg whites – 1 c sugar – ¼ tsp salt – ½ tsp vanilla – 1 can bakers coconut (about 1 ½ cups) beat egg whites until foamy throughout, add sugar 2 tsp at a time, beat after each addition until sugar is blended. Then continue beating until mixture will stand in peaks. Add salt, vanilla and coconut. Drop from tsp on ungreased heavy paper. Bake in slow oven 325* for 20 minutes. Cool 5 minutes before removing from paper.
Olga Peters
Salem, OR

Crisp Pastel Jell-O Cookies

¾ c butter – ½ c sugar – 1 (3 oz) pkg Jell-O – 2 eggs – 1 tsp vanilla – 2 ½ c flour – 1 tsp salt – 1 tsp baking powder; make in balls and flatten with glass dipped in sugar. Bake at 375* for 6 to 8 minutes.
Mabel
Scappoose, OR

Diabetic Cookies

½ c flour – ¾ tsp baking powder – ½ tsp salt – 2 ½ tsp sweeten or equal – 2/3 c shortening – 2 eggs – 1 ½ c oatmeal – 1 tsp vanilla – 1 c dates – ¾ c nuts. Mix together form ball and flatten slightly. Bake at 400* for 10 to 12 minutes.
Beverly
Beach, ND

Drop Choc Cookies

1 c sugar – ¼ c lard – 2 eggs – ½ c sour cream – 2 c flour – 2 tbl cocoa – 1 tsp soda (sour milk is better than cream) cream sugar and lard add eggs and than the cocoa. Add soda to the cream or milk. Add to the sugar mixture. Add flour. Bake at 350* for 8 to 10 minutes.
Mary
Portland, OR

Egg Yolk Paint

Not sweet but good and fun; blend well – 1 egg yolk and ¼ tsp water. Divide among several small mustard cups. Add a different food coloring to each cup to make bright colors. Paint designs on cookies with small paint brushes. If paint thickens on standing add a few drops on water. Cut a dozen cookies at a time, then paint, so unbaked cookies don't dry out before they are painted. Use your imagination be creative. For clear colors, let brown. Just start to turn around edges.
Barbara
Emmett, ID

Filled Cookies

1 ½ c sugar – 1 ½ c shortening – 2 eggs – ½ c milk – 4 c flour – 1 tsp soda – 1 tsp salt – 1 tsp vanilla; bake at 350* for 8 to 10 minutes. Press dent in middle of cookie and fill with what ever you wish. (Like jam, jelly, dates, etc)
Edith
Lake Preston, SD

Frosted Molasses Cookies

1 c sugar – 2 egg yolks (save whites for icing) 1 c lard – 1 tsp cinnamon – 1 tsp ginger – 1 c molasses – 1 c boiling water; dissolve 3 tsp soda in water, mix sugar and lard. Add rest of ingredients. Drop by tsp on cookie sheet and bake at 350* for 8 to 10 minutes. When cool frost.
Mary
Portland, OR

Frosted Pineapple Cookies

1 ½ c flour – ¼ tsp soda – 1/8 tsp salt – 6 tbl softened butter – 1 ½ c sugar – 1 egg – ½ c undrained crushed pineapple – 1/3 c chopped fine nuts; sift flour, soda and salt. Beat butter, sugar and egg at high speed. At low speed beat in flour mixture, alternately with pineapple. Add nuts. Beat until just blended. Drop by top 2 inches apart on ungreased sheet. Bake at 350* for 10 to 12 minutes. Turn to other side for frosting; frosting white butter – 2 tbl oleo – 2 tbl milk – 1 c powdered sugar – 1 tsp vanilla – flaked coconut. Heat butter with milk. Gradually add sugar beating until smooth, beat in vanilla. Spread on cookies.
Vivian
Hillsboro, OR

Ginger Cookies

Mix together; 1 egg – 1 c sugar – ¾ c shortening – 4 tbl molasses; sift together twice; 1 tsp cinnamon – 1 tsp ginger – ½ tsp salt – 2 ½ tsp soda – 2 c flour. Add to 1 st mixture. Roll into small balls, roll in sugar, and do not press down. Bake 375* for 12 minutes. This dough should be chilled overnight.
Irene
Richardton, ND

Ginger Crinkles

Stir together; 2 ½ c flour – 2 tsp baking soda – 1 tsp ginger – 1 tsp cinnamon – ½ tsp cloves – ¼ tsp salt. combine; 1 c brown sugar – ¾ c shortening or oil – 1 egg – ¼ c molasses; add dry ingredients to beaten mixture, beating well. Form one inch balls. Roll in graduated sugar, if desired. Place two inches apart on an ungresed cookie sheet. Bake in 375* oven about 10 minutes.
Sylvia Garner
Emmett, ID

Gingersnaps

Combine; 1 c packed brown sugar – ¾ c oil – 1/3 c dark molasses -1 egg – beat well; stir together 2 c flour – 2 tsp soda – 1 tsp cinnamon – 1 tsp ginger – ½ tsp cloves – ¼ tsp salt; gradually blend into molasses mixture; using about 1 tbl for each form into 1 tbl for each, form into 1 ¼ in balls. Roll in graduated sugar, place 2 inches apart on greased cookie sheet. Bake at 375* for 10 to 12 minutes.
Tina
Emmett, ID

Graham Cracker Toffee

Grease lg cookie sheet. Fill cookie sheet with graham crackers, cut in half. Boil 1 minute ½ c butter – ½ c oleo – ½ c sugar – 1 tsp vanilla. Add 1 c sliced almonds. Spoon or pour over crackers. Bake at 325* for 10 minutes. Loosen edges. Set till firm, cut where lines of crackers are.
Barbara
Emmett, ID

Gum Drop Cookies

Omit black ones; 1 c gum drops cut in small pieces – 4 eggs beaten – 1 tbl cold water – 2 c brown sugar – 2 c scant flour -1 tsp cinnamon – ½ tsp salt – ½ c nuts; mix eggs and water. Add brown sugar and beat well. Sift dry ingredients together and beat into egg mixture. Add gum drops and nuts mix well. Spread in sheet pan which has been lined with wax paper. Bake 30 minutes at 350* turn out pan and remove paper. While still hot spread with icing ,f 3 tbl orange juice - 2 tbl oleo and enough powdered sugar to thicken.
Vivian
Hillsboro, OR

Ice Box Cookies

3 eggs – 1 c sugar – 1 c brown sugar – 1 c nuts – 4 ½ c flour – ¾ c melted butter – ¾ c melted shortening – 2 tsp soda – 1 tbl sour cream put soda in cream. Cream sugar, shortening and butter. Add eggs and than add the flour and sour cream. Fold in nuts. Roll in wax paper and refrigerate over night. Cut and bake at 350* for 8 to 10 minutes.
Mary
Portland, OR

Jell-O Cookies

Cream together. 1 c sugar – 3 eggs – food coloring – 1 (3 oz) pkg Jell-O – 1 c shortening. Add; 3 c flour – 1 tsp baking powder – pinch of salt. Roll out and cut into shapes. Bake at 350* for 8 to 12 minutes.
Lisa
Emmett, ID

No Bake Choc Fudge Cookies

2 c sugar – ½ c milk – ½ c oleo – 3 to 4 tbl cocoa – ½ c peanut butter – 2 ½ to 3 c oatmeal – 1 to 2 tsp vanilla – 1 c chopped nuts; boil sugar, milk, oleo and cocoa for 1 to 1 ½ minutes (start timing after the mixture reaches a full boil) remove from heat. Add peanut butter, oatmeal, vanilla and nuts. Beat until blended then drop on wax paper by tsp.
Barbara
Brooks, OR

No Bake Cookies

In 2 qt sauce pan mix – 2 c sugar – 4 tbl cocoa – 1 cube margarine – ½ c milk; bring to boil over med high heat. Boil 2 minutes. Remove from heat right away. Stir in; ½ c peanut butter – 1 tsp vanilla – 3 c quick oats; drop by spoonfuls on cookie sheet. Chill 1 hour.
Viola Coates
Emmett, ID

No Bake Cookies

2 c sugar – ½ c of cocoa – 1 stick butter (½ c) – ½ c milk
Let boil two minutes, remove from heat and add; 2 ½ c oatmeal – ½ c nuts (opt) – 1 tsp vanilla – 1/3 c peanut butter. Drop by teaspoons on wax paper, let set. Enjoy.
Debbie Green
Keizer, OR

No Bake Chocolate Peanut Butter Snack

1 (16 oz) pkg granola cereal – 2/3 c corn syrup – 3 tbl butter – ½ of (12 oz) pkg (1c) peanut butter morsels – 1 (16 0z) pkg (1c) semi sweet choc morsels; place cereal in large bowl; set aside in heavy sauce pan combine corn syrup and butter. Bring to full rolling boil over medium heat stirring occasionally. Remove from heat. Add peanut butter morsels. Stir until morsels are melted and mixture is smooth. Pour over cereal. Mix well. Press into foil lined 13x9 inch pan. Melt over hot (not boiling) water the semi sweet choc morsels and stir until smooth. Spread evenly on top. Chill to set. (About 10 minutes) cut into 2x1 inch bars. Makes 4 ½ dozen.
Thea
Emmett, ID

No Bake Fudge Cookies

Boil 3 minutes; 3 c sugar and 1 c milk. Pour over 45 crumbled soda crackers – 9 tbl peanut butter and 12 oz pkg choc chips. Stir till blended. Put on wax paper by tsp.
Sandy
Scappoose, OR

Peanut Blossom Cookies

1/3 c peanut butter – 1 egg – ½ c sugar – ½ tsp salt – 1 tsp vanilla – ½ c shortening – ½ c brown sugar – 1 tsp soda – 1 ½ c flour; cream sugar, shortening and peanut butter. Add egg, vanilla and dry ingredients. shape into balls, dip into sugar. Bake at 375* for 8 minutes. Press choc kiss in center and bake 2 minutes longer.
Elenore
Sentinel Butte, ND

Peanut Butter Cookies

Cream together; ½ c sugar – ½ c brown sugar – ½ c shortening – ½ c peanut butter – 1 egg; stir in 1 ½ c flour – ¾ tsp baking soda -½ tsp baking powder – ¼ tsp salt; shape dough into balls and flatten with criss cross (using fork) or put choc kiss on top. 375* 10 to 12 minutes.
Julia
Emmett, ID

Peanut Butter Kisses (no bake)

2 c dry milk – 1 c peanut butter – ½ c honey – ¼ c coconut. Mix all together and drop by tsp on wax paper.
Jackie
Sentinel Butte, ND

Peanut Butter Blossoms

Prep: 25 min bake: 10 min oven: 350* makes: about 54 cookies - ½ c shortening – ½ c peanut butter – ½ c sugar – ½ c brown sugar (packed) – 1 tsp baking powder – 1/8 tsp baking soda – 1 egg – 2 tbl milk – 1 tsp vanilla – 1 ¾ c flour – ¼ c sugar – milk choc kisses or stars (about 54) preheat oven to 350*. In a large mixing bowl beat shortening and peanut butter with an electric mixer on medium to high speed for 30 seconds. Add the ½ c sugar, brown sugar, baking powder, and baking soda. Beat until combined, scraping sides of bowl occasionally. Beat in egg, milk, and van until combined. Beat in as much of the flour as you can with the mixer. Stir in any remaining flour. Shape dough into 1 – inch balls. Roll balls in the ¼ c sugar. Place 2 inches apart on an ungreased cookie sheet. Bake for 10 – 12 min. or until edges are firm and bottoms are light brown. Immediately press a chocolate kiss into each cookie's center. Transfer to a wire rack and let cool.
Elizabeth Frolov
Salem, OR

Petticoat Tails

Mix together; 1 c butter – 1 c powdered sugar – 1 tsp vanilla – sift together and stir in 2 ½ c flour – ¼ tsp salt; mix all together with hands. Press and mold into a long smooth roll about 2 inches in diameter. Wrap in wax paper and refrigerate. Cut in thin slices. Place on ungreased pan. Bake until lightly brown, in oven at 400* for 8 to 10 minutes.
Mable
Scappoose, OR

Portzille (New Years Cookies)

2 c milk – 1 tsp salt – ¼ c butter – 2 c raisins – 3 eggs – 1 compressed yeast cake – ¼ c sugar 4 to 5 c flour; scald the milk. Cool to lukewarm and add remaining ingredients. Mix. Let rise until double in bulk. Drop into deep fat by spoonful and fry until brown.
Olga Peters
Salem, OR

Powdered Sugar Cookies

2 sticks oleo – 1 ¾ c powdered sugar – 1 egg – 1 tsp van. – ¼ tsp almond extract – 2 ½ c flour – 1 tsp soda – 1 tsp cream of tarter – 1 c chopped nuts – cream oleo and sugar, add egg and flavorings. Beat till fluffy. Stir in soda and cream of tarter, add and mix well. Stir in nuts. Add flour with soda. Take some dough and form into ball roll in sugar put on pan flatten thin with glass. Sprinkle with sugar. Bake at 400* for 8 to 12 minutes.
Audrey
Lake Preston, SD

Pumpkin Cookies

½ c shortening – 1 c sugar – 2 eggs – 1 c pumpkin – 2 c flour – 4 tsp baking powder – 1 tsp salt – 2 ½ tsp cinnamon – ½ tsp ginger; can add raisins and nuts. 350*
Olga Peters
Salem, OR

Rock Cookies

1 c sugar – 2 eggs – 1 c shortening – 2 c oatmeal – 2 c flour – 4 tbl buttermilk – 1 tsp salt and soda – 1 lb candied fruit; mix together drop by tsp on ungreased cookie sheet. Bake 12 minutes at 350*
Olga Peters
Salem, OR

Russian Teacakes

1 c soft butter – ½ c powdered sugar – 1 tsp van. – 2 ¼ c flour – ¼ tsp salt – ¾ c nuts. Mix together chill. Roll into balls. Bake at 400* for 10 to 12 min. roll in powdered sugar while warm. Roll again when cool. Makes about 48.
Donita Adams
Emmett, ID

Sand Dabs Cookies

¾ c butter – 4 tbl sugar – 2 tsp cold water – 2 tsp vanilla – 2 c flour – 1 c finely chopped nuts. Mix all together. Roll dabs as lg as your finger about 2 inches long or roll into balls. Bake in a slow oven 275* or 300*. While warm roll into powdered sugar. I bake about 10 to 12 minutes. I also sometime add a little more water to make dough easier to work with.
Lucille
Shakopee, MN

Smor Bullar

1 c butter – 3 tbl powdered sugar – 1 tsp vanilla – 2 c flour – 1 c chopped pecans; cream butter, add sugar and vanilla. Add flour and nuts. Make into small balls and bake on ungreased cookie sheet in 350* oven for 20 min. Roll in powdered sugar while hot.
Beverly
Beach, ND

Snickerdoodles

2 eggs beaten – 1 ½ c sugar – 1 c shortening – cream above together and add 1 tsp soda – 2 tsp cream of tartar – ½ tsp salt – 2 ¾ c flour. Mix well. Form into balls and dip into topping. Topping; 2 tbl sugar and 2 tsp cinnamon. Bake at 350* for about 12 minutes.
Freda
Taylor, ND

Snickerdoodle Cookies

Mix. 1 c shortening – 1 ½ c sugar – 2 eggs. Stir in; 2 ¾ c flour – 2 tsp cream of tarter – 1 tsp soda ½ tsp salt. Chill dough. Roll into balls the size of small walnuts. Roll in mixture of 2 tbl sugar and 2 tsp cinnamon. Put 2 inches apart on ungreased pan. Bake at 400* for 8 to 10 minutes.
Barbara
Emmett, ID

Spritz

1 lb butter (2 c) – 1 ¾ c sugar – ¼ tsp almond flavoring – 3 egg yolks – ¼ tsp salt – 4 ½ c flour; mix all ingredients and chill. Put in cookie press. Bake 350* for 10 minutes
Kathy
Emmett, ID

Stained Glass Cookies

Mix thoroughly; 1 c butter – 1 ½ c sugar – 1 egg – 1 tsp vanilla – ½ tsp almond extract. Blend in; 2 ½ c flour – 1 tsp soda – 1 tsp cream of tarter. Divide dough in half, color portions of one half with colors. Cover dough; chill 2 to 3 hours. Heat oven to 375*. Roll plain half of dough 1/8 inch thick on lightly floured cloth covered board. Cut with tree, star, ball or other decorating cookie cutter. Place on lightly greased baking sheet. Roll colored dough's cut out different shapes to fit on top of each plain cookie shape. If you wish to hang the cookies on your x-mas tree, insert small pieces of paper drinking straw through top of each cookie before baking. Bake 7 to 8 minutes or until golden brown on edge. About 2 dozen cookies.
Julie
Emmett, ID

Sugar Choc Chip Cookies

1 c butter – cream and add 1 c sugar – mix well. Add 1 egg – 1 tsp vanilla together. Add 2 ½ c flour – 1 tsp soda – 1 tsp cream of tarter; sift and add to first mixture. Add chips. Form ball on greased cookie sheet and flatten with bottom of glass dipped in sugar. Do not roll dough. Bake 350* for 8 to 10 minutes.
Gretie
Beach, ND

Sugar Cookies

2 c butter – 1 c sugar – 1 c powdered sugar – 1 egg – 1 tsp vanilla – 1 tsp cream of tarter; make into balls and flatten with glass dipped in sugar. Bake 10 minutes in a 350* oven.
Mabel
Scappoose, OR

Sugar Cookies

2 c sugar – 1 c butter – 1 c plain yogurt – 3 eggs – 1 tsp soda – ½ tsp nutmeg – 1 ½ tsp vanilla – ¼ tsp salt – 6 c flour; mix well, roll out to ¼ in thick, cut with cookie cutter. Bake at 350* on foil for 7 minutes. Bottoms will turn slightly brown but tops won't. Don't over bake. Cool. Icing; 2 pd powdered sugar (7 ½ c) 1 c shortening – 1 tsp salt – ½ c water – 1 tsp vanilla – ¼ tsp rum flavoring. (Divide and add different food coloring)
Colleen Coates
Emmett, ID

Sugar Cookies (doubled)

2 c sugar – 1 c shortening – 3 eggs – 1 c milk – 1 tsp soda – 1 tsp vanilla – 5 or 6 c flour – pinch of salt; mix well. Refrigerate for 2 hours. Roll out dough and cut with cookie cutters. Bake at 350* for 5 to 10 minutes or until golden brown.
Loreen Korell
Emmett, ID

Sugar Cookies (paintbrush)

Mix thoroughly; ¾ c shortening (part butter) – 1 c sugar – 2 eggs – ½ tsp lemon flavoring or 1 tsp vanilla. Sift and mix together; 2 ½ c flour – 1 tsp baking powder – 1 tsp salt. Blend together and chill at least 1 hour. Heat oven to 400*. Roll cold dough 1/8" thick on lightly floured board. Cut with 3" cookie cutters. Place on ungreased baking sheet or on a greased baking sheet if painting them. Paint with egg paint recipe if desired. Bake 6 to 8 minutes or until cookies are delicate golden color around edges.
Barbara
Emmett, ID

Super Sugar Cookies

1 c oil – 2 eggs – 1 c powdered sugar – 1 c butter – 1 c sugar – 1 tsp soda – 1 tsp baking powder – 1 tsp lemon extract – ½ tsp salt – 4 c flour (maybe a little more) cream oil and butter with eggs, sugar, salt and extract. Add flour, soda and baking powder. Mix well. Roll into balls, the size of a small egg. Press down and bake at 350* for 10 to 12 minutes.
Cora
Sentinel Butte, ND

Whatever Cookies

½ c butter – ½ c sugar – ½ c brown sugar – 1 egg – ½ tsp soda – ¼ tsp baking powder – ¼ tsp salt – 1 c quick cook oatmeal – 1 ½ c rice crispys – 1 c choc chips. Preheat oven to 375* mix butter, both sugars, egg, vanilla then stir in the rest. Bake until browned, best to under cook some. Any dry cereal can be used in place of rice crispys (frosted flakes, cherrios ect) any candy type pieces can be used in place of chocolate chips. (m&ms, toffee, peanut butter chips ect) add whatever you want to make them yummy!
Diana Brown
Keizer, OR

Zucchini Cookies

2 c honey – 1 c oil – 2 eggs – 5 c flour – 2 tsp soda – 1 tsp cloves – 2 tsp cinnamon – 1 tsp salt – 2 tsp vanilla – 2 c choc chips – 2 c grated zucchini – 2 c walnuts chopped. Mix all. Drop by tsp onto cookie sheet. Bake at 350* for 10 minutes.
Viola Coates
Emmett, ID

Zucchini Cookies

1 c shortening –1 ½ c brown sugar – 2 eggs – 2/3 c shredded zucchini – 2 c flour – 1 c oatmeal – 1 c uncooked wheat cereal -1 tsp cinnamon – ½ tsp ginger – ½ tsp nutmeg – 1 c chopped walnuts; cream shortening and brown sugar. Add eggs beat until light and fluffy. Stir in zucchini add the rest. Drop by tsp onto greased sheet. 375* for 10 to 12 minutes.
Olga Peters
Salem, OR

Choc Frosting

4 rounded tbl cocoa – 1 ½ c sugar – 7 tbl milk – ¼ tsp salt – 2 tbl oleo – 2 tbl shortening – 1 tbl white syrup – 1 tsp vanilla; mix all ingredients except vanilla and bring to a hard boil (rolling) cool 1 minute. Remove for heat. Add vanilla and cool.
Thelma
Richardton, ND

Creamy Choc Frosting

6 oz semi sweet choc – 3 eggs – 6 tbl oleo – 5 c powdered sugar; melt choc in top of a double boiler over boiling water. Cool. Beat oleo in lg bowl until softened. Blend in 2 c sugar 1 c at a time. Stir in eggs, then choc. Beat until blended. Add remaining sugar beat until smooth.
Lola
Lake Preston, SD

Cream Milk Choc Frosting

¼ c shortening melted – 1/3 c cocoa – ¼ tsp salt – 1/3 c milk – 1 ½ tsp vanilla – 3 1/3 c powder sugar. Mix all together.
Judy
Lake Preston, SD

Icing

½ c shortening – ½ c oleo – 1 tsp vanilla – 4 c powder sugar – 2 tbl milk. Cream shortening and oleo until fluffy, add vanilla. Gradually beat in powdered sugar alternating with milk.
Polly
Candy, OR

Pistachio Frosting

2 pkg dream whip – 1 ½ c milk – 1 sm instant pistachio pudding – nuts or coconut. Mix together the dream whip and milk. Fold in pudding. Frost cake and sprinkle with nuts or coconut.
Wilma Coates
Emmett, ID

Seven Minute Icing

1 egg white - ¾ c sugar – ¼ tsp cream of tarter – 1 tsp vanilla; mix together and add ½ c boiling water. Beat until stiff. Barbara
Cornelius, OR

Topping for Oatmeal Cake

1 cube butter – ½ c brown sugar – ½ c milk – 1 c coconut – ½ c chopped nuts. Melt oleo; add sugar and milk bring to a boil. Cool slightly and add nuts and coconut. Pour on top of hot cake and place in broiler until topping is bubbly. Oatmeal cake is under cakes. This can be used on any cake with broiled frostings.
Melba
ST Helens, OR

Almond Rhubarb Coffee Cake

2 ½ c bisquick – 1 c packed brown sugar – 1 c milk – 1 egg – 1 tsp vanilla – 1 ¼ c finely chopped rhubarb (1 ½ c frozen rhubarb finely chopped thawed and well drained can be used for the fresh) ½ c sliced almonds – ½ c sugar – ¼ c sliced almonds – 1 tbl firm oleo; grease and flour an jelly roll pan 15 ½ x 10 ½ x 1 inch. Mix bisquick brown sugar, milk, egg and vanilla. Beat vigorously 30 seconds. Stir in rhubarb and ½ c almonds. Pour into pans. Mix sugar oleo and ¼ c almonds. Sprinkle over batter. Bake at 350* for 25 to 30 minutes or until tooth pick comes out clean.
Helen
Richardton, ND

Applesauce Cake

1 c sugar – 1 egg – 2 tsp soda – 1 tsp cinnamon – ½ tsp cloves – ½ c butter – 2 c applesauce – 2 c flour – 1 c raisins – ½ tsp allspice – 1 c nuts. Cream butter, sugar, add eggs. Put 1 tsp soda in applesauce. Add alternately with flour, to creamed mixture. Bake at 350* for 35 minutes or till done.
Thelma
Beach, ND

Banana Cream Cake

½ c short – ¾ tsp salt – ½ tsp ginger – 1 ¾ tsp van – 1 c sugar – 2 eggs – 2 c flour – 2 tsp baking powder – ¼ tsp soda – ¼ c sour milk -1 c mashed bananas – 1 c heavy cream – ¼ c sifted conf sugar – 2 bananas sliced. Combine short, salt, ginger, and 1 ½ tsp van. Add sugar cream until light and fluffy. Add eggs 1 at a time beating thoroughly after each addition. Sift flour, baking powder and soda together. Add beating after each addition. Pour batter into two 8 "layer pans, greased. Bake at 350* for 25 to 30 minutes. Whip cream. Add sugar and remaining ¼ tsp van. Put layers together with whipped cream and sliced bananas. End with whipped cream.
Olga Peters
Salem, OR

Better Then Sex

Choc cake mix. Cook as directed. 21 oz can cherry pie filling – 1 cup sugar – 1 large pkg choc instant pudding – 8 oz cool whip topping – coconut optional – nuts optional. Cook cake by directions. Cook cherries, and sugar with water to thin. Cook for about 3 minutes. When cake is done make holes with a wooden spoon and pour mixture over cake while its hot. Let cool completely. Make pudding by directions and let set a little, then spread over the cool cake. Spread cool whip on the sprinkle coconut and nuts if desired.
Tina Hansford
Emmett, ID

Bucke de Noel

2 c heavy cream – ½ c confectioners sugar – ½ c unsweetened cocoa powder – 1 tsp vanilla – 1 egg yolk – ½ c sugar – 1/3 c unsweetened cocoa powder – 1 ½ tsp vanilla – 1/8 tsp salt – confectioners sugar; preheat oven to 375*. Line a 10x15 "jelly roll pan with parchment paper. In a large bowl, whip cream, ½ c confectioners sugar, ½ c cocoa and 1 tsp vanilla until thick and stiff. Refrigerate. In a large bowl use an elec mixer to beat egg yolk with 1/2 c sugar until thick and pale. Blend in 1/3 c cocoa – 1 ½ tsp vanilla and salt. In large glass bowl, whip egg whites to stiff peaks. Gradually add ¼ c sugar, and beat until whites form stiff peaks. Immediately folding yolk mixture into the whites. Spread the batter evenly over the parchment paper. Bake for 12 to 15 minutes in the preheat oven or until the cake springs back when lightly touched. Dust a clean dish towel with confectioner's sugar. Starting at the edge of the cake, roll the cake up with the towel. Cool for 30 minutes. Unroll the cake and spread with the filling to within 1 inch of the edge. Roll the cake up with the filling inside.
Tasha Murray
Middleton, ID

Carrot Cake

1 ½ c Wesson oil – 2 c sugar – 4 eggs – 2 tsp baking powder – 2 tsp baking soda – 2 tsp cinnamon – 2 c flour – 1 tsp salt – 3 c grated carrots – ½ c nuts chopped; mix sugar and oil, beating after each egg, be sure to add one egg at a time. Stir in dry ingredients into mixture, stir in carrots and nuts. Bake 1 hour at 350*.
Helen
Pacifica, CA

Carrot Cake

3 c flour – 2 tsp vanilla – 1 tsp soda – 2 ½ c sugar – 2 tsp baking powder – 3 eggs – 2 tsp cinnamon – ½ tsp salt – 1 ½ c oil – 2 c grated carrots – 1 c crushed pineapple – 1 c nuts; mix dry ingredients together. Add the rest and beat thoroughly. Bake in an lg pan greased at 350* for 50 minutes. Cool serve with whip cream.
Mabel
Scappoose, OR

Carrot Cake

2 c sugar – 1 1/3 c oil – 4 eggs – 2 tsp soda – 2 c flour – 2 tsp baking powder – 2 tsp cinnamon – 4 c grated carrots – ¾ c broken nuts. Beat sugar and eggs until thickened and pale. Stir in oil. Sift together flour, baking soda, baking powder and cinnamon. Stir into egg mixture. Fold in carrots and nuts. Spoon batter into greased and floured 13 x 9 x 2. 350* 35 to 40 minutes. Cream cheese frosting; 8 oz cream cheese at room temp – ½ c butter – 1 tsp vanilla – 1 lb powdered sugar. Beat all ingredients until well blended and velvety.
Pearl Cavender
Salem, OR

Carrot Cake Best Ever

1 ½ c oil – 2 c sugar – 5 eggs – 2 ¼ tsp bkg powder – 1 tsp soda – 2 tsp cinnamon – 1 tsp salt – 2 tsp vanilla – 1 c crushed pineapple – 1 c chopped walnut (or pecans) – 3 c grated carrots (add more for more moist cake – up to 5 c) beat oil & sugar in a large bowl. Beat in eggs one at a time. Sift dry ingredients; add them alternately with vanilla, carrots, pineapple and nuts to the sugar mixture. Pour into 14x10 pan. Bake 1 hr at 350*. Icing—
1 8oz package cream cheese – ½ stick melted butter or margarine - 1 box powdered sugar – 2 tsp vanilla mix well together and frost cake.
Carole Lloyd
Letha, ID

Cheese Cake

20 graham crackers – 6 tbl sugar – 6 tbl butter – 1 pkg dream whip – 8 oz cream cheese – 6 tbl powder sugar – ½ tsp vanilla – 1 ½ c milk – 1 can fruit pie filling. Roll crackers to crumbs, mix with 6 tbl sugar and butter. Put in bottom of pan. Whip dream whip as directed on pkg. Add cream cheese and powdered sugar. Spread over crackers. Spread pie filling on top of cream cheese. Chill until ready to eat.
Eva
Sioux City, IA

Choc Sheet Cake

2 c flour – 2 c sugar – ½ tsp salt; mix all together. Bring to a boil and pour over flour mixture – 1 c butter – 1 c water – 3 tbl cocoa. Then mix together and mix well. 2 eggs well beaten – 1 tsp soda – 1 c buttermilk. Mix everything together and bake in a greased and floured pan 15 ½ x 10 ½ x 1 inch for 20 minutes at 350*.
Mabel
Warren, OR

Choc Sheet Cake

2 c sugar – 2 c flour in sauce pan; 1 stick oleo – ½ c oil – 4 tbl cocoa – 1 c water. Bring to a rapid boil. Continue cooking for a few min. Pour into sugar and flour. Add ½ c buttermilk – 1 tsp soda – 2 eggs slightly beaten 1 tsp vanilla, pour into greased pan. Bake at 350* for 20 minutes. Icing 5 min before cake is done make this icing. 1 cube oleo – 4 tbl cocoa – 6 tbl milk, bring to a boil, remove from heat and add 1 box powdered sugar and ¼ tsp vanilla and 1 c chopped nuts. Spread on hot.
Louise
ST Helens, OR

Cherry Cake

¾ c shortening – 3 eggs – 5 tbl milk – 1 ½ c sugar – 1 tsp soda – 2 c flour – 1 tsp salt – 1 tsp cinnamon – 1 tsp nutmeg – 1 tsp vanilla -½ tsp cloves – 1 c pitted cherries well drained – 1 c nuts; blend shortening and eggs. Add sugar and milk blend well. Add remaining ingredients. Bake at 350* for 50 minutes.
Helen
North Platte, NE

Christmas Fruit Cake

2 c seeded raisins – 4 c seedless raisins – 2 c uncooked prunes – 2 c halved candied cherries – 4 c sliced citron – 1 c sliced candied pineapple – ½ c ground candied lemon peel – 1 c ground orange peel – 30 chopped nuts – 1 lb grated orange rind – ½ c fruit juice – 5 c flour – 1 ½ tsp salt – 3 tsp baking powder – 1 lb shortening – 2 c sugar – 1 c brown sugar – 3 tsp baking powder – 1 lb shortening – 2 c sugar – 1 c brown sugar – 3 tsp cinnamon – 2 tsp cloves – 1 tsp allspice – 2 tsp mace – 1- eggs well beaten – 1 tbl vanilla – rinse raisins, drain dry on a towel and slice seeded raisins. Pour boiling water over prunes. Cover and let stand 10 minutes drain dry and cut form pits into very small pieces. Rinse and drain dry cherries and citron before slicing. Combine fruity nuts and orange rind. Pour fruit juice over combine fruits. Sift flour, salt and baking powder together. Cream shortening, sugar, and spices until fluffy. Add beaten eggs and mix thoroughly. Add flour mix when adding prepared fruit mixture and flavoring and stir until fruits are well distributed. pour into 1 (10") tube pan and 1 loaf pan 10x5x3 lined with 2 thickness of brown paper, greased smooth tops and decorate if desired. Bake in slow oven 3 to 3 ¼ hour. Test with a toothpick or cake tester before removing from oven.
Ellenore
Rock Away Beach, OR

Cinnamon Ripple Cake

1 angel good cake mix – 1 tbl cinnamon; mix cake as directed on package. Spoon one forth of batter into a ungreased tube pan and spread evenly. With a fine small sieve, sprinkle one third of cin over batter. Repeat layering 2 or 3 times ending with batter. Bake and cool as directed. cinnamon cream sauce; ¾ c whip cream – ½ c milk – 1/2 c sugar – 1 tsp vanilla – ½ tsp cinn. Mix cream and milk in a chilled bowl. Beat with chilled beaters until thick. Blend in confectioner's sugar, vanilla and cinn.
Wilma Coates
Emmett, ID

Coffee Cake

Mix like pie crust; 1 c sugar – 1 c brown sugar – 1 c shortening – 3 c flour – 1 tsp salt – 1 tsp soda; save 1 c of crumbs for topping. add 2 eggs beaten well with 1 c sour milk or buttermilk (thick) - 1 tsp vanilla – 1 tbl cornstarch, mix all ingredients, gently till well blended. Bake at 350* for 45 minutes or done.
Alice
Coolidge, AR

Coffee Cake

Mix together; 2 c flour – 4 tsp baking powder – ½ tsp salt – 1 c sugar – ½ c shortening (save a ½ c for topping) mix; 1 tbl orange peel – 1 egg beaten – 1 c milk; add to above mixture. Put in lg flat pan. Topping; ½ c of the flour mixture, add 2 or more tbl brown sugar – ½ tsp or more of cinnamon. Sprinkle over dough. Put nuts on top and melted butter if you wish. Add peaches or pears on top before baking. Bake at 350* for 25 minutes.
Mary
Portland, OR

Cookie Sheet Cake

2 c flour – ½ tsp salt – 1 tsp soda – 2 c sugar – ½ c buttermilk – 2 eggs – mix and beat, add 1 tsp vanilla. Melt 2 cubes of oleo and add 1 c water and 3 heaping tbl cocoa. Pour into greased cookie sheet. Bake at 350* for 20 to 30 minutes.
Marge
Emmett, ID

Cottage Cheese Cake

1 c plus 2 tbl flour – 1 tsp baking powder – 1 egg – 6 tbl sugar – 5 tbl butter; Combine and mix well and pat into a 9x13 pan; filling – cream the following 2 c dry cottage cheese – 1 c sugar – 2 beaten eggs – ½ tsp salt – 2 tbl corn starch – ½ c sweet cream – 1 c sour cream – 1 tbl lemon juice – 1 tsp vanilla – 1 tsp cin. Pour over crust sprinkle with cinnamon. Bake 350* 45 to 50 minutes.
Lorrane
Richardton, ND

Crazy Cake

Mix all together; 1 ½ c flour – 1 c sugar – 1 tsp soda – 1 tbl vinegar – 3 tbl cocoa – 1 c cold water – ½ tsp salt – 1 tsp vanilla – 6 tbl milted oleo – do not use mixer just to blend together and bake at 350* for 25 to 30 minutes.
Vivian
Hillsboro, OR

Crazy Cake

3 c flour – 2 c sugar – 2 tbl vinegar – 1 tsp soda – 6 tsp cocoa – 1 ½ c oil – 2 tsp vanilla – 2 c water. Mix well. Bake 350* for 25 to 30 minutes.
Dorletta
Corvillis, OR

Danish Coffee Cake

1 c flour – ½ c butter – 1 tbl water; cut butter into flour as for pie crust. Mix in water with a fork make into 2 balls. Pat into 2 long strips 3x12. 3 inches apart on ungreased pan or cookie sheet. Make like a cream puff, ½ c butter – 1 c water – 1 tsp almond extract – 1 c flour – 3 eggs. Heat butter, water and almond extract, when hot stir in flour. Remove from heat and stir in 1 egg at a time and divide and spread on each strip of pastry. Bake at 350* for 60 minutes until nicely brown. Frost with powdered sugar icing like a glaze, sprinkle nuts on top.
Mabel
Scappoose, OR

Dream Cake

1 box layer cake mix yellow or white – 1 pkg dream whip mix dry -1 c cold water – 4 eggs. Blend all ingredients until moist. Beat on med. speed 4 minutes. Fold in 1 (12 oz) pkg choc chips. bake at 350* in either long or angle cake pan.
Pearl Cavender
Keizer, OR

Fruit Cake

1 Sara lee pound cake – 1 lg vanilla pudding made and cooled – 2 banana's sliced – 1 lg can pineapple tidbits drained – 2 c fresh strawberries cut in fourths – whipped topping; use ½ of each and layer as wrote down. Ending with whipped topping. Can use different fruit or more fruit.
Tina Ellenwood
Salem, OR

Fruit Cocktail Cake

1 c sugar – 1 c flour – 1 tsp soda – ½ tsp salt; sift together into bowl, add a can of fruit cocktail. Pour into cake pan. Cover with ½ c brown sugar and ½ c nuts or coconut. Add vanilla. Bake at 350* for 35 to 45 minutes.
Doris
Beaverton, OR

German Apple Cake

2 eggs – 2 c flour – 1 tsp soda – 2 tsp cinnamon – ½ tsp salt – 2 c sugar – 1 c oil – 1 tsp vanilla – ½ c nuts – 4 c diced apples; mix all ingredients (do not use a beater) batter will be stiff – spread into floured greased 9x13 pan. Bake at 350* for 50 to 60 minutes.
Melba
ST Helens, OR

German Choc Cake

(use 2 round cake pans) 1 c shortening – 3 eggs – 2 tsp vanilla – ½ c cocoa – dissolve in 1 c hot water – 2 c sugar – 2 tsp soda – 1 c buttermilk – 2 ½ c flour. Filling; ½ pt heavy cream or canned milk – 2 eggs – 1 c nuts – 1 c sugar – 1 c coconut – 1 tbl butter. Beat eggs add cream and sugar. Cook slowly until thick. Add nuts, butter, and coconut. Bake cake at 350* for 35 to 40 minutes -spread filling between layers then ice.
Melba
ST Helens, OR

Ginger Bread Cake

¼ c shortening – ¾ c sugar – 1 egg – 2 ½ c flour – 1 ½ tsp soda – 1 tsp ginger – 1 tsp cinnamon – ½ tsp cloves – ½ tsp salt – ¾ c molasses – 1 c water. Cream together shortening, sugar. Add eggs beaten. Sift flour, soda and ginger. Combine water and molasses. Alternate with flour to creamed mixture. Mixing well. Pour into greased 9 inch sq pan. Bake at 350* for 50 to 60 minutes. Cool for 5 minutes.
Glenda
ST Helens, OR

Hurry Up Cake

1 white or yellow cake mix - 1 pkg dry Jell-O; make cake as directed adding Jell-O to batter. Bake as usual no frosting.
Barbara Jeans
Emmett, ID

Italian Cream Cake

1 c buttermilk – 1 tsp soda – 2 sticks oleo – 2 c sugar – ½ c shortening – 2 tsp vanilla – 2 c flour – 5 eggs – 1 c nuts – 1 c coconut – 8 oz cream cheese – 1 box powdered sugar; cream 1 stick oleo and shortening together. Add sugar, eggs, buttermilk, soda, 1 tsp vanilla, flour, coconut and nuts. Beat well. Bake at 350* till done. Done if toothpicks come out clean. Icing; whip together cream cheese – 1 stick oleo – 1 tsp vanilla and powdered sugar. Spread on top of cake.
Vivian
Lake Preston, SD

Lemon Rhubarb Cake

Mix a lemon cake as directed on box. Pour into 9x13 greased and floured pan. Mix 4 c rhubarb – 2 c small marshmallows -1 ½ c sugar. Mix all together until well blended. Spoon over cake mix in pan. Bake at 350* for 45 minutes. (If using frozen rhubarb pour hot water over it and drain.
Florence
Richardton, ND

Mashed Potatoes Cake

¾ c shortening – 1 ½ c mashed potatoes – 3 eggs – 1 c buttermilk mixed with 1 tsp soda – 2 c flour mixed with 1 tsp cin. a ½ tsp of each; nutmeg, allspice, ginger and salt – ¾ c nuts. Cream short and sugar, add eggs, and cream together. Add milk with flour alternately. Add nuts. Bake at 350* for 50 min. Can be baked in layer pans. Frost.
Odette
Salem, OR

No Bake Cheese Cake

1 lb cream cheese – 8 oz cool whip – ½ c sugars – 3 tsp vanilla; mix well with elec mixer. Put in cooked pie, crust or graham cracker crust cool to set.
Rodney Murray
Middleton, ID

Oatmeal Cake

1 c quick oatmeal – 1 ½ c boiling water – ½ c butter – 1 c firmly packed brown sugar – 2 eggs – 1 1/3 c flour – 1 tsp cinnamon – 1 tsp soda – ½ tsp salt -1 tsp vanilla. Pour water over oatmeal and set aside. Cream in butter and sugar until fluffy. Add eggs one at a time, beating well. Add oatmeal mixture. Sift dry ingredients together and add beating well. Bake in greased and floured loaf pan or tub pan at 350* for 30 to 35 min. Good with boiled frosting.
Melba
ST Helens, OR

Orange Slice Cake

1 lg or 3 sm loaf pans. Sift together 3 ½ c flour – ½ tsp salt. Combine; 1 lb orange slices candy cut up. 1 pkg pitted dates chopped – 2 c chopped walnuts – 1 c (3 1/2 oz) flaked coconut. Add flour (½) mixture to this. Blend with spoon until light. Take 1 c oleo and add 2 c sugar one at a time. Add 4 eggs beat well after each egg. Combine 1 tsp soda to ½ c buttermilk, than add alternately with rest of flour and salt, mixture to sugar and eggs. Add candy mixture and mix well. Bake in greased pan, also flour them. Bake at 300* for 1 hour and 45 min. Combine 1 c orange juice and 2 c powdered sugar and pour over hot cake. Cool and store in refrigerator overnight before removing from pans. Keep a long time in the refrigerator.
Stella
Warren, OR

Pineapple Upside Down Cake

½ c butter – 1 c brown sugar – 1 (#2) can sliced pineapple – 2 tbl whole pecans – 1 c flour – 1/8 tsp salt – 1 tsp baking powder – 3 eggs separated – 1 c sugar – 5 tbl pineapple juice; melt butter in 9x9 pan. Spread brown sugar evenly in pan. Arrange pin. slices on top filling in spaces with pecans. Mix flour, baking powder and salt together. Beat egg yolks until light, adding sugar gradually, add pineapple juice and flour. Fold in stiffly beaten egg whites. Pour batter over pineapple. Bake at 375* for 30 to 40 min. Turn upside down on cake platter. Serve with whipped cream.
Ellenore
Rockaway Beach, OR

Pig Cake and Frosting

1 sm can mandarin oranges – ½ c coconut – ½ c oil – 4 eggs – yellow butter cake mix; mix and bake at 325* for 25 minutes or until done. Icing; (sm) cool whip – (sm) crushed pineapple – (sm) instant vanilla pudding.
Viola Coates
Emmett, ID

Popcorn Cake

Mix 4 qts popped popcorn and 1 lb m&m's together. Boil together – ½ c butter – 1 pkg marshmallows. Pour over popcorn and m&m's. Press into 9x13 pan. Cut into squares.
Marie
Beach, ND

Popcorn Cake

9 qts popcorn – 1 lb sm gum drops (no black) – ½ lb salted peanuts – 1 lb marshmallows – ½ c oil – ½ c butter; melt in top of double boiler over low heat pour over warm popcorn. Stir quickly into well buttered pan using wooden spoon and pack firmly and quickly into well buttered tube pan. Refrigerate for ½ hour before removing from pan. I cut gum drops into small pieces for more color.
Dorothy
Richardton, ND

Prune Cake

1 ½ c sugar – ¾ c shortening – 2 c ground up fresh prunes – 1 heaping tsp soda – 1 tsp cloves – 1 tsp nutmeg – 1 tsp cinnamon -2 ½ c flour – 1 c nuts – 1 egg; mix all ingredients together. I use the egg. I sprinkle sugar and cinnamon on top instead of frosting. Bake at 350* for 35 to 40 minutes.
Virginia Quenzer
Emmett, ID

Pumpkin Cake

1 lg can pumpkin – 1 can milk – 1 tsp salt – 1 tsp cin. – 1 c sugar – ¼ tsp cloves – 4 eggs beaten – nuts – whipped topping; beat and pour in greased 9x13 pan. Mix with fork ½ c melted butter and 1 pkg cake mix dry crumble this over pumpkin. Bake at 350* for 50 to 60 minutes.
Paula Starcher
Emmett, ID

Raw Apple Cake

½ c shortening – 1 c sugar – ½ c brown sugar – 2 eggs – 2 ½ c flour -1 tsp salt – 1 tsp baking powder – 1 tsp soda in 1 c milk – 2 c raw chopped apples. On top sprinkle ½ c nuts – 2 tbl brown sugar. Bake at 350* for 45 minutes.
Olga Peters
Salem, OR

Rhubarb Cake

1 c brown sugar – ½ c sugar – ½ c shortening – 1 egg – 2 c flour – 1 tsp soda – 1 ½ c rhubarb – 1 c sour cream or buttermilk; mix all ingredients together, sprinkle with sugar and cinnamon.
Mabel
Warren, OR

Rhubarb Cake

first layer; ½ lb butter – 2 c flour – 2 tsl sugar ; second layer; 4 tbl four – ¼ tsp salt – 1 c cream – 2 c sugar – 5 c cut rhubarb – 6 egg yolks – 2 tsp vanilla; third layer; 6 egg whites – ½ c sugar – pinch of salt and coconut; crumble ingredients from 1st layer and put in a 9x13 pan. Bake 10 min. at 350*. Mix ingredients for 2nd layer. Pour over baked crust. Bake 45 to 50 min at 350*. 3rd layer; beat egg whites well with salt and sugar, put meringue on top of baked custard. Then sprinkle with coconut and bake about 10 min. longer or until light brown.
Kate
Arvada, CO

Romanian Refrigerator Cake

2 cups milk – 1 tsp vanilla – 2 tsp sugar (or 1 packed sugar substitute) – 1 pint whipping cream – 1-2 cups raspberry jam – 1-2 tsp water – 1 package Italian lady fingers. Mix milk, vanilla and sugar together in large flat bottom bow. Dip lady fingers on both sides in mixture (quickly) and layer into bottom of glass cake pan. Mix whipping cream and layer half of mixture over the lady fingers. Mix raspberry jam and water together until mixture is thin and easily spread able. Layer jam mixture over the top of the whip cream. Repeat lady finger layer. kTop off with the remaining whip cream. Put in the refrigerator over night and then serve. (You can serve the cake at any time but it sets up more firmly if it is refrigerated over night.)
Randy Wilson
Emmett, ID

Ruby Slipper Cake

1 pkg yellow cake mix or pudding cake mix – 2 eggs – 1 c sour cream – ¼ c water – 1 pkg (3 oz) Jell-O, raspberry flavor. Combine cake mix, sour cream, water, eggs in a large bowl. Beat on med. speed for 2 minutes until creamy. Spoon 1/3 of batter into a well greased and floured 10" fluted tube pan. Sprinkle with ½ the gelatin. Repeat layers; spread remaining batter over gelatin to cover. Bake at 350* for 45 to 50 minutes until cake springs back when lightly pressed. Cool in pan on rack. Sprinkle with powdered sugar if desired.
Pearl Cavender
Keizer, OR

Skillet Cake

Preheat oven to 450*. Mix together in mixing bowl. 1 ¼ cups flour – ¾ cups sugar – 2 tsp baking powder – ½ tsp salt. Then ass. 2 tsp melted lard – ½ cup milk – 3 tbl cocoa – 1 tsp vanilla. Mix together and press in bottom of skillet/dutch oven. Then add ½ cup sugar (white) – ½ cup sugar (brown) – ¼ cup cocoa – sprinkle over top of dough in skillet then pour 2 cups of coffee over top. Bake in oven for 20 to 25 minutes.
Randy Wilson
Emmett, ID

Sour Cream Choc Cake

2 eggs – 1 ½ c sugar – 1 ¼ c sour cream – 4 tsp cocoa – ½ c hot water – 2 c flour – 1 tsp soda – 1 tsp vanilla. Mix together. Bake at 350* for 45 minutes.
Sandi
Dwight, ND

7 Up Cake

1 pkg yellow cake mix – ¾ c oil – 1 can 7 up – 1 pkg instant vanilla pudding – 4 eggs. Beat all ingredients for 2 min. at med speed with mixer. Makes a large cake and should use layer pans to bake it in. Topping; 1 ½ c sugar – 1 tbl flour – 1 cube oleo – 2 eggs – 1 c drained crushed pineapple – ½ c chopped nuts. Combine and cook till thick. Cool and spread between cakes.
Francis
Richardton, ND

Texas Chocolate Pecan Sheet Cake

2 c sugar – 2 c flour – ¼ c cocoa – 1 tsp baking soda – 1 tsp ground cinnamon (I omit this) – ½ c butter (1 stick) melted – ½ c buttermilk – ½ c canola or other vegetable oil – 1 c water – 2 eggs lightly beaten – 1 tsp vanilla: preheat oven to 375*. Grease and flour a 13x9x2inch baking pan. (I use a bigger sheet pan, it is up to you) sift together the sugar, flour, cocoa, baking soda and cinnamon, and set aside. Stir together the remaining ingredients. Mix the wet ingredients with the dry ingredients, stirring until you have a smooth, rather thin batter. Pour into your prepared pan, and bake at 3758 for 20 to 25 min, or until a toothpick comes out clean. While the cake is baking, prepare the frosting. ¼ c plus 2 tbl milk – ¼ c cocoa – ½ c butter – 1 lb confectioners sugar, (about 4 cups) – 1 tsp vanilla – 1 c chopped pecans: mix the milk and cocoa in a heavy saucepan (stir, stir, stir) add the butter and over medium heat, stir until the butter melts. Remove from heat and gradually stir in the sugar and vanilla until smooth. Add the pecans. When the cake is just out of the oven, spread the frosting evenly on the hot cake.
John & Tracy Nunez
Huskie Pizza
Emmett, ID

Wacky Cake

1 ½ c flour – 3 tbl cocoa – 1 tsp soda – 5 tbl oil – 1 c cold water – 1 c sugar – 1 tsp salt – 1 tbl vanilla – 1 tbl vinegar; sift all dry ingredients in the pan. Make a hole and pour in the liquids and mix well. Bake at 325*.
Olga Peters
Salem, OR

Yellow Jell-O Cake

1 pkg lemon Jell-O – 1 pkg yellow cake mix – ¾ c hot water to dissolve jell-o – ¾ c oil – 1 tsp lemon juice – 3 eggs beaten; mix at high speed for 3 to 4 min. Bake at 350* for 35 to 40 min. in a 9x13 pan. Remove from oven, let stand 10 min. poke holes all over cake and pour this glaze over it. glaze; 1 c powdered sugar in juice of one lemon.
Mabel
Scappoose, OR

Yum Yum Cake

Yellow cake mix - 1 use flatter and bigger cake pan
topping---- 1 8oz pack phil cream cheese soft – 1 box instant vanilla pudding - 1 c milk – 9 oz wool whip – medium size can crushed pineapple (drained) sprinkle on top.
Barbara Travis
Halsey, OR

Yum Yum Cake

2 c flour (don't sift) – 2 c sugar – 2 tsp soda – ½ tsp salt – 2 eggs – 20 oz can crushed pineapple (don't drain). Put 2 level tsp cornstarch in cup and fill with flour, add soda and salt. Add to the rest of ingredients. Bake at 350* for 40 to 45 minutes. When cake is still hot pour the following hot icing over it. Icing; 1 stick oleo – 1 c sugar – 1 sm can milk. Cook until thick; add 1 c chopped nuts and 1 c coconut. Spread on cake.
Melba
ST Helens, OR

Zucchini Cake

3 eggs – 2 c sugar – 1 c oil – 2 c grated zucchini – 3 tsp vanilla – 2 c flour – ¼ tsp baking powder – 1 tsp salt – 2 tsp soda – 1 tsp cinnamon – 1 c raisins. Mix all ingredients together and bake at 350* for 45 min. Frosting; 2 ½ c powdered sugar – 1 stick oleo - 3 oz creamed cheese whipped with elec. beater.
Dorothy
Richardton, ND

Zucchini Cake

1 c butter – ½ tsp nutmeg – 2 c sugar – 1 tsp soda – 1 tsp cinnamon -3 eggs – ½ tsp allspice – 2 c shredded zucchini – 2/3 c nuts – 3 c flour – 2 tsp baking powder – ½ tsp salt. cream butter & sugar until light & fluffy adding spices & rind. Add eggs, zucchini and nuts. Combine remaining ingredients. Cake will pull from sides of pan when baked 350* for 35 to 40 minutes.
Olga Peters
Salem, OR